PERU

PERU

VICTOR ALBA

WITHDRAWN

WESTVIEW PRESS
Boulder, Colorado

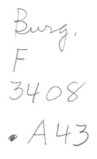
The author wishes to thank Michael Abel Fernandez for his work in translating from Spanish the final chapter of this book.

Published 1977 in the United States of America by
 Westview Press, Inc.
 1898 Flatiron Court
 Boulder, Colorado 80301
 Frederick A. Praeger, Publisher and Editorial Director

Library of Congress Cataloging in Publication Data

Alba, Victor.
 Peru.

 Bibliography: p.
 1. Peru. I. Title.
F3408.A43   985   77-666
ISBN 0-89158-111-1

Printed and bound in the United States of America

Contents

1

Between the Abyss
and the Summit

The traveler in Peru frequently has the impression that he is suspended between a summit and an abyss. A voyage into the history of the country produces the same sensation: Peru seems to be on the edge of a precipice, halfway between the heights and the depths. One needs only a nodding acquaintance with the different regions of the country to see that some inhabitants are in an abyss of poverty, isolation, and ignorance, and that others live on the heights of wealth, knowledge, prestige, and power.

Peru is neither one of the smallest nor one of the largest of the twenty countries of Latin America. But, despite distinct differences, at least half of the Latin American countries—those that have a large proportion of Indian population and a mountainous terrain—may be considered similar to Peru; so that, by learning about that country, one acquires a good introduction to the other countries of the Andean *cordillera,* the spinal column of South America. In Peru the common characteristics, problems, and hopes appear as if magnified, perhaps because everything there is looked at either from the topmost heights or from the lowest depths. The essence of Latin America is brought into focus in Peru.

If a traveler wants to know Peru, he cannot shut himself up in Lima, which is so easily accessible by plane. One must enter the Sierra and travel the winding roads—some of them 9,000 feet or more above sea level. One must go by car over the desert-like coastal zones, hauling oneself from city to city. One must fly over the endless jungles of the eastern region and see the Peruvians tilling the soil with wooden ploughs and smelting metal in tall, modern blast furnaces, and then descend into mines that operate at a height of nearly 10,000 feet. One must observe desolate stretches from some mountain, where miles seem like yards, and everything appears within reach. One must spend long hours going through ruins that antedate the arrival of the Spaniards and try to imagine the life, thoughts, and feelings of the men who built these astonishing cities, fortresses, temples, and terraces.

The traveler must make up his mind to go through the museums and palaces—the former offices and residences of the colonial era. He must go into the matting huts, the adobe houses, and the concrete mansions of the Peruvian country-side, cities, and slums. He must patiently leaf through the periodicals and look at the television programs—and he will need great patience in both cases, for much that they offer is needlessly redundant.

It is essential to stroll around Lima at three in the morning in the vicinity of the Plaza San Martín and to get up at day-break to see the people going to work. One must attend cockfights and *corridas,* political rallies, and masses in the cathedrals and observe Peruvians in the salons, at the market-places, in luxurious restaurants, or within the retreats of the university. One must learn to catch the hidden humor of their speech and nicknames. One must learn to recognize the prehistoric survivals in their speech, their way of hearing mass, and in the way a peasant family sits down to meals or behaves at a fiesta.

The visitor should not let himself be put off because Lima, a city that has a free and easy air, makes the reserved atmo-sphere of the country's other cities and towns depressing by comparison. He would do better to recall what the German traveler Baron Alexander von Humboldt perceived when he toured Peru early in the nineteenth century. "In Lima," he wrote in his memoirs, "I learned nothing about Peru. No subject concerning the public well-being is ever discussed there. A blind egotism governs everyone." Lima has not changed; what Humboldt said of it is even truer today than it was a century and a half ago.

The French painter Gauguin passed through Lima on the way to his Polynesian island. He visited the cemetery and was told that an enterprising Frenchman had, for his own profit, set the fashion of marble tombs. "So they are all heroes," he wrote to a friend. Lima's cemetery has not changed—everyone is a hero. Men of ordinary size are found far from the capital, and, if one doesn't know this, one cannot lay claim to the vaguest notion of what Peru is like.

Peru presents a typical case of the symbiosis of an internal oligarchy and foreign capital. In its largely oligarchic society, power is exercised by a limited number of landholding families. The relationship between peasant and landowner is still, practically speaking, one of servitude; similarly, the relationships between the big landowners and the urban population—and between both and the state—are those of lords and vassals. This adds a feudal element to the picture. But Peruvian society is also neocolonial because the middle class, which owes its existence and prosperity to foreign investments, now finds itself hampered by those investments. Moreover, despite its continued growth, the middle class still lacks sufficient power or development to justify saying that it has formed a capitalistic society. On the other hand, private initiative and economic freedom persist to a degree that would seem incredible in the United States, where laissez-faire is adulterated sometimes by the state, sometimes by the great size of the enterprises themselves.

Peru has been, and still is, a country whose share of social injustice, indifference to the well-being of the people, covert racism, and social immobility puts one's hair on end. Anyone might think that, of all the countries of the world, Peru is the one in which revolution would be not only justified but necessary. And yet, there has never been any true revolution, although the country's history abounds in mob action, military coups, riots, and even guerrilla warfare.

This alone would justify one's interest in knowing Peru, because that country's experience leads to a reexamination of customary theories concerning the causes and motives of revolution. In any event, it has given the country another peculiar trait: Peru is the only nation in Latin America that has reached the point of having a revolutionary party that, although weakened, aged, and appeased, is capable of reaching the submerged masses and mobilizing them. In a country so profoundly elitist, this is something of an anomaly. To those who talk incessantly of revolution, it offers lessons in areas ranging from the technique of organizing the masses to the philosophy of social change.

Whatever force, movement, or party that wishes to bring about a transformation in Peru must ask itself what the socieity it wants to change is like. Peru today seems extraordinarily like China in the past century; for, as was the case in China, the elite among the landholders find that the profitability of their possessions is declining. To compensate for this, they turn to politics to obtain fiscal privileges and the aid of the local police in the management of their lands.[1]

There is another reason for studying Peru—contemporaneity. Since 1968, Peru has had a military government that is outwardly different from traditional dictatorships, self-described as a revolutionary government of the armed forces. This government has effected agrarian reform, expropriated one North American enterprise and given concessions to another, and adopted various measures affecting industry, foreign trade, and education—measures that would be deemed moderate in a society less immobile than Peru's, but which, in Peru, seem radical. These measures, imposed from above, with the people being neither consulted nor given any part in their application, make the revolution—if such it is—paternalistic. The object is to effect—or, at least, hasten—Peru's transformation from a landholding oligarchy to a capitalist society. Marxists would call it a "bourgeois" revolution.

Peru's experience poses a series of questions, and in studying it with a view toward resolving them, we can perhaps find answers applicable to other Latin American countries as well, at least to those with similar characteristics. For example, Peru's experience poses the problem of explaining the apparent contradiction of the new Latin American generation of technicians and intellectuals who have adopted the terminology of the New Left to follow a characteristically technocratic policy. In another area, the Peruvian situation obliges us to face the problem of the roots of Latin American anti-imperialism (meaning anti-Americanism) and of the social strata in which it is most evident. Forces commonly considered pro-American (such as the military and the bourgeoisie) have turned out to be the most aggressively Anti-American. We have to see why and to what extent this sentiment influences politics—or whether it is only a screen held up before the mass of the population.

The occurrences of recent years in Peru seem to trace a pattern for other Latin American countries, in which a bourgeois lives as a parasite on the oligarchic landholding system and aspires to turn the feudal society into a capitalistic one, but without a real revolution—that is, without admitting the masses to the exercise of power. This experiment has received favorable response in the United States and in Europe, as much among businessmen and diplomats as among the New Left. Knowing the reasons behind this experiment, the truth about how it is carried out, and the alternatives offered in the future to the young military men of Peru can help us understand not only much that is happening in Latin America but also whether fundamental social change effected from above without participation by the public can be called revolution. The entire question of elitism and paternalism in revolution, which for decades has been poison to many theorists, is put to the test in Peru. So is the function of foreign capital; for, though profoundly nationalist and anti-imperialist, Peru's "revolution from above" needs foreign investment to help it avoid the extreme totalitarian methods of capitalization used in the Soviet Union, Cuba, and, in the past, Peru itself (by the landholding oligarchy and the Spanish colonizers). Thus, on the plane of political analysis and revolutionary theory, Peru's case is one that, if it were not for the hardships it entails for Peruvians, could be called ideal.

The future will tell us whether it is possible, in the twentieth century, to produce a capitalistic society by decree without it resulting in democratic forms of political power, or whether the latter will ultimately prevail. We shall then be able to tell, also, whether the issue of a "progressive" dictatorship will be a collective ideal—one that will give a national identity to a country—or whether, on the contrary, such a system will emphasize obstacles to the country's integration of the various social strata now on the outer fringes of political life into a national unit.

Latin America has tried a number of different methods for bringing about changes in its social structure—politics in a representative democracy, popular violence, violence on the part of the elite, and dictatorship by the elite. Many people, disappointed by the failure of previous methods, have now put their confidence in change by decree—revolution without popular participation. What happens in Peru will greatly influence the other countries' choices of avenues toward modernization. Study of the Peruvian situation is no mere academic exercise; rather, it provides a foundation for the understanding and forecasting of Latin America's course for the near future.

2

An Oppressive Topography

Peru's landscape is oppressive. Grandiose in beauty and in ugliness, immense in size and in menace, it reduces man to insignificance and instills the feeling that merely staying alive is a feat. The dominant impression produced by the country is one of silence and loneliness. Human traces are scattered, as if concealed by the dimensions of the topography.

Peru today is 496,222 square miles in area, or twice as large as the Spain of which it was a viceroyalty for three hundred years. In Latin America, only Argentina, Brazil, and Mexico are larger. It is bounded on the north by Ecuador and Colombia, on the east by Brazil and Bolivia, on the south by Bolivia and Chile, and on the west by the Pacific. The eastern boundaries are still quite imprecise; those on the north have been the cause of conflict, and they are still disputed by Ecuador.

Diversity

Two hours' flight in a plane enables one to see four or five different kinds of landscapes. Two days' journey in a car, traveling from east to west, permits one to see four or five

7

different types of people. A brief look at the overpowering quality and variety of the countryside will help us understand Peru and the great diversity of Peruvians.

The terrain is very irregular: lofty mountains, deep valleys, desolate plateaus, rugged seashores, rolling forests crossed by many rivers. Sometimes the forest extends right down to the sea. Sometimes the desert rises right up into the mountains. The world's highest lake, Titicaca, is bordered by extensive wastelands. From tropical, humid, exhausting heat one passes to the eternal snows, climbs to the high, cold Puna, the desert-like plateau, and descends to the coastal valleys, agreeable and hospitable when close to cities, isolated and dismal otherwise. Among the cities, one finds some that are outworn, boring, and provincial, seemingly living in the past, and others that are forward-looking, modern, and vibrant.

The Three Zones

The major geographical zones are the coast in the west, the inter-Andean region in the center, and the *selva,* or forest, in the east. The forest extends for thousands of miles. The Andean peaks rise as high as 23,000 feet, with passes between the valleys at 13,000 feet.

Perhaps what most marks the country's character is the inter-Andean region. Here are geologically young, solid mountains, neither eroded nor sculptured by the winds, the waters, or man. Because they are young, they are susceptible to the changes brought about by earthquakes, washouts, and eruptions.

There are two *cordilleras* in this region, both of which descend from Ecuador. One, the "red," goes toward Chile and discharges its rivers into the Pacific; the other, the "white," which is much more massive, goes toward Bolivia and permits the drainage of only one river—the Santa. The other waters flow eastward, to form the sources of the Amazon.

Between the two *cordilleras* are numerous chains uniting them from east to west. These, less lofty than the *cordilleras* themselves, form the valleys in which human life asserts itself. But even the valleys are from 6,000 to 10,000 feet above sea level. In one of them lies Lake Titicaca, shared by Peru and Bolivia, with more than 500 miles of *meseta* bordering it—the widest part of the *meseta* lying between the two *cordilleras*.

Also between the two *cordilleras* is the Cuzco region, imprisoned, as it were, between the two great Andean masses, which here are only about 200 miles apart. This corridor narrows toward the north until it is only 115 miles wide. In this region, there are seven lagoons of frozen waters among snowy peaks.

Those who live in these regions have the sensation of being prisoners of the mountains. This sensation is reinforced when one looks down. All around, there extends, at an altitude that varies from 10,000 to more than 16,000 feet, the *Puna*, a true desert, covered with weeds and brush and apparently interminable. There is no greenery; there are no sounds; there are scarcely any men or animals. There is neither twilight nor dawn but a sudden transition from sunlight to darkness, and vice versa.

From time to time, however, the *Puna* descends to about 7,000 feet, and then the landscape alters: there are cultivated fields, pasture lands, hamlets clinging to the slopes, and pockets of vegetation where the rivers have deposited their silt. Peruvians call this inter-Andean region the Sierra. It has historical, anthropological, and social peculiarities of its own, which we shall consider later.

The coastal region extends a mere 50 miles inland and stretches, from north to south, 1,500-odd miles along a part of the Pacific that is as deserted as the *Puna*. Although the region is characterized by drought, there is a great deal of drizzle—called the *garúa* by Peruvians—from the Humboldt current. Somewhat colder than the surrounding mountain air, and somewhat less salty than the bordering ocean, this current favors the multiplication of plankton. As a result, the region abounds with fish—one of the real riches of the country—and sea birds, whose droppings form the enormous masses of *guano*, a source of wealth to Peru when it was used as a fertilizer. The Humboldt current, whose greenish outline can be seen when one flies above the Pacific, makes the coast desolate but provides it with a means of sustaining life and with breezes that refresh the tropical climate enough to make it habitable. The coast is without bays and its only beauty is the impression produced when some promontory of the Andes extends down toward the waters and separates the dry beaches. The cities are almost always a short distance inland, close to the rivers that descend from the Andes and (if the sand does not absorb all their water) plunge into the ocean. On the shore, one finds only harbors and fishermen's houses.

Water has been Peru's chief bugaboo. As ocean, it isolates the country. On the coast and in the Andes, it is scarce. In the forest, it brings floods. Nowhere does it serve to bring people closer. Rivalries that have lasted for centuries sprang up between communities for its possession. Peruvians have never been sailors and only in very recent times has fishing become important.

The forest region is as isolated as the coast once was, and as the *Puna* is now. The many rivers have steep banks and are so swift that navigation is undertaken at the risk of one's life. Cultivation is difficult, because the forests are so fertile that it takes as much effort to defend the fields against their encroachments as it does to raise crops. The region is a typical Latin American jungle, with small animals more dangerous than the big ones, death-dealing plants, and stifling heat and humidity that can be withstood only by those searching desperately for something: the missionaries, for God; the conquistadors and the contemporary adventurers, for wealth; and the Indians of the forest tribes, for mere survival.

Flora and Fauna

In such a country, life is present in isolated patches. A map showing the flora, fauna, and demography of Peru looks like the map of an archipelago, one in which diversity and abundance are by no means the predominant characteristics.[2]

The geography has not changed since the arrival of the Spaniards, who found this world so astonishing. But the flora and fauna are not like those they found. Today, for example, eucalyptus trees, which had not then arrived in America, line most of the roads; and cows are found on many *haciendas*—big farming operations—where earlier only the llama browsed. The llama is a domestic animal, but two of the same family—the vicuña, from whose wool very fine and very warm fabric is woven, and the guanaco—are still wild. On the other hand, the alpaca, also a source of textiles, is now domesticated; the Indians knew it only in the wild state. Although the llama appears on the shield of Peru, it is in no way a true symbol of the country. For the llama, while permitting light loads to be placed on its back, stubbornly refuses heavy ones; it responds to goadings and beatings by launching a stream of saliva at the offender. Such vigorous resistance and swift retaliation are not characterteristic of the Peruvian people, who are long-suffering and patient.

Like the camel, the llama is capable of going for many days without food or water, but, except for its wool and its dung (which, when dried is used for fuel on the treeless *altiplanos*), it has no use, because its flesh, when the animal is grown, is bitter, apparently because of the weeds on which it lives.

Among the Incas, only the small, heavy-set dogs, the falcon, and the guinea pig were domesticated. The wildcats and other beasts of the forests—the terrors of the peasants—are useful only decoratively, as sculptured images or for garments. Horses, cattle, sheep, deer, and poultry came from Europe. It is very likely that their use was the aspect of the Spaniards' civilization to which the Indians adapted themselves most rapidly and completely.

The natives' adoption of exotic plants was slower. Indian corn was, and has continued to be, the chief staple. It is a plant of such hardiness that it will grow even on the heights where human beings can scarcely live. The Incas also had another grain called *manco*—one of the few examples of a food plant that has disappeared, apparently because the Spaniards, who did not like it, replaced it with wheat. But the Spaniards quickly became fond of the *papa* ("potato"), which they took back to Europe. The potato was eaten raw or cooked and could be buried in the frozen earth of the heights to preserve it as food for the winter.

The Indians have always had beans and millet, which the Spaniards called *arroz chico* ("little rice"). They have traditionally grown *aji*, a very hot pimiento, which today plays a part in most local recipes. Millet has a supplementary use: the ashes of its stalks are mixed with the leaves of the coca plant, from which modern chemical methods extract the alkaloid cocaine. The Indians chew the mixture to escape the miseries of their existence and also, it seems, to strengthen themselves—to supply the energy for which their diet is insufficient.

It is in the tropical valleys that one finds besides the fruits brought from Europe, those characteristic of Peru or other American tropics: the *guayaba* ("guava"); the alligator pear; the cherimoya; the yucca, from which a highly nourishing flour is made; and the *mani* ("peanut"), from which oil is derived. There are carob beans, which serve as fodder and, in the past, furnished a gum made from their juice. Other plants were used by the Incas not for food but as conveniences: the *opuntia*, a variety of cactus, which had thorns so tough that they were used as needles; and the ichu grass, which was mixed with clay to reinforce bricks and was used as thatch and llama fodder. Other plants were used (as they still are in many villages) for dyeing and as medicine. The *totora*, or giant reed mace found in the banks of Lake Titicaca, is still used to make the rafts so attractive to tourists who want to take home picturesque snapshots. Maguey, which is still found in Mexico and other parts of Latin America, was a textile source.

It has been said that one may cross Peru without ever getting into the shade. Certainly there are few trees—mostly European varieties that have been acclimatized. The *ceibas*, or silkcotton trees, whose wood does not decay and is used for boats, are quite majestic; some grow to a height of more than thirty feet. The birch that grows in the Cuzco region is even taller and is well suited for construction. The Spanish were the first to exploit the valuable woods that are comparatively plentiful in the Amazon forests, where the cedars attain a height of sixty-five feet. None of this, however, makes the landscape any more cheerful. Darwin, when visiting the country, said, "I am weary of writing the words 'desert' and 'barren.' "

Mountains and Rivers

The geography of Peru gives an impression of discontinuity, of lack of system. There is no natural center, and even the two *cordilleras,* which appear as its spinal column, are like stairways that lead nowhere and obey no design. As a result, communication is difficult and laborious. The general impression is one not of a geography composed by terrestrial forces, but rather of something that was already in existence and now is being toppled, battered, and destroyed. This impression is not far from the truth, for earthquakes in the Andean regions are frequent and at times devastating. In 1970, there was one near Chimbote that claimed 50,000 lives and destroyed 60 percent of that city, as well as several other towns.

The Andes attain their ultimate magnificence in the south with such volcanoes as Chachani (20,000 feet), Misti (19,500 feet)—which, in spite of its height, is never covered with snow—and Tutucapa (19,000 feet). In this region, the mountains extend to the sea, but they are separated from it in the central and northern zones, where we find the *cordilleras* of Huayhuash and Blanca ("White"), the latter so named because of the glaciers that adorn it. Mount Huascarán (22,500 feet) could be seen above these *cordilleras* if a fog did not nearly always obscure the view, as it does in the Sierra Negra, which constantly exceeds 17,000 feet. Near the Ecuadorean frontier, the Andes are less lofty, with passes and defiles usually no higher than 8,500 feet. There, too, the Puna gives way to high marshy flatlands (like the pampa of Junín), in which rivers of modest size, the Mantaro and the Santa, have their source.

More impressive are the rivers of the forest regions, such as the Marañón, the Napo, and the Ucayali, which rise in these steep zones and then, widening, flow through this part of the country that accounts for half of the national territory.

The Climate

Peru's climate is one of great diversity, and there are violent constrasts between the dryness of the coast and the humidity of the jungle, between the heat of the latter and the cold of the Andean region. The coast is terribly deserted—some parts are literally deserts; for example, the Sechura in the north, near the city of Piura. The coast consists mainly of wide, rocky beaches, with intermittent oases of stunted vegetation at the mouths of the rivers and streams that flow down from the Andes, passing through the *páramo,* a small, treeless plain with sparse vegetation about 1,600 feet above sea level. There is a minimum of seasonal variation, although changes of temperature during the day can be abrupt and considerable. In Lima, which is only a few miles from the coast, the annual mean rainfall is less than 1.5 inches, and most of that comes from the *garúa.*

In the Amazon region, the rainfall is torrential, about ten feet a year, and the heat is such that air rising from the jungle tempers the cold of the eastern Sierra. In Cuzco, for instance, despite its altitude, the mean temperature is 40°F. The western Sierra, closer to the coast, is much colder. In the Andean region, rain falls from December to April; the rest of the year is entirely dry. Oddly enough, it rains more in the north (as much as thirty-six inches a year) than in the south, where the rainfall is only about twelve inches.

The Cities

In terms of miles, the distances in the interior of the country are not enormous. But, in terms of time, they prove interminable. A postcard takes longer to go from Lima to a city in the Amazon region than it takes to go by air from Lima to New York, or even to Moscow! Every city is isolated, content to be the center of the little world of its valley. To the inhabitants, the people of the city in its neighboring valley seem farther away than those in the capital—to which they must turn for the solution of their problems.

Peru, besides being composed of the regions previously described, may also be viewed as consisting, more generally, of two elements: Lima, the capital, and the rest of the country. Lima has 2 million inhabitants (in 1940, there were only half a million)—a sixth of the entire population of Peru. It is not only the seat of the government, but the center of the economy and the culture of the country as well. The metropolitan area spreads out toward the coast in rich suburbs (some, such as Miraflores, are insolently rich) until it reaches the port of Callao, destroyed by an earthquake in 1940 and promptly rebuilt. Toward the interior, however, Lima assumes a markedly different aspect: clustered together in abject poverty are countless little huts, some with only matting as outer walls; there are no utilities, no schools, no modern conveniences. Lima is a city of contrasts, in which vast colonial palaces stand side by side with modern skyscrapers.

The other cities of Peru—on the coast, beside rivers, or in the Andean valleys—are provincial and less modern, although their rate of growth is accelerating. In the north are Chiclayo, Trujillo, and Piura. In the center are Pisco, on the coast, and Huancayo, at a distance from it; the other settlements are towns rather than cities: Ica, Cajamarca, Huancavelica (in the eighteenth century, center of the most significant Indian rebellion in the history of Latin America). In the south are two cities: one modern and close to the coast—Arequipa, whose passion for politics seems to be a local characteristic; and the other in the Sierra—Cuzco, the great religious center of the Incas, which has preserved an immense treasure of pre-colonial and colonial monuments. In the Amazonian region is Huánaco, once a center of drug traffic—for much coca was harvested in the vicinity. Among the Amazonian towns, there are still remnants of a fleeting splendor, when rubber and quinine attracted adventurers and capital; today, with both products in declining demand, the villages that were a center of the trade in them have returned to their erstwhile somnolence.

To the north of this region is Iquitos. Situated on the bank of the Amazon, it is a gathering point for adventurers in search of uranium. It is easier to reach by going up the Amazon from the Atlantic than by land via Lima, although today even the poorest mineral prospector would use an airplane.

None of these cities have more than a quarter of a million inhabitants, which shows the centripetal power of Lima. The traveler, the student of history, the archaeologist, and the economist are familiar with still other names: Puno, on Lake Titicaca; Ayacucho, where a decisive battle for the independence of the country was fought; Talara, with its oil wells; Cerro de Pasco, with its mines; Tacna, bordered by Chile and the desert; as well as a hundred sites of ruins, a hundred settlements of native communes, a hundred picturesque corners—all incredible in a topography in which, logically, there should be no human life at all.

3

A Troubled History

The landscape, the distances, and the silence of Peru seem oppressive to visitors. It is certain that Peruvians have felt the effects of their environment, but this has not prevented them from developing a history that can be described, without exaggeration, as troubled or even tempestuous. The country's history may be divided into precolonial, colonial, independence, and national periods.

The Pre-Inca Period

There are many theories about the origin of the "indigenous" Americans. Some say they came from Asia, via what is now the Bering Strait; others, that they arrived from Polynesia in balsa rafts or canoes five hundred or more centuries ago. The region that is now Peru was probably a landing platform from which the earliest arrivals made their way to other parts of the continent. In any case, it appears that this people was of either Upper Paleolithic or Neolithic Culture. Archaeological findings (in Lauricocha, Ancón, and Chivateros) have furnished proof that the land was inhabited ten thousand years before the Christian era. Further discoveries indicate

that the first groups either underwent a change or were
conquered by others. All that is known is that they tilled
the soil, built hamlets, wove rushes, molded rude pottery,
and erected altars and shrines. It is not clear what or whom
they worshipped.

The earliest culture seems to have been that of the Chavíns,
who came down from the sources of the Marañón River and
Cordillera Blanca in the west and spread over all of what is
now Peru. It is believed that they spoke a language called
Akaro, from which were derived Aymará—still spoken by
millions of Andean Indians—and other less used and now
extinct tongues. Their gods were the moon and the sun,
symbolized respectively by a fish and an eagle; the cougar,
or puma, symbolized a supreme being who held dominion
over the moon and sun.

The Chavíns cultivated the soil and dug irrigation canals.
An unknown cataclysm—an earthquake or a volcanic eruption—abruptly buried their culture, destroyed their temples,
and scattered the survivors. Legends about them were transmitted orally from generation to generation by their suc-
cessors and were collected many centuries later by the friars
of the Spanish Conquest. These legends have now been
partially confirmed by archaeology.

We do not know the period in which the Chavín culture
flourished, but carbon-14 tests indicate that its remains are
more than twenty-two centuries old. Neither do we know the
period of the Tiahuanaco culture, of which the only evi-
dences are majestic ruins situated on a lonely *altiplano* near
Lake Titicaca. From the skulls that have been found, we are
able to surmise that the Tiahuanacas practiced deforming
the head, probably by means of bands drawn around it in
infancy. Because it is not found in all the skulls, it is supposed that this deformation was a mark of distinction, a
sign of membership in the ruling class. Concerning their
religion, we know only that they worshipped a supreme
being, Wiracocha, to whom the tutelary deities—the condor,
the puma, and the serpent—were subject. All are sculptured
on the huge ruins, which have outlasted the memory of the
people that built them. In fact, even the name of the people

has not come down to us, for "Tiahuanaco" is an Inca name. Legend has it that, when an Inca king was visiting these ruins, a messenger arrived with such speed that the king, by way of praise, commanded, *"Tia, huanaco!"* ("Rest, *huanaco!"*)—that being the name of the swiftest animal then known.

These cultures had all become part of the past by the time a fleet of canoes with multicolored sails arrived on the coast. A chief and his followers—cupbearers, warriors, servants, and women—disembarked and, at what is now Lambayeque, near the city of Chiclayo, founded a temple to their god, Chot. This tribe, which archaeologists call the Mochicas, widened its dominions and taught the peoples it conquered gold- and silversmithing, pottery making, and weaving. But, according to legend, the demon, envious of this happy people, sent the monarch a wife who led him into vice. Angered, Chot hurled a rain of fire upon the Mochicas that destroyed them. Thus, the prehistoric "Peruvians" gave to a volcanic eruption the same explanation the Hebrews gave to the destruction of Sodom and Gomorrah.

The survivors were absorbed by the Chimús, whose capital was Chan-Chan, and of whose history whole centuries remain unknown. In the fifteenth century, the Incas came and conquered them, but they did not extirpate them, for the Spaniards later found groups of this people extant and were able to describe their arts and customs.

Another tribe flourished in the same period as the Chimús, but in a different part of the territory, near today's city of Pisco (on the coast, to the south of Lima). This people trepanned the skulls of their men, wove cloth of astonishing sheerness, and wrapped their dead in cone-shaped bundles for burial. Their culture is called Paracas, from the name of the bay near which many of the mummies have been found. The tombs found there were shaped like inverted cups and were usually built in caves. At some later period a change of style occurred, and this obscure tribe began constructing great necropolises—underground "dwellings" in which they left their dead wrapped like Egyptian mummies. Various cadavers have been found with skulls trepanned and with plates of silver and gold in place of the destroyed bone. No one knows whether this trepanation was done to live people, as a religious rite or surgery, or performed on corpses.

In the region of Ica, in the valley of the Grande River, there flourished the Nazcas, who spread over the surrounding valleys—over a territory that would contain any of the average-sized countries of Europe. Like the Paracas, the Nazcas left no great monuments. Instead, they left very beautiful tombs and ceramics—as well as canals and dams, which indicate that they must have been an agricultural people with relatively advanced techniques. A polytheistic tribe, the Nazcas were exceptional in that, instead of representing their supreme being as a star or an animal, they gave it a human form. They must also have been navigators, for they had a sea god and left, in a huge field, a series of gigantic geometric tracings that supposedly constitute an almanac—undeniably the largest in the world. Being well informed about the weather, however, did not protect the Nazcas against a series of internal rivalries that decimated the population and broke the territory into small dominions.

In what is now Lima and its vicinity have been found the remains of a tribe, probably of fishermen, called the Tribe of the Valley of Rimac. They buried their dead wrapped in matting and were apparently ruled by priests. Their sanctuaries and cemeteries have yielded crude pottery and textiles, as well as utensils of wood and bone but none of metal.

These various peoples, who lived in different eras, probably shared a legend that produced in time one of the most impressive pre-Inca monuments—the sanctuary of Pachacámac. The legend was that the god Kon, creator of man, disgusted by the vices of his creatures, changed them into cats and other black-furred animals and made darkness reign over the earth. But Kon's son Pachacámac took pity on the men who had been changed into animals and restored their human form. Moreover, to prevent their falling again into vice, he surrounded them with fertile valleys so that they might live with ease. To show their gratitude, the people raised a sanctuary to Pachacámac on the crest of a nearby hill. The monument has six platforms, and on the top one stands an enclosure that once contained the image of the benevolent god.

That these pages sound like a catalogue indicates the complexity of the many cultures in Peru that preceded the only one we really know through reliable witnesses. Books have been written about each of these cultures, and every museum has wings devoted to them. Condensing information about them into a few lines here may lead the reader to assume that they were of very small importance. In reality, the opposite is true, for every one of them lasted as long as any of the great Western empires.

The Incas

Legend also surrounds the origin of the Incas, the people who, by the time of the arrival of the Spaniards in the sixteenth century, dominated the survivors of all the other tribes. According to fable, two children of the sun, a brother and sister who were also man and wife, emerged one day from Lake Titicaca. They had been charged by the sun to found a city at a place where a bar of gold he had given them would bury itself. They journeyed many days until the bar of gold escaped from their hands and buried itself in the hill where the city of Cuzco now stands. There, the heir of the sun, named Manco Capac, taught men to become warriors and planters, while his sister-wife Mama Ocllo taught the women the household arts. But what developed was less poetic. Four tribes converged on what is now Cuzco and fought for supremacy. The one led by Manco Capac emerged victorious, founded the city of Cuzco, and ruled the other three tribes. The Inca empire was born.

The word "empire" is no exaggeration; for, given the vast amount of territory that they ultimately came to dominate and the many races over whom they held sway, what the Incas established, despite technological limitations, was indeed an empire. At the time of the Spanish Conquest, the Incas governed a territory of about 1.25 million square miles—four times the size of Spain. It included what is now Bolivia, the northern parts of Argentina and Chile, all of

Ecuador, and part of Colombia, in addition to Peru.

We lack the basic facts necessary for tracing the history of the Incas. It appears that they had fourteen sovereigns. These had symbolic names such as Manco Capac ("Mighty Chieftain"), Sinchi Roca ("Prudent Warrior"), Lloque Yupanqui ("Memorable Man of the Left Hand"), Yahuar Huaca ("He Who Weeps Blood"), and even so metaphysical a name as Mayta Capac ("How Far, My Lord"). There were three pre-Spanish dynasties, and, under the Spaniards, five nominal monarchs survived. Mayta Capac was the king who most fully extended the Inca dominions, and it was in his reign that they first reached the sea. Apparently, at some point, the people finally wearied of warlike adventures, and a revolution (perhaps only of the palace variety) took place that gave rise to the second dynasty, inaugurated by Inca Roca ("Prudent Lord"). Instead of making conquests, he dedicated himself to establishing schools and opening irrigation canals. But, two or three reigns later, the expeditions of conquest were renewed. This time, in advance of the warriors, *amautas*— whom we would call propagandists—arrived in the enemy territory and tried to persuade the peoples they planned to conquer to submit without a struggle.

The third dynasty which resulted from internal strife was concerned with administration rather than conquest. Rival camps arose when the brothers Huascar and Atahualpa fought a civil war over the throne. It was during this war that the Spaniards arrived, and they took advantage of the division to do away with the empire.

Little is known of the realities of the Inca empire, because the custom was to use what might be called "double historical bookkeeping"—a chronicle of heroic legends for the common people and a true and even critical history for the instruction of the ruling Incas. This duplicity was not confined to history, but extended even to language: the common people spoke differently from the governing classes, and the latter were able to communicate among themselves by using words of which the public was ignorant.

The basis of the society was the *ayllu*—a group of families united by consanguinity and by communal possession of land. The *ayllu,* with modifications, has survived colonialism and independence and still exists under the label of *comunidad* ("indigenous commune").

The land belonged to the Inca chief, but each member of an *ayllu* was entitled to a specific quantity of it (females to half of that); this land was not considered theirs, however, but the community's. The *ayllu* was much more than an agricultural commune. It really constituted the entire world of the peasant, a magic world in which there were local gods, baleful charms, and both harmful and propitious spirits. The protecting spirits lived on the nearest and topmost height, and the caves sheltered the spirits from whom the people of the *ayllu* descended. Today, we still find such beliefs among the inhabitants of the Indian communes.

The first Inca nation was a kind of confederation of *ayllus,* just as their empire, in the beginning, was a confederation of tribes dominated by the Incas. It was only with the third dynasty that imperial forms were adopted. During this time, too, the *ayllu* lost its autonomy and became an arm of the Inca chieftain's power.

As with all empires, that of the Incas had a religion that united the gods and beliefs of the subject peoples. Inti, or the sun, was the supreme god, followed in the hierarchy by Quilla, the moon; Illapa, the ray; and Mama-Pacha, the earth. The nobles kept a private cult of their own—that of Wiracocha, the old god of Tiahuanaco, who was considered to be the creator of the other gods relegated to the common people. "Be you whom you may be, Lord of Divination: Where are you?" was one of the prayers offered to Wiracocha.

For the people, religion was a trifle less metaphysical. They worshipped, first of all, the *huaca,* the founder of the clan or *ayllu,* and the *pacarina,* or genius loci of their *ayllu.* The dead were also worshipped: they were buried mummified, surrounded by goods and foods, and when a dead man had been a great lord, his servants were sacrificed, so that they might accompany him to the Uca Pacha, or inner world. There were several other central temples, all very rich, and many shrines and oratories. The walls were apparently covered with silver or gold leaf.

The Inca (name of a clan or, in this case, title of the chief, which by extension came to mean the people he governed) had every power—political, military, and religious. He was the supreme chief of the priests—although, in the period immediately before the advent of the Spaniards, this function was transferred to a different person, the Willac Uma ("Talking Head"), who was a magician and augur—and always a relative of the Inca. Subject to the supreme high priest were priests of various ranks, all diviners and magicians. For the worship of the sun (who was the god of the Inca's clan), women, called *acllas,* were chosen from infancy for their beauty and consigned to perpetual virginity of a sort: living immured in the temples of the sun, they kept the sacred fires burning, wove the Inca's robes, prepared his meals, and slept in his bed—for it was held that carnal relations with the Inca did not affect their virginity. The Inca's authority was derived from his status as child of the sun. In order to keep power within the clan, it was decreed that the Inca could marry only his sisters.

Animals were sacrificed to appease inimical gods. Sea shells were considered adequate substitutes for any gift or sacrifice, probably because they were hard to obtain. The calendar and the festivals were closely related to the land; there were ceremonies to give thanks for the harvest, to render tribute or homage to the nobles, to bring rain, and to ask for fertility of the earth and of women.

The Inca empire was divided into four great zones, corresponding to the four cardinal points of the compass. The population was divided into thousands and hundreds; at the head of each of these parts, there was a representative of the Inca, who was himself superintended by one of the various Tucuyricus ("Those Who See Everything"), the ears and arms of the sovereign. Only by the discipline these functionaries were able to impose can we explain the fact that, without the wheel, iron, or beasts of burden, the Incas were able to extend their dominion over such a great area—nearly double the Peru of today—in which, shortly before the advent of the Spaniards, there were about 6 million people.

Thanks to this organization, it was possible to carry

out such great public works as the paths that crossed the empire. The foot messengers, or *chasquis,* ran a kind of relay race along them, carrying the *quipus,* or knotted cords, that served as a means of communication, since writing was unknown. The knots were arranged in a code, from which the message was deciphered. There were two great roads—one along the coast and another through the Sierra—united by a series of paths from east to west. At the end of each day's journey, the traveler could find an inn or supply station. The *chasquis* went from Cuzco to Quito—about 1,250 miles—in only five days of relays. There were also many broad canals constructed, to carry the small amount of available water to arid places.

Interestingly, the Incas were the only indigenous people who built terraces on the mountainsides to make use of the land there. This peculiar practice may be ascribed to the scarcity of land rather than to the fear of erosion, because it is unlikely that the latter concept existed then. These terraces can still be seen by travelers passing through the Andes.

The social organization of the Incas has been termed socialist, but, in reality, it was a communal theocracy with a tinge of enlightened despotism. The land belonged to the Inca, who distributed a third of it among the *ayllus.* They had to pay what we would call their rent by working the remainder of the land, the second third of which was directly owned by the Inca—that is, by the state—and the final third of which belonged to the sun, or to the temples and priests. What the sun left was used to support the aged, the children, and so on. There was no family inheritance, since the land belonged to the community, and such personal goods as clothing and furniture were buried with their owners.

This organization was extended to the *mitimacuna,* or subjects of the conquered tribes, as well, who were made to learn Quechua, the language of the Incas that is still widely spoken in the Andes. Plainly, the peasant was a serf who owed his lord, or Inca, labor as well as armed service. While the nobles or warriors, who formed a separate class, constituted the army cadres, the ranks were filled by soldiers from the *ayllus.* Although in the cities there were some artisans in the service of the Inca, each peasant family produced what it needed: it wove its clothes and made its own tools, furniture, and other necessities. Maintenance of dominion over these people was probably aided by the Incas' custom of frequently uprooting and isolating conquered populations by ordering their transference from one region to another.

Education was confined to the nobility and was given at Cuzco. The common people received no education at all. There were specialists in teaching the use of the *quipus,* as well as specialists in poetry, in which the nobles were also instructed. This poetry could not have been written; it was transmitted orally, so that we know nothing of it apart from a few songs and fragments preserved by the Spaniards. Music and dance were subject to strict rules. Because the Incas used these two forms of artistic expression as means of communicating with the people, they had at once a ritual content and a political objective.

At the beginning of the fifteenth century, the empire had already passed the peaks of its splendor and was beginning to decline. Legend attributes this to the life of ease adopted by the Inca Huayna Capac, who was in love with a princess of another tribe. This couple's son was Atahualpa (1500-1533), Huayna Capac's second son. His first, Huascar, should have been the heir, but the Inca divided his empire between the two sons, and this led to civil war. Atahualpa defeated Huascar (d. 1532) but was overthrown, in turn, by the Spaniards, who put him in prison. He was the last legitimate Inca.

In reality, the empire's decadence had causes more profound than the brothers' rivalry for the throne. If the empire had had a healthy society, it is very probable that no civil war would have broken out. At any rate, there would have been greater ability to resist the invasion. But the society was no longer healthy. With the extension of the Incas' dominions, not only did hatreds spring up among the conquered tribes, but trade increased and the bureaucracy grew. As a result, there emerged what we would call a mercantile and bureaucratic middle class, which in time felt frustrated at the requirement of constant obedience without any share in the real power. This restive middle class expressed its discontent by taking sides with Atahualpa, who, because he was the pretender, offered a greater hope of change than the legitimate, and therefore more traditionally inclined, Inca. Thus the cause of the civil war was basically social.

The Conquest

In 1502, about ten years after the first voyage of Christopher Columbus, the Spaniards established themselves in Tierra Firme, as they named the point at which the Isthmus of Panama meets South America. They improvised little cities, which were sometimes besieged by the Indians, and organized expeditions of discovery, conquest, and trade. Although these expeditions had to be authorized by representatives of the Spanish crown, they were really private undertakings. An adventurer would persuade a capitalist—sometimes a priest, sometimes the agent of a Spanish bank, sometimes another expeditionary who had already become rich—to join forces and set about finding men for the expedition. Each expeditionary was promised a certain percentage of the profits—booty, land, or Indians—and the partners reserved for themselves not only the command of the expedition but also the major share of the profits.

In 1513, Vasco Nuñez de Balboa discovered the western ocean, which he named the Pacific. He hoped to go toward the south, where it was said there was a very rich empire. But he was accused of treason by the governor, who was envious of his success, and was beheaded. Francisco Pizarro (1470? -1541), one of the twenty-six men who had been with Balboa when he discovered the Pacific, remained in Panama. For several years, he listened to tales of a fabulous region, Peru (which, in actuality, was the region of the Virú River, much farther north than present-day Peru). In 1522, Pascual de Andagoya set out with an expedition to the fabulous region, but he fell ill and had to return to Panama.

Pizarro decided to undertake what Andagoya had failed to accomplish, and in 1524 he formed a partnership with the cleric Hernando de Luque (d. 1532) and another soldier, Diego de Almagro (1475?-1538). In November of that year, they set off, but the expedition was attacked by Indians at one stage and had to return to the isthmus. Pizarro, however, who did not wish to enter Panama, waited for Almagro to return with reinforcements. The latter was also attacked by the Indians, and one of his eyes was put out by an arrow, after which everyone called him El Tuerto ("The One-Eyed"). Finally, the expedition was resumed with 160 men and one ship. They had crossed the equator and, disillusioned, were about to turn back when they captured an Indian vessel laden with cloths and objects of gold. Pizarro remained with his men on the Isla del Gallo, and Almagro returned with the ship to Panama to seek reinforcements. The governor, disappointed over the expedition's failure, ordered Pizarro to return and, to see that his orders were carried out, sent a lieutenant. When Pizarro heard the message, he drew his sword, traced a line on the ground, and said to his men, "This way you'll go to Peru to be rich; that way, to Panama to be poor. Let any good Castilian say which would be better for him." Thirteen soldiers followed him.

After six months of wandering and suffering, they reached what is now the port of Guayaquil. The inhabitants, astonished by the white skins, the beards, and the horses, submitted without resistance. It appeared that the expedition had been successful. Some of the Spaniards remained to live with the Indians, and some went back to Panama with Pizarro and the two native youths he took with him.

When Pizarro returned to Spain, Carlos I appointed him governor of the new-found land, which was called Peru (because of the mispronunciation of the name of the Virú River), or New Castile. Almagro was named *adelantado,* which was the title given to the governor of a border zone (some of whose lands had not yet been explored), and Luque was elevated to bishop. They prepared for a new expedition. Upon arriving in the New World, the explorers founded San Miguel—today called Piura—in the northern part of present-day Peru. They left their ships there, and, having learned of the existence in the Sierra of a ruler who had an army, Pizarro climbed the Andes.

In November, 1532, Atahualpa, who had finally defeated

his stepbrother Huascar, was taking his ease at the baths of Cajamarca. When Pizarro arrived there, he invited the Inca to come see him. The emperor was no doubt surprised by such a haughty visitor, but, perhaps frightened by what he had heard of the earlier conquest of Guayaquil, he agreed to go and meet Pizarro. He was received by a priest who showed him the Gospels and began talking to him about Christ. The Inca, angered by what he considered lack of reverence—according to Inca ritual, no one was allowed to speak to him without asking permission—struck the priest and dashed the Gospels to the ground. The priest then ordered the soldiers to attack the blasphemer, and the Spaniards opened fire. Atahualpa was dragged from his golden litter and taken prisoner. Pizarro, mindful of the consequences, protected the Inca against a group of soldiers who wanted to kill him, and was wounded in doing so. The rest of the conquest is, so to speak, a matter of record. The Inca empire had come to an end; headless as well as divided, it could have no hope of successful resistance. From prison, Atahualpa ordered his followers to execute Huascar, whom he had made a prisoner shortly before he himself had been taken captive by the Spaniards. This prompted Huascar's supporters to join with the Spaniards. In exchange for his own freedom, Atahualpa offered to fill two rooms with gold as high as his head. Pizarro agreed, but once the ransom had been paid, he accused the Inca of assassinating Huascar and plotting an insurrection. Atahualpa was condemned to be burned alive, but, since he had been baptized, the sentence was commuted to strangulation, which took place in 1533.

With his chief enemy out of the way, Pizarro marched to Cuzco, which the Incas called the "navel of the world." Not feeling powerful enough to oppose the people, he sought instead to neutralize them by naming another Inca—a brother of Atahualpa, who died shortly thereafter on the march. Pizarro quickly replaced him by another Manco Inca (1500?-1544), and went on to found the city of Jauja, in a spot so fertile that even today the Spanish phrase *"estar en Jauja"* is the equivalent of "to be in paradise," to feel completely happy.

In January of 1535, Pizarro arrived at a pleasant valley, where he founded the city of Lima on the banks of a river called Rimac by the Incas. There he persuaded his associate Almagro to march toward the south—today's Chile—and to conquer the people there. In this way, he got rid of a possible rival, since Almagro was more popular than Pizarro among the men.

Manco Inca was not as subservient as the Spaniards had hoped he would be. He escaped from Cuzco and, to the cry of "Into the sea with the bearded ones!," led a revolt. Cuzco and Lima were besieged, but Pizarro emerged victorious and Manco was assassinated in 1544 by a Spaniard to whom he had given asylum.

The country was conquered. What remained now was to explore it. Gonzalo Pizarro (1506-1549), brother of the expedition's leader, marched as far as the site of Quito, believing that he would find the fabled Eldorado. But, as the jungle journey had exhausted them, Francisco de Orellana (ca. 1490-1596) built a brigantine and commenced coasting the rivers in search of food. In this way, he discovered the Amazon and traveled down the river to the Atlantic Ocean. Fever and hunger caused him to have hallucinations, in which he saw the mythical Amazons—single-breasted women mounted on horses.

Meanwhile, Almagro had returned to Cuzco after exploring the lands north of Chile. Ambitious for power, he imprisoned Pizarro's two brothers, Hernando and Gonzalo, the latter upon his return from Quito. He then marched on to Lima, where Francisco Pizarro exchanged Cuzco for his brothers' freedom. But, in 1538, the struggle between the two factions was renewed, and Almagro was defeated, tried, and beheaded.

Almagro's supporters were eager to avenge their captain. Pizarro had left them in such a wretched state that they were living in one large tumbledown building and, with only one cape among them, had to take turns going out into the streets. Finally, in 1544, they made a surprise attack on the palace and killed Francisco Pizarro, then a marquis, by stabbing him in the throat with a dagger.

The Almagro faction was not triumphant for long, for the

court sent over a viceroy. There was a battle in the Sierra, in which Almagro el Mozo ("Almagro the Younger"), son of the beheaded captain, was captured. He suffered the same death as his father.

At last, there was peace among the Spaniards. They had land, and the Indians that lived on it made it productive. But the Council of the Indies, established by Carlos I to legislate for the new colonies, abolished Indian slavery and created the system of *encomiendas,* under which the care of the Indians was entrusted to the Spaniards with the object of protecting them and making them work for the person who received the charge.

The conquistadors did not resign themselves to the loss of their Indians. Gonzalo Pizarro, named captain general by the conquistadors, overthrew the viceroy sent by the court and cut his throat. But a new viceroy was more resourceful; he won over Pizarro's soldiers, and the deserted captain general was thus captured and put to death in 1549. The conquest, and the wars among the factions of the conquistadors, had lasted eighteen years. Finally, Peru entered upon a period of peace. From this time on, for two and a half centuries, it had scarcely any history.

The Colony

The Spanish colonies were organized in viceroyships: that of New Spain (Mexico) and that of New Castile (Peru). Within each, there were captaincies general and *adelantados,* as well as archbishoprics and *audiencias* ("territorial courts"). The king promulgated the laws, as they were proposed by the Council of the Indies seated in Seville. In that city there was a *casa de contratación* ("board of trade") in control of the commerce between Spain and the Indies, which by law was limited to a few ports in America (the one in Peru was Callao, near Lima) and to Seville and Cadiz in Spain. Emigration was limited to Castilians; foreigners and Jews were excluded.

As in the rest of the colonies, the church not only converted the Indians to Christianity but, until the seventeenth century, defended and protected them. Nevertheless, the Indians in Peru found themselves in a worse situation than

those in New Spain. This was undoubtedly because the conquistadors chosen by Pizarro were a more adventurous and
greedy group than those of Hernándo Cortéz in Mexico.
Racial integration in Peru was much slower and much more
limited than in Mexico. In Peru the Spaniards mingled less
with the Indians, and *mestiźaje* ("mixture of blood") pre-
vailed among smaller groups of the population. Today, there
is a much higher percentage of *mestizos* among the Mexican
population than there is in Peru. The difference was still
greater in the colonial period.

Naturally, there was a steady disappearance of the native
cultures. We know about them through ruins and exhuma-
tions by explorers, especially in the last century, and through
the chronicles of the Spaniards themselves. At the same time
that they were destroying the native cultures, the Spaniards
were trying to preserve in writing the memory of what they
had seen. By royal order, each expedition had to include a
veedor ("inspector") who was supposed to keep a journal
of the adventure. There are chronicles of the conquest, such
as those of Miguel de Estete, Pedro Pizarro (written in his
old age), Pedro Sancho de la Hoz, and various others. Other
archaeological and geographical records are devoted to de-
scribing the customs of the Incas; for example, the work of
Pedro Cieza de León (1518-1560). Finally, there are chronicles we may label polemic; some were written at the behest
of the viceroy Francisco de Toledo (ca. 1515-1584), an
implacable governor who ordered the execution of the last
Inca, Tupac Amaru (1544?-1571)—for which he was later
punished by Philip II. Toledo directed that the Indians live
in villages under colonial control and brought in the Inquisition. Later, other chroniclers appeared, a number of whom
were *mestizos* seeking to refute the "Toledans."

The Viceroyship of Peru, organized in 1542, comprised,
at the beginning, all of South America except Venezuela and
the Portuguese colony of Brazil. Then, in the eighteenth
century, came the creation of the viceroyships of the Plata
(Argentina and Uruguay) and of New Granada (Colombia and
Venezuela). There were forty viceroys—from the first, Blasco
Nuñez de Vela (d. 1546), who was overthrown by Gonzalo

Pizarro and had his throat cut by the latter's order, to the last, José de la Serna (1769-1833), who lost the decisive battle of Ayacucho to the independent forces and signed the surrender by which Spain recognized the independence of her South American colonies.

As the representative of an absolute monarch, the viceroy enjoyed absolute authority but was responsible to the tribunal of the royal *audiencia.* He was also head of the land and sea forces; but, when his appointment came to an end, so did his immunity. He had to write an account of his stewardship and was subject to the so-called *juicio de residencia,* a sort of impeachment hearing set up by the Council of the Indies, before which all who had grievances against the viceroy might appear. Finally, the council either approved or disapproved of the performance of his duties—and disapproval was by no means rare, for several viceroys went from the castle to the jail. Neither the viceroy nor the members of the *audiencias* were allowed to acquire property in the Indies or to make contracts.

The viceroy could scarcely have any voice in economic matters, which were in the charge of the Tribunal of the Consulate, a kind of bank that received deposits of money and made loans. The interest from these loans was earmarked for charity. The tribunal likewise controlled trade with the metropolis as well as the system of taxation. Taxes were, as a rule, rigid and high, and their collection served as the cause of most of the rebellions marking the three centuries of colonialism. In an effort to protect the Indians from the colonists, the crown established the office of *corregidor* ("magistrate"); but, in reality, the *corregidors* almost always took the side of the *encomenderos.* Not until Carlos III replaced them with *intendentes* ("directors") in 1783 was a modicum of respect won for the laws that protected the Indians.

In the social structure of the colony, the lines of race and class were parallel because the society had, after all, been established by immigrants and imposed upon the autochthonous population. At the top of the structure were the Spaniards, who, ever since the generation of the conquistadors, had been functionaries of the crown. Below them were the Creoles (*criollos*), children of the Spaniards, who were born in America and lived and died there. They formed a white aristocracy, although there were great differences of caste and fortune among them. Their ranks included great landholders, personages of the church, intellectuals, artisans, merchants, and even some peasants who owned small farms or ranches. They could not, however, assume public office above the local level, and this was a cause of resentment.

Even greater resentment was felt by the *mestizos,* who formed the bloc we now call the middle class—artisans, small landowners, and petty merchants. Offspring of Spanish men and Indian or *mestizo* women or of *mestizo* couples, they formed the bulk of the population in many regions. In other areas, however, the Indians, or the *mestizos* who shared the Indians' lifestyle constituted the majority. The *mestizos* had no voice in local government, and, of course, none in the general government either, although many were bureaucrats or were in the lower echelons of the army and clergy. Among them, especially toward the close of the colonial era, were many families that had become wealthy. In regions with a Negro population, there were also mulattos, but, because of the social stigma of slavery, they were more sharply segregated than the *mestizos.* Another type of exploitation was carried on in the workshops where wool was woven; the Indians worked in them under extremely hard conditions. Although this first local industry did not prosper—for the Spaniards and the Creoles preferred to wear textiles imported from Spain—there were important workshops in Lima, Puno, and Jauja.

At the bottom of the social structure, as the basic producing groups, were the Indians of the Sierra and, later, the Negroes of the coast. They had no share in government and found themselves legally disadvantaged under the tutelage of the authorities and the church (a tutelage that often constituted a means of supplementary exploitation). The Indians had to pay tribute—the collection of which caused numerous rebellions and local uprisings. Besides being subject to the *encomienda* system, they were collected into *mitas*, groups subject to compulsory service in the villages and employed in road and church construction, mining, and similar activities—a de facto tribute of labor. The Negroes were slaves (although, in the eighteenth century, there were a good many freedmen), and, while it may be true that they were given a measure of legal protection, in reality they were treated merely as property—except when they were domestic slaves. Then, owing to the closer relationship that developed with their owners, and particularly with the latter's children, they were accorded some consideration.

Thus, there were plenty of reasons for discontent: the practical impossibility of filling official posts for the Creoles; the lack of social mobility among the *mestizos* and the mulattos; the rigid exaction of exhausting tribute from the Indians; and the abject condition of the Negro slaves. The French and English pirates more than once entertained the hope that this discontent would yield them allies in their incursions into the coasts of the viceroyships, but they were deceived. Instead of open arms, they met fierce reistance, not just from the authorities but from the Creoles and the population in general.

In the seventeenth century, discontent provoked by the Spanish commercial monopoly—which prevented the enrichment of the Creoles and furnished great opportunities to smugglers—reached a peak. A series of rebellions broke out and developed into the movement for independence. This movement was not to be appeased by the measures of modernization ordered between 1760 and 1790 by the Spanish court, especially under Carlos III. Such measures included the creation of *intendencias,* the dispatching of inspectors to receive the complaints of the people, the expulsion of the Jesuits, the suppression of the *encomienda,* and even an abortive project to make the monarch's sons the kings of the viceroyships, to form a kind of community of Spanish-speaking kingdoms.

The life of the colony, however, was generally placid. The chief events, except for the rebellions and the attacks of the pirates, were the struggles between the viceregal and ecclesiastical authorities. In the seventeenth century, the city of Lima had twenty-two convents, twelve monasteries, and four houses of retreat for laywomen. There were religious orders of Dominicans, Franciscans, Mercedarians, Augustinians, and Jesuits. Many of the members of these orders were dedicated to study and teaching; others, to missionary activity. The church was powerful, and Catholicism, with its pompous ritual, was the common religion; but, among the Indian masses, old pre-Columbian beliefs persisted beneath the Catholic ritual. But Indian beliefs and practices were not the prime object of the Inquisition, which was established in Lima in 1579. The chief targets were captured Protestant pirates, possible heretics—Judaizers and Protestants—and, later, the rationalists, who were influenced by the French Encyclopedists.

In the eighteenth century, the monotony of colonial life was varied now and then—at least among the cultivated groups in the cities—by scientific expeditions. The Frenchman Charles Marie de la Condamine came to Peru to measure the arc of the meridian at the equator. The Spaniards Jorge Juán and Antonio Ulloa studied the flora and fauna and reported to the king on conditions in the colonies. The Frenchman Aimé Bonpland collected more than six thousand plants in Peru. The German Baron Alexander von Humboldt visited the viceroyship and described it in detail. A number of Peruvian Creoles were also prominent in scientific activity, among them Hipólito Unanúe (1755-1833), who founded the school of medicine in Lima and fought against the belief that the American races were inferior to those of Europe.

While scientific expeditions were fostering the propagation of rationalist ideas among the cultured nuclei of society, discontent was growing among the masses because of profound disappointment with the reforms ordered by the Spanish court. This disappointment found expression in a dramatic rebellion of the Indians in 1780, when José Gabriel Condorcanqui (1740-1781)—who claimed descent from the Inca emperors, had an education from the *colegio* in Cuzco, and was *cacique* of several villages—decided to put an end to the abuses of a local *corregidor*, Antonio de Arriaga. After capturing de Arriaga and ordering his execution, Condor-canqui raised an army of six thousand Indians and led it against Cuzco. The Indians, believing him to be a new Inca, gave him the name of Tupac Amaru. After a year of battles, however, he was overthrown, captured, and put to death after being forced to witness the quartering of his attendants and lieutenants.

All Peru had been shaken by news of the rebellion. Other similar rebellions in what is now Bolivia and the north of Argentina were suppressed after long and bloody struggles. Meanwhile, the Creoles were also protesting. In Peru, these protests did not assume the intensity of those in Paraguay and Colombia, but they convinced the Spanish authorities that the time was drawing near when they would no longer be able to maintain order.

Independence

In 1808, King Ferdinand VII was carried off to France by Napoleon, who had invaded Spain. To maintain loyalty to the king and to rebuff Napoleon, whom many called the Antichrist, gubernatorial juntas were organized. The viceroy, José Fernando Abascal (1743-1821), who was old and shrewd, reinforced the army and crushed such juntas, not only in Peru but also in the north of Argentina and Bolivia, Ecuador, and Chile. While the partisans of independence—who had by now ceased to mention Ferdinand VII—were having success in Colombia, Venezuela, Chile, and Argentina, in Peru they were reduced to organizing conspiracies that were constantly being detected. Several conspirators were executed and many were imprisoned. There were some uprisings (in Tacna and Huanaco, for example) that were also suppressed. When two Limeños were appointed representatives of the viceroyship in the Spanish Cortes, or Parliament, which had reassembled at Cadiz in opposition to the Napoleonic forces, celebrations were organized, and an attempt was made to take advantage of them and capture the viceroy by surprise. But the plot failed. Abascal, despite his years, assumed leadership of an army when a new uprising was set afoot in Cuzco by the Indians—who succeeded in capturing that city and also La Paz, the capital of present-day Bolivia—and crushed that rebellion.

The Cortes at Cadiz had abolished the Inquisition and proclaimed freedom of speech. Many gubernatorial juntas abandoned the king and declared the colonies independent. But Peru, center of the colonial authority in South America, remained loyal to the crown; as long as royal troops remained in command there, none of the new countries could consider its independence assured.

In 1820, José de San Martín, the Argentine general who had freed Chile, organized an expedition to Peru. Lima was besieged by land and sea; finally, on July 9, 1821, San Martín entered the most prosperous city of the Indies. On the twenty-eighth, Peru's independence was proclaimed.

San Martín assumed the title of protector and became the head of the new state. He leaned toward the establishment of a monarchy, but the Constituent Congress decided in favor of a republic. After a meeting in Guayaquil with Simón Bolívar, the liberator of Venezuela, Colombia, and Ecuador, San Martín decided to withdraw. Laden with honors and titles, he left the country in 1822.

The Constituent Congress named a governmental junta (council) which was finally ousted after defeat in several battles. The ousting of the junta was the first case of militarism in the new country; it had been demanded and carried out by a group of military leaders.

The president who succeeded the junta, José de la Riva Agüero (1783-1858), obtained the support of several of Bolívar's generals. Lima was threatened by the royalist troops, and the Congress took refuge in the fortress of Callao in the city's harbor. Bolívar arrived in 1823, only to find the Congress and the president at loggerheads, alternately ousting each other. When the royalists took possession of Callao, the situation became grave, and the Congress appointed Bolívar dictator.

The Peruvian independent forces defeated the royalists in the battle of Junín—which was fought by the cavalry with lance and sabre—and at Ayacucho. When that battle ended in December of 1824, the viceroy (Abascal had been succeeded by José de la Serna) signed the capitulation, which recognized Peru's independence and that of the other regions of his viceroyship.

The country was independent; what remained was the difficult task of organizing it. The people were divided; most of the Creoles and the middle class were happy with independence, but many Indians, who looked upon the king as their protector against exploitation by the Creoles, had fought with the Spanish forces and were willing to continue the struggle. The rich Creoles wanted political change, but many of the middle class, inspired by the Encyclopedists and the revolutions in North America and France, wanted social change as well. The history of Peru, from 1821 to the present, is the story of the struggle between these two concepts—the strictly political (advocated by the great landholders) and the social (advocated by the middle class and, on occasion, the Indians).

The Republican Era

As soon as independence was secure, Bolívar marched to Upper Peru where he organized the country that is now Bolivia. A Constitution proclaimed him president for life. The Peruvian Congress adopted the same constitution and similarly proclaimed Bolívar president. But many who had taken part in the struggle for independence were dissatisfied, and they took advantage of a visit Bolívar made to Colombia to abolish the constitution and depose him.

The new leaders tried to intervene in the affairs of neighboring countries—first in Bolivia, from which one of Bolívar's lieutenants, Antonio José de Sucre, was forced to flee before the Peruvian army; then in Gran Colombia (a country formed of what is now Ecuador, Colombia, and Venezuela), this time under the pretext of a disagreement over borders and debts for the war of independence. A Peruvian squadron occupied Guayaquil, but was defeated, and when peace was signed in 1829, the Peruvian president was ousted.

During the six years that followed, there were several presidents—sometimes more than one simultaneously—and a short "civil war." Not a shot was fired; for, when the two armies met, the soldiers embraced and deserted their leaders. Finally, in 1835, Felipe Santiago Salaverry (1806-1836), a romantically inclined young soldier, seized power. But one of his opponents, Luis José de Orbegozo (1797-1847), who had been elected president, won the support of the Bolivian president, Marshal Andrés Santa Cruz, and defeated Salaverry, who was tried and executed. As the price for Bolivian aid, Orbegozo agreed to form a confederation of Bolivia and the three states of North, Central, and South Peru. Santa Cruz became president of the new confederation, while Orbegozo continued as president in North Peru. Santa Cruz encouraged the formation of a navy, reorganized the army, and tried to establish an administration that would replace what was left of the colonial system.

The Chileans were alarmed, and, in December of 1836, Chile declared war on the confederation, using as a reason some assistance that had been given to an exiled adversary of the Chilean president. Two expeditions composed of exiled Peruvians eventually triumphed, and the confederation was broken up. Augustín Gamarra (1785-1841), who had commanded the expeditionaries, assumed power in 1840 and ordered that a new conservative constitution be drafted. He declared *guano* a public asset—in other words, he nationalized it—and established the first steamship lines. But, fearing that Santa Cruz would return to Bolivia, he invaded that country, only to be killed in battle. Two presidents arose to fill the vacuum created by Gamarra's death, and a brief civil war ensued, followed by a period of autocratic governments and constant disorder. Finally Marshal Ramón Castilla rebelled, and, after several battles, established control over the country in 1845. He governed for six years with little opposition. During his presidency, he established the first state budget, obtained steam-propelled ships for the navy, founded intermediate and high schools (but not elementary ones), and built the first railway in South America, which extended from Lima to the nearby port of Callao. Finally, he reorganized the exportation of *guano* to Europe. Political elements profited by this period of order to create the country's first liberal and conservative parties. Castilla left office in 1851, but under his successor José Echenique, the country was beset by several financial scandals. In 1854, Castilla overthrew Echenique and once again assumed the presidency, this time as leader of the Liberal party. During his second term in office he abolished slavery, suspended the payment of tribute by the Indians, and obtained approval of a liberal constitution. In 1859, Castilla personally led an expedition of Peruvian forces to Guayaquil, Ecuador, to settle a boundary dispute, and he occupied the city until a peace treaty was signed in 1860. In 1862, his second term came to an end.

Miguel San Ramón, who succeeded Castilla, died in office in 1863 and was succeeded by the first vice-president Juan Antonio Pézet. Shortly after he had been sworn in, Pézet found himself involved in a strange conflict with Spain. In 1864, a Spanish squadron arrived at Lima to demand the payment of a debt claimed by Spanish subjects for property destroyed during a minor riot. When the Peruvian government refused to receive the squadron's envoys, the fleet took possession of the islands along the coast. In 1865, the government negotiated a treaty with Spain, but this angered a number of military men who were against any payment to the Spaniards. Col. Mariano Ignacio Prado (1826-1901) staged a coup in Arequipa, the southern city in which most of the military revolts occurred, and proclaimed himself supreme head of the republic—a title adopted before and after him by most of the dictators.

The neighboring countries—Chile, Bolivia, and Ecuador—alarmed at the presence of the Spanish squadron, allied themselves with Peru, and, in 1866, declared war on Spain. After two indecisive naval engagements, the Spanish squadron was forced to withdraw. Once the danger was past, Prado was ousted by a new *pronunciamento* in Arequipa.

In 1872, after the assassination of another military president and a coup, Manuel Pardo (1834-1878), founder of the civilian party and the country's first bank, became the first non-military president. Opposed by the army, he was able to assume the presidency with the support of the navy. During his four years in power, he had to suppress twenty-eight *pronunciamentos.* After his term expired, Pardo became president of the Senate, but was assassinated when Mariano I. Prado—promoted meanwhile to general—again assumed the presidency.

Pardo had signed a defensive alliance with Bolivia. In 1879, Bolivia claimed a duty on the exportation of nitrate from Antofagasta, a coastal region that, at the time, was Bolivian territory. Protesting on the grounds that the nitrate concessionaires were Chileans, Chile sent troops to occupy the region. When Peru offered to mediate, Chile invaded her territory, too. Discontent was aroused when General Prado went to Europe to buy arms for a war with Chile. Nicolás de Piérola (1838-1913), founder of the conservative Democratic party, took advantage of the situation to have himself proclaimed supreme head. He had made two previous unsuccessful attempts to seize power.

In 1880, the Chileans occupied Lima, and Piérola withdrew his forces to the Sierra; a civilian government was formed in the occupied territory, and Piérola resigned. Finally, a peace was signed, by whose terms Peru lost a part of her southern territory, and Bolivia lost her route to the sea via Antofagasta.

After a succession of military presidents, Piérola managed to have himself elected in 1895. During his four years in office, he was able to attract foreign capital, stabilize the economy, reorganize the demoralized army, and begin expansion toward the *selva.* He also established civilian supremacy. The military men had lost so much prestige in their defeat by Chile that they were unable to oppose several consecutive civilian presidents, who turned out to be generally good administrators, although none succeeded in carrying out the social reforms that the country needed.

Actually, the great mass of Peruvian people—the Indians—remained subject, in effect, to the same institutions they had endured before the coming of independence; some, it is true, had been abolished, but enforcement of the laws favorable to indigenes was rare. In Lima, Arequipa, and a few other cities, the textile industry had begun to develop, as well as some light industry. Mining began to develop increasingly in Cerro de Pasco and other regions (nearly all of which are at very high altitudes). Thus, there emerged a proletariat, composed of artisans replaced by machinery (although skilled labor remained the principal source of production of everyday articles), of peasants transplanted to the cities, and immigrants. (Peru, however, because of her isolation, was not one of the countries to which great currents of immigration flowed; before the Panama Canal opened, Peru could be reached only overland, via the Isthmus of Panama, or by sailing around Cape Horn.) This first proletariat was soon organized into unions, under the direction of a group of anarcho-syndicalists, among whom the ideological influence of the Spanish anarchists was strong. But strikes were forbidden, and the unions, which were illegal, were often persecuted by the police. Peru needed agrarian reform that would convert the Indian masses into citizens, and social legislation that would protect the workers. But neither Democrats, civilians, nor the military *caudillos* had any doubts about the prevailing social system of agrarian feudalism. Soon, however, there would be forces and movements demanding change.

These movements began to develop under one of Peru's toughest and most effective presidents, Augusto B. Leguía (1863-1932), a businessman, who, after serving as minister of finance, was elected president in 1908. He promoted industry, improved the customs system, and brought about other reforms, but in doing so, he incurred the ill will of many politicians. A year after he had taken office, he was kidnapped from the presidential palace. Ransomed by the army, he completed his term and then went abroad.

In 1914, militarism again reared its head when Colonel Oscar R. Benavides (1876-1945) seized power. This was an unprecedented move for a colonel, since palace coups had been carried out in the past only by generals. The Congress promptly elevated him to general and proclaimed him provisional president. He called an election and turned power over to an elected civilian, who established the eight-hour day and recognized the unions.

In 1919, Leguía returned and was elected president. Fearing that he would not be allowed to take office, he seized the palace by force, dissolved the Congress and launched the slogan "New Fatherland," under which he sought to change the political but not the social system. Although he drew up a new constitution, he governed as a dictator. He suppressed all opposition and did not hesitate to deal harshly with students when they began demanding university reforms. When he tried to have the Sacred Heart of Jesus enthroned as "Protector of Peru," violence erupted in the streets; nevertheless, he managed to have himself reelected in 1924. Leguía founded banks, built highways, repaired ports, and settled the frontier problem with Colombia and Chile. But his regime became more and more a police state, and when he sought reelection for a third time in 1930, Luis M. Sánchez Cerro (1899-1933) led an uprising in Arequipa. Leguía handed power over to a military junta, which then sent him to prison, where he died.

Modernization

The end of Leguía's dictatorship saw the birth of a series of parties, the reorganization of the unions, and the establishment of the APRA (Alianza Popular Revolucionaria Americana—American People's Revolutionary Alliance), a movement founded in 1924 by the former student leader Víctor Raúl Haya de la Torre (1895-   ) when he was in exile. Its ideology, which has had considerable influence on other Latin American populist movements, attracted many intellectuals, isolated the Communists (who had founded a party of their own some years earlier), and reached the Indian masses, who, for the first time, heard mention of their rights. From now on, Peruvian politics would revolve around the problem of either putting the APRA into power or keeping it out. Meanwhile, the country was to go on being modernized, at least as far as the cities were concerned.

The military junta soon found itself threatened by an uprising of naval officers, which it successfully put down; its power was subsequently assumed by two successive juntas. In 1931, elections were held with Sánchez Cerro and Haya de la Torre as the candidates. The count of votes was altered when it became obvious that Haya had received a majority,

and Sánchez Cerro was proclaimed the victor. He immediately began a campaign against the APRA, and this led to
the imprisonment of Haya until 1933. In the same year,
Sánchez Cerro was assassinated in Lima's Hippodrome. His
term was completed by Benavides, who tried to pacify
popular opposition by declaring amnesty for political prisoners and granting a measure of freedom to the press. But his
military supporters urged continued suppression of the
APRA, which they regarded as a "party of assassins." The
army had never forgiven the fact that several officers were
killed when a group of Apristas rebelled in Trujillo in 1932.
Haya, as leader of the party, was considered personally
responsible for the incident, even though he was absent
from Trujillo at the time.

In the 1936 elections, Haya was again a candidate, but the
APRA was immediately outlawed. The Apristas then gave
their support to the Democratic candidate, Luis Antonio
Aguiguren (1887-   ), who won. But because he had re-
ceived Aprista votes, his election was annulled and Congress
prorogued Benavides' term. Finally, in 1939, with the APRA
still outlawed, the engineer and banker Manuel Prado (1889-
) was elected. During his term of office, Peru and
Ecuador agreed to have the question of boundaries arbi-
trated; the result was the Protocol of Rio de Janeiro of 1942.
Persecution of the APRA continued almost until the end of
World War II, in which Peru, though declaring war on the
Axis, did not take part. Peru's participation in World War I
had been confined to breaking off relations with the Central
Powers.

In 1945, the candidate of a hastily formed Democratic
Front, José Luis Bustamante y Rivero (1894-   ) was
elected with Aprista support. He restored the APRA's legality
and appointed several of its leaders to his cabinet. But, in
1948, alarmed by Aprista pressure for reform, he reorganized his cabinet to exclude the party's members. This
move, however, backfired; for, without their support, he
could not check a revolt by General Manuel Odría (1897-
1974), who had been his minister of the interior. Odría
headed a military junta until 1950, when he had himself

elected president. He bore down hard on the Apristas, whom he accused of being Communists—even though the Communists, who supported him, had themselves criticized the Apristas with blind fury. Haya de la Torre thereupon took asylum in the Colombian embassy; it was five years before Odría finally granted him safe conduct in compliance with an order by the International Court at The Hague.

Odría's term ended in 1956. Although still outlawed, the APRA indirectly took part in that year's elections by supporting Manuel Prado, the only candidate who promised it political coexistence. Despite his persecution of the party during World War II, Prado now had embarked on a policy of political pacification, and, if the Apristas were willing to forget the past, so was he.

But, by giving him its support, the APRA—which, following Odría's election, again became legal—drew critical fire from the young members of the extreme Left. It met the challenge head on, and ousted the Communists from the unions they had led with Odría's backing. In 1962, the party offered Haya as its candidate in that year's elections.

When it became apparent that Haya would win, the army staged a coup, ousted Prado, and set up a junta. There were no reprisals, and the junta called an election in 1963. The architect Fernando Belaúnde Terry (1912-   ), whom the candidate Haya had defeated the year before, was elected president. He governed against the opposition of the APRA, which allied itself in Parliament with the supporters of General Odría, who had also been a presidential candidate. The APRA's alliance with Odría's supporters damaged its prestige, but it did not lessen the party's hold upon the masses.

In October, 1968, a series of smuggling scandals involving military and government figures which the APRA refused to allow the government to ignore led to another military coup. General Juan Velasco Alvarado (1917-   ) emerged as chief, and the new junta's first act was to expropriate the International Petroleum Corporation, which was disputing the government over back taxes. Although this was the junta's pretext for the coup, it realistically can be attributed to the military's fear of having its high chief's involvement in the scandals exposed, and to the fear that the APRA's candidate would emerge as the winner in the elections scheduled for June, 1969.

From 1956 to 1968, Peru became considerably industrialized. There were fiscal reforms, Parliament passed a moderate agrarian reform law proposed by APRA, the unions became stronger, and industry grew. But the vast majority of the people still had no share in the government or in the nation's wealth.

Just as the history of Peru, since her independence, has been the history of the struggle for power among rival factions of the oligarchy, so its future history will probably be that of the struggle of the new elites to keep the masses isolated and submerged. That, however, and the role of the military junta of 1968 will be discussed later.

4

An Unshakable Political System

Peru has had fewer political vicissitudes than other Latin American countries. There have been no civil wars waged over federalism versus centralism, since the centralist tendency has predominated from the beginning. Neither have there been civil wars over relations between church and state, since, except for brief periods of liberalism, it has always been admitted that the Peruvian state is Catholic. Civil wars in Peru have involved very small armies and have been brief and personality-oriented. Theoretically, the system has been democratic ever since independence, but the practice of democracy is sui generis; even the most unbending dictators have had themselves elected after holding power for a time.

As heir of the two highly centralized Inca and Spanish empires, Peru was from the beginning a centralized state; all attempts at decentralization have failed. Municipal autonomy is very weak, and politicians have looked upon it as a disintegrative factor. Peruvian politicians have regarded the country as being so varied, so heterogenous in its geography, ethnology, and economy, that they have almost always considered it essential that the state counter the centrifugal tendencies produced by this diversity. Today, there is no one who does not consider centralization best suited to the country.

The Constitutions

Since becoming independent, Peru has had twelve constitutions: those of 1823, 1826, 1828, 1834, 1837, 1839, 1856, 1860, 1867, 1868, 1919, and 1933. Today, although the constitution of 1933 is technically still in force, it has been suspended by the military government that assumed power in 1968.

These frequent changes of constitution—not untypical of Latin American history—had two causes: first, the nature of many dictatorships, and, second, the bitter rivalry between the liberals and the conservatives. Since, ideologically, there were no appreciable differences among the various dictators, the only way each could mark his personal rule was by promulgating a new constitution of his own. Similarly, when the liberals and conservatives followed each other in power, they preferred drawing up a new constitution to merely amending the existing one; although, in the latter case, the reason for doing so was more basic. For there were three principal areas of difference between liberal and conservative constitutions: in civil rights or guarantees, which were fuller in the liberal constitutions; in the relations between church and state, liberal constitutions providing for separation between the two; and, finally, in the disposition of immediate interests, such as the length of the president's term, decentralization, and the greater or lesser influence of Parliament. But, no matter what their tendency, the basic elements have been identical in all the constitutions. Religious liberty, however, was recognized for the first time in 1915, thanks to a constitutional amendment.

All Peruvian constitutions have been presidentialist. Of the three traditional powers—executive, legislative, and judicial (to which some constitutions, like that of 1933, added the electoral)—the executive, personified by the president, is the strongest.

There have been brief periods, however, in which Parliament has made itself felt. This has been the case particularly when there have been parties of distinct ideological content. In the last thirty years, APRA, which has often been close to being a majority party, has given Parliament a mission of censure and initiative which had not often been previously exercised, even though it figures in the constitution. Thus it can be said that before the 1968 coup, the Peruvian system was presidential but modified by an active Parliament. This distinguishes Peru from the rest of Latin America where the systems are presidential with more or less passive parliaments (except Chile, sometimes Argentina, and Costa Rica).

In addition to being presidentialist and centralist, all Peruvian constitutions, even if democratic in name, are in fact elitist. All limit the right to vote. An example is the denial of the franchise to illiterates. In a country where a high percentage of the adults are illiterate—80 percent or more in certain rural regions—this is equivalent to restricting the vote to the urban population (and not all of that) and to the politically privileged: the skilled working class, the middle class, the bourgeoisie, and, of course, the upper class. Elections by constitutional mandate have never reflected the will of all Peruvians.

Under the most recent Peruvian constitution, written in 1933, the president of the republic is the titular holder of the executive power and personal representative of the country. He is politically self-sufficient (that is, he does not have to give an account to Parliament) and, during his term, may be accused only of treason, impeding parliamentary or presidential elections, having dissolved the Congress or impeded its meeting, or having impeded the functioning of the national electoral board. Obviously, the constitution endeavors to protect the legislative power; yet, in the time it has been in effect, there have been several military coups, and none of the instigators have been accused of these crimes. The president is elected for six years, by direct and general vote of all citizens (native or naturalized) over twenty-one years of age, illiterates excepted. All presidential candidates must have been born in Peru, have the right to vote, be over thirty-five, and have lived continuously for ten years in national territory. The president may not be reelected at the end of

his term, but may not be elected again after another president's term has elapsed.

His cabinet is composed of ministers, whose number, however, is not fixed. They are responsible to the Congress, and,
if this body censures them by majority vote, they must
resign. Peru is one of the few Latin American countries with
the office of president of the council, or premier. The ministers are responsible as a group for any unconstitutional
acts on the part of the president—unless they resign immediately—as well as whatever presidential acts they endorse.

The requirements for ministers and deputies are the same.
No member of the judiciary or of the clergy may be named a
minister, although members of the armed forces may. Traditionally, the minister of defense is a military man. Besides
naming his ministers, the president designates functionaries,
diplomats, and so forth; the armed forces are subject to his
disposition, although he is not their head; and he directs
international relations. If, for any reason, the Congress delays
in carrying out its duties or fails to convene, he may govern
by decree. There are two vice presidents, elected at the same
time as the president.

The Congress is composed of a chamber of deputies,
elected by direct vote, and a senate, elected by universal
suffrage on a regional basis. The last chamber of deputies
(dissolved by the military in October, 1968) was composed
of 156 members; the senate had fifty-two. All enjoy parliamentary immunity—that is, they may not be arrested or tried
without the authorization of their respective chamber.

The constitution anticipates the existence of a consultative economic council, but none has been designated. In
June, 1950, a consultative mission from the United States—
the Klein mission—recommended that this council be established and function as a planning agency, but the recommen-
dation was never put into effect, and the planning bodies
created by the executive power, in 1964, were solely technical and administrative in character.

The constitution also provides that the municipalities be
headed by elected councils; yet, the first municipal elections
in thirty years were held in 1963.

The judicial power is independent. The Supreme Court, seated in Lima, is composed of 11 judges and 4 prosecutors. There are nineteen superior tribunals (courts of appeal), with 156 judges and 42 prosecutors. The judges of the Supreme Court are designated by the Congress on the basis of lists presented by the government, but the dictators have not hesitated to change them at will. The judges of the superior tribunals, as well as those of the courts of petty sessions, are appointed by the government from lists furnished by the Supreme Court and the superior tribunals, respectively.

Finally, there is a national electoral jury, or committee, constituting, in effect, a fourth independent power. Its members are appointed by the Congress. This jury—on which also sit representatives of the various parties that have candidates—establishes rules, in each election, to guarantee the fairness of the voting. Its decisions concerning the validity and results of the elections are not subject to appeal. Voting is compulsory for all citizens of both sexes from ages twenty-one to sixty, with the exception of illiterates. Women were granted the right to vote by constitutional amendment in 1955.

In emergencies, the constitution permits the executive branch to suspend constitutional guarantees, after submitting a report to Congress and asking its approval. At such times, most of the civil rights provided by the constitution are suspended. Generally, when the military stage a coup, their first act is to suspend constitutional guarantees—almost as a matter of course—by declaring a "state of siege," which often lasts as long as the military remain in power. Since, in such event, Parliament is usually dissolved, with the president either in exile or under house arrest, the means to legalize such a move disappear; and force becomes law.

The Administration

The Peruvian bureaucracy is diffuse and complicated, like all Latin American bureaucracies. In recent years, the normal administrative system has acquired, through the ministries, a series of more or less autonomous branches, dealing specifically with petroleum, agrarian reform, and so forth.

The country is divided into twenty-three departments, each of which is headed by a prefect. The departments themselves are divided into provinces—a total of 144—with a subprefect in each. In turn, the provinces are divided into districts, of which there are 1,616, each with a governor. These offices are designated by the president. There is also a so-called constitutional province, in Callao, with departmental functions but without any subdivisions. There are 78,274 population centers, governed by municipal councils that were elected only from 1963 to 1968. Foreign residents of a town are eligible to vote and to fill posts in the municipal council.

The national unit of currency is the sol. Legally, the golden sol weighs .421264 gram, but none has been coined for many years. The common coins are of base metal. The national flag has three vertical stripes—red, white, and red. The national anthem, which dates from 1821, is *"Somos Libres"* ("We Are Free").

The budget is prepared by the president and approved by the Congress—a requirement ignored during dictatorships. The government's income, of course, is derived from taxes—sales taxes, customs and tariffs, taxes collected through monopolies, and various indirect taxes. There are almost no land taxes in Peru.

Military service is obligatory and theoretically universal, but only a limited number are drafted—mostly from among the poor. The term of service is two years. The country is divided into five military districts. There are about 35,000 soldiers, to whom must be added 18,000 police, civil guards, and republican guards (the latter are responsible for guarding the prisons). The police force is national, and is responsible to the minister of government, although the municipalities may have their own city police. The navy consists of 7,500 men. It is composed of four submarines, two cruisers, two destroyers, and thirty-seven smaller units. The aviation department has three combat groups; in addition, there are training and transport systems and six military airfields. Recently, several French Mirages have been added to the stock of planes.

It is not unusual, when Chile acquires planes or vessels, for the Peruvian armed forces to demand the purchase of planes or vessels of the same type—and vice versa. In this way, there is a perpetual arms race between the two countries, explained, in part, by memories of the war between them and, in part, by the desire of the armed forces to show their influence over the national government.

On the whole, the Peruvian administration is rather cumbersome and antiquated. The bureaucracy is poorly paid; many government employees work only a half day and spend the other half at a different job. Although minor employees remain in their posts after a change of administration takes place, the number of high-ranking officials replaced by every new president is proportionately much greater than it is in the United States.

International Relations

Constitutionally, the president of the republic directs international relations. But he is subject to two decisive influences: on the one hand, that of the raw material exporting interests (*guano* in the past, minerals and fish meal, today); and, on the other, that of the armed forces, which bring pressure to bear for newer and better weapons and which, at certain times, have urged an armed settlement of border problems.

There are two constant factors in Peru's international policy, as there are in that of any other Latin American country of any importance: fear of the neighboring country, or the wish to make the neighbor country feel such fear; and the presence of some foreign power that is looked upon as a menace.

Peru is one of the Latin American countries that has been involved in the most foreign wars—with Bolivia at the beginning of its national existence and then with Chile and Spain. Its border disputes with Colombia and Ecuador have come close to war. The memory of this history, always present in the armed forces, whose officer cadres receive a strongly nationalistic education, leads the army to think constantly in terms of competition with Chile—the nearby country

that has a military strength most nearly comparable to
Peru's, and which, in the nineteenth century, severely defeated Peru. It may be said that, in certain traditional military
circles, and possibly in those of very young elements, known
as progresistas ("progressives"), there exists an unacknow-
ledged desire to retaliate for this defeat, which military men
resent as if it were of recent occurrence.

Not a few Peruvians still resent the fact that Chile and
Argentina opposed the confederation of their country with
Bolivia, which, in retrospect, is viewed as having offered
Peru the possibility of extending its frontiers toward the
heart of the continent, with the same boundaries as the
Spanish viceroyship.

This resentment is much greater, at least among the educated, than that felt toward the ancient mother country. In
Lima, for example, there is a statue of Pizarro right beside
the Palacio Nacional; and the colonial past, which left mag-
nificent works of art, especially in architecture, is regarded
with pride. In Peru, Spain is still referred to by many people
as the "mother country." Spanish cultural influence persists
partly because Peru is considered the typical Catholic, conservative country of Latin America—that is, the one that has
tried the hardest to keep alive the values of the colonial
epoch. But that has not kept Peru from entertaining a long-
standing attitude of mistrust toward postcolonial Spain.

Peru's participation in the various attempts to coordinate
the Latin American countries—from the Panama Conference
called by Simón Bolívar in 1828 to the various conferences
of the Pacific countries—can be attributed to her desire to
win alliances or support in the event of Spanish aggression.
Following the short war with Spain in 1866, however, this
threat appeared to diminish, especially after the peace treaty
with Madrid in 1879; the loss, in 1898, of the last of Spain's
American colonies caused the threat to vanish completely.
Since then, Spain has never been in any condition to intervene—at least by force of arms—in the affairs of her former
American possessions.

Although Great Britain made considerable investments and
opened credit to Peru in the nineteenth century, which led

to some conflicts, no tense situations with London ever materialized. On the contrary, the tensions that did occur were with the United States, although it was then far behind Great Britain in investment in Peru and only in the twentieth century became an important factor in Peru's economy.

In the last half century, relations with the United States have been the axis of Peruvian foreign policy. These relations have been generally called amicable, although not entirely free from resentment and friction. The first time the United States intervened in the affairs of Peru was during the latter's conflict with Spain. Washington informed Madrid that the occupation of Peru by Spain would prejudice Spain's relations with the United States. Not long afterward, Peru signed a series of contracts with an American citizen, Henry Meiggs, to build railways in the Andean zone; but this required so much capital that, in 1876, the country suspended payments on its foreign debt.

At the beginning of our century, the Grace Company and the Cerro de Pasco Company were formed in Peru—the first concerned with shipping and mines and the second, with copper mining.

These and other American enterprises, after some initial conflict with the government (during which the mines were put temporarily under state control), succeeded in obtaining privileges equal to those enjoyed by the British investors, in having extended one of the railways Meiggs was building to the mines. Negotiations were carried out by the American legation. The influence Washington had acquired in Peru was also evident in the diplomatic field. For example, Peru was one of the first countries to recognize Panama.

During World War I, Peru broke off diplomatic relations with the Central Powers after the sinking of a Peruvian vessel by German submarines. But it was during Leguía's second term (1920–1930) that the United States acquired real influence in that country. Before becoming president, Leguía had represented some American and British interests. He favored American investments and could rely on active support and sympathy from the United States government and the great American firms. He issued many bonds on the

American market and gave important concessions to American mining interests, especially oil firms, under conditions
that are still a source of conflict.

During Sánchez Cerro's dictatorship, the United States
maintained a policy of watchful waiting. American diplomats
were completely unaware of the growing influence of the
APRA among the masses—although it was an American citizen who, at his own personal risk, concealed Haya de la Torre
when the latter was being harassed by the police. Sánchez
Cerro broke off relations with Mexico when that country
aided some Apristas who were fleeing the police, and perhaps
to punish the United States for its neutrality, Sánchez Cerro
decreed a limit of 20 percent on the number of foreign
employees in any foreign firm.

Sánchez Cerro's successor, Marshal Benavides, was accused
of having supported the economic and even the political interests of the Axis powers, but this was never proved. When
Benavides relinquished the presidency, American influence increased. His successor, Manuel Prado, lost no time in accepting
President Roosevelt's Good Neighbor Policy and signed agreements with the United States for the sale of cotton, linseed,
and rubber on conditions highly favorable to Peru. Peru
entered World War II in 1941 on the side of the Allies, but
the country did not take any active part in the struggle.

The sympathy for Washington and American investors that
had become widespread under Prado was somewhat re-
strained under Bustamante, probably because he owed his
election to the APRA, and because he had, for a while, two
Apristas in his cabinet. This, added to the postwar business
recession, created an atmosphere favorable for a coup by
Odría and the military. The latter, who bore down harshly
on the APRA, enjoyed the favor of American businessmen
and diplomats, who failed to realize (or did not wish to see)
that the Communists had also supported the dictator and
opposed the APRA. Odría received important aid that
enabled him to modernize the army and keep the officers
contented. One of his first acts was to ask the United States
to send an economic assessment mission (the Klein mission) to Peru; but when it did, he did not follow any of its

recommendations concerning social matters.

In view of this, it is not surprising that anti-Americanism (stirred up by the Communists, who, although officially outlawed, were free to propagandize under Odría) found violent expression during Vice President Nixon's visit in 1958. Nevertheless, relations between the two countries were not dampened. In 1962, when the military staged a coup to block Haya's triumph, President Kennedy refused to recognize the military regime and cut off aid to Peru until the junta called new elections. It was thanks largely to American influence that the coup became the first in Peru's history not followed by reprisals.

There was another military coup in 1968, but this time recognition of the junta by the United States came swiftly. A delicate situation arose when the junta expropriated the property of the American-owned International Petroleum Company (IPC). Washington would have invoked the Hickenlooper amendment to the foreign aid measure—which provides that aid be withdrawn from any government that expropriates American holdings without compensation—but, when the military regime allowed IPC to appeal to the Peruvian courts, Washington accepted this as equivalent to negotiations for compensation. As a result, the junta was deprived of an effective means for winning public approval though an open confrontation with Washington.

Relations between Peru and the United States are now cordial, despite the military's deep resentment of the United States' refusal to sell it jets in 1968, forcing it to turn, instead, to France. However, the military junta has not refrained from giving obvious support to the many anti-American campaigns in the country. This ambiguity is reflected, too, in its dealings with American business: while expropriating IPC's holdings, on the one hand, the government signs accords with American oil and mining interests, on the other.

In international organizations, especially in the United Nations, Peru has generally voted in line with Washington's diplomatic policy. Several Peruvians hold high posts in the United Nations, and former president José Luis Bustamante y Rivero is a judge on the International Court at The Hague. Peru is also a member of the World Bank, the International Monetary Fund, and the Inter-American Bank for Development. Peruvian delegates to the Organization of American States (OAS) have also usually supported the position of the United States; this was especially true in the case of Cuba until 1972. In that year the junta, in a show of diplomatic independence, suggested that Cuba be readmitted into the OAS, and when the suggestion was rejected, reestablished diplomatic relations between Lima and Havana.

The Peruvian diplomatic corps is not a highly professional one. Frequently, posts are held by politicians whom the government is anxious to keep out of the country; by poets or artists it wants to treat as protégés (or to isolate); and by friends of the president. In recent years, however, there has been a tendency toward the gradual creation of a career diplomatic corps. It is too soon to say whether this will continue under the military government that took over in 1968.

Political Mores

What the constitution and the laws prescribe is one thing; the way political life develops is quite another. One's name, prestige, family, and wealth can modify the application of the law, which the high cost of justice makes unequal. The same inequality is found in military life. The sons of the rich and, in general, those of city families serve less frequently than do the sons of peasants. As for education, there are few schools for the children of peasants and slum dwellers. Most of the students still come from the upper middle class, although in recent years admission to the university has been made easier for the children of the working and middle class.

In the past century, the political struggle was between personalities supported by oligarchic families. Many parties were formed to support particular candidates. An ideological party organized along modern lines only appeared with the development of the APRA; but even in the APRA the influence of the founder is preponderant. Recent years have seen the emergence of parties which, although still somewhat personalistic, have shown a tendency to survive between elections. At least this was the case before 1968, when the military coup deprived the parties of any possibility of winning power.

Elections were usually rigged. The *caciques* of the villages (strong men at the bidding of the administrators of big *haciendas,* or of political parties that offered them the most) decided which candidate was to carry their district or region. Campaigns ran into difficulties when they were for opposition candidates not acceptable to the local *caciques.* And, of course, the mass of Indians, being illiterate, did not have the right to vote. Only in cities, and among the middle class and organized workers, were there elections in the true sense of the term.

The electoral process itself is relatively clean. When voters cast their ballots, the back of their hands or their fingertips are marked with ink that remains indelible for several hours, so that they can vote only once. The army usually watches the polling places, to prevent the breaking, substitution, or disappearance of the urns containing the ballots.

In former years, the church had considerable influence on elections. This is still true in certain very backward regions. The unions do not really pressure their members to vote for a particular candidate, but through their influence with their membership union leaders contribute many votes to chosen parties, mainly the APRA.

One element that the voters always take into account and that limits their freedom of choice is the army. Often voters who would have given their ballots to a certain candidate (Haya de la Torre is a concrete example) have given them to another, knowing that, if their preferred candidate were elected, the army would only stage a coup to prevent him from taking office. Masses of citizens take part in electoral campaigns when it is felt that the elections will be clean, and rallies attended by 50,000 or more are not unusual. Participation in the voting, however, is not very high. In the last elections held—those of 1963—the country had somewhat fewer than 10.5 million inhabitants. Half were not old enough to vote. Of the other half, only 2.3 million had registered—913,600 in Lima.

The Political Parties

In the first half of the nineteenth century, liberals and conservatives struggled for power whenever it was not held by the military. Then these groups left the field to the Civilians and Constitutionalists (whom we today would describe as centrists) and the Democrats (whom we would call rightists). At the end of the century, Manuel González Prada (1848–1918) tried to form a regenerationist party, the National Union, which failed but greatly influenced later generations.

Most of the parties of this century have been personalistic; that is, they have arisen around individuals during campaigns and administrations. To combat this tendency, it was decreed by law that a party must have a minimum of 60,000 members in order to enter a candidate for the presidency and 20,000 to enter candidates for other offices. Small parties can form electoral coalitions to attain these figures.

There were Pradistas (friends of Manual Prado), the partisans of the Miro Quesada family (ultraconservatives and owners of an influential newspaper), the adherents of Pedro Beltrán (1897–   ), a centrist and newspaper owner. After the fall of General Odría's dictatorship, a party of his supporters was formed. The centrist Party of Popular Action (Acción Popular), whose language was technocratic and leftist, was formed around the architect Fernando Belaúnde Terry. The Social Christian party (Christian Democrats) was divided over two different personalities.

All these parties are favorable to political changes (more or less democracy and freedom, more or less reform of the administration), but all accept the status quo and do not seek any change in Peru's social structure. At best, they offer timid agrarian reforms—awarding lands to the peasants, but retaining the large latifundia. Since these parties have no body of doctrine, as such, it is impossible to describe their ideology.

The Marxist groups of various leanings are, of course, much more doctrinaire. Most important is the Communist party, descended from the Socialist party founded in 1928 by the writer José Carlos Mariátegui (1895-1930). Much of its activity has consisted of struggling against APRA, for it believed that, so long as the latter remained influential, its own influence would be severely limited—as has, indeed, been the case. Having collaborated with the Odría dictatorship and having criticized the United States for not supporting the dictatorship of 1962, the Communist party now backs the military regime of 1968.

The Communist party, which remains faithful to Moscow's line, is influential only among intellectuals, students, and some sections of the middle class. It has not infiltrated the peasantry, and it has managed to control only for a time a few workers' unions. It knows how to make capital out of anti-Americanism, particularly among the young; but it has lost a large segment of its student following, who now consider it part of the establishment.

Various small groups have separated from the Communist party (the Trotskyites before World War II, the Titoists and Maoists, among others, after), but none has succeeded in forming a strong party. The Trotskyites have instigated guerrilla warfare in connection with peasant agitation in the Cuzco region, and their leader, Hugo Blanco, was put in prison in 1966 as a result of such activities. A group of Apristas who seceded from the APRA—which they considered conservative—also engaged in guerrilla activities under Luis de la Puente Uceda; most of them were killed in battle. Less activist than the organizations mentioned above are the numerous small groups—Neo-Marxists, dissident Christian Democrats, Maoists, Guevarist-Castroites, Fidel-Castroites, and so forth. Their membership includes intellectuals, and they publish books, manifestos, and weeklies. This gives the impression that the movements are extensive, but they are actually more verbal than organizational.

Among political groups we must include various factions of the armed services that, especially in recent years, have taken ideological stands. For example, there is a group of young officers from the higher military academy who are more or less Marxist. We must also take into account several factions of industrialists who hold technocratic views. Many such industrialists have collaborated with the present junta.

Finally, there are the progressivist Catholic priests who, although they do not participate directly in politics and are not affiliated with any of the parties, nevertheless have some influence, through their writings and sermons, both among the youth trying to organize the slum dwellers and among peasants. Generally, they support the concepts of the New Left. These concepts are not based on classical Marxism, but on the writings of Ché Guevara and Régis Debray concerning the importance of guerrilla activity for creating revolutionary situations, formulating the program of a revolution, and forming a party to lead it. Although many of the New Left collaborate with or support the 1968 military regime—because its elitist and paternalistic tendencies agree with theirs, and because it is anti-American—some denounce what they call the "demagogy of the military."

The Case of the APRA

Much more important than these groups and, in fact, than any other Peruvian party, present or past, is the APRA, often called, simply, the People's Party. In 1918, a strike broke out in a textile mill in Lima over the demand for an eight-hour day. As a gesture of solidarity, a general strike was declared. On the initiative of their leader, Victor Raúl Haya de la Torre (1895–   ), son of a landowning family in Trujillo, the students who were agitating for university reform attended a union meeting and then persuaded the minister of the economy to accept the workers' demands for an eight-hour day. The strike had succeeded. The students then organized *universidades populares* (people's universities) in the local unions and taverns of the workers' districts, among other places. From the strike arose the Textile Federation—still the most powerful union in Peru—and from the people's universities sprang most of the future union and APRA leaders. Shortly thereafter, the Leguía dictatorship began, and Haya de la Torre was forced into exile. From Mexico, he set forth his idea for the APRA—a movement of continental dimensions, which would be the first attempt, not only in Peru but in all Latin America, to look at the realities of that continent with Latin American eyes rather than through the prism of imported European ideologies. This accounts for the great effect that Haya's ideas have had. They have since been adopted, in their general lines, by a series of movements that may be called populist or leftist-democratic (Acción Democratica of Venezuela, Febrerismo in Paraguay, the PRD of the Dominican Republic, Liberación Nacional of Costa Rica, and others).

According to Haya, imperialism in Latin America is not the final stage of capitalism, as Lenin held, but the first. It becomes dangerous because the oligarchies of the various countries open the gates to it. The best way to combat it, therefore, is to combat the local oligarchy with parties that include all classes (peasants, intellectuals, students, the middle class). The parties should seek the aid of liberal elements in the United States, and should have as their goal the union of the Latin American peoples in a supranational body. Agrarian, fiscal, educational, and other reforms must be made, and the masses must be allowed to participate first in the party and then in government. Basically, the idea calls for a revolution that will establish a democratic form of capitalism.

In 1930, when Haya de la Torre returned to Peru and founded the Peruvian APRA, he met with immediate success. Haya ran for the presidency against Colonel Sánchez Cerro, but when it became apparent that he was about to win, the election was falsified. Then came a period of harsh repression, during which the Communists joined in attacking the APRA; then another campaign, again voided when it became clear that the candidate supported by the APRA was going to win; followed by another period of repression, and still another campaign, in which an outside candidate (Bustamante) ran, and won, with Aprista backing; and, finally, a third period of repression. All this meant a constant growth in the prestige for the APRA—and also many years of prison or exile for its leaders and militants, as well as a significant number of tortures and assassinations during the years of repression.

In 1956, a third outside candidate (Prado) won with Aprista support. Haya himself was victorious in 1962, but a military coup prevented his inauguration; in 1963, he was defeated by a narrow margin; and, in 1968, to keep him from winning the approaching election, a new coup was staged. Probably the oligarchy would not have been able to block the APRA's triumph by merely political means at any time after 1930. The army took charge, on the oligarchy's behalf, of closing the doors of power to the APRA.

Their constant frustrations have not been without consequences. The APRA has remained faithful to its program, and has modified its tactics where necessary, always with a view toward appeasing the military and finding support that would permit Haya to win the presidency. The leadership of the APRA has grown old in the double activity of building these bridges (which always, however, at the last moment, have proved useless) and of maintaining the adherence of the masses (in which it has succeeded, although not without some loss of influence among the youth and the intellectuals). In its years of struggle, the Aprista movement's democratic character has become more marked, and its revolutionary character has been softened. Today, many consider the APRA a left-center party and not, as in earlier years, a party of the extreme Left. Although the military government of 1968 was aimed against the APRA, the regime has not forbidden the party to remain active. As a result, the APRA is today the most powerful force in Peru opposed to the military—more, it must be admitted, by propaganda than by action—and continues to demand a return to a democratic system.

In its brief periods of influence in the cabinet or in the Congress, the APRA has brought about the passing of significant reforms, the modernization of the labor laws, and so forth. But none of this has satisfied its more activist elements.

What is exceptional about the case of the APRA is that it is the first Latin American party that has arrived at the threshold of power without achieving it, yet has continued to be active for more than three decades without losing its unity or the adherence of the masses. It was also the first Latin American party to reach the public at large and to mobilize the masses. In this respect, few others have surpassed it. Although it is personalistic, in the sense that Haya's decisions are respected by all, the APRA is a party of the masses; its activists organize party schools and head unions, cooperatives, universities, and so on—always having before their eyes the interests of the party, and knowing how to speak the language of the people. To a certain degree, the APRA accomplished, in the service of democratic ideals, what the Communists wanted to do but were unable to do in Latin America, in the service of their own ideology. The APRA organization is always functioning—not only at election time—and reaches out to all parts of the country, although the north—called by the Apristas "the solid north"—is its strongest and most secure base. Most union leaders are Apristas; and the Apristas still exert a good deal of influence in the universities, although from time to time some student groups have dissociated themselves to move farther to the left or right.

No one can say whether the APRA will be rejuvenated, whether the military will succeed in eradicating it, or whether it will end triumphant. But, in any event, it is undeniable that in the last quarter of a century all Peruvian politics have revolved around the APRA.

The Pressure Groups

The concept of pressure groups implies the existence of a center, subject to pressure, that functions as an arbiter between different groups. In Peru, this center, rather than being an arbiter, is controlled by what in another country would be one of the pressure groups—the landholders. The pressure of the various groups is, actually, exerted upon the oligarchy, although the body responsible for receiving it directly, on the oligarchy's account, is the government. At least, that was the situation up to the time of the 1968 military coup. Even when there are anti-oligarchic elements in the government, they must pay so much heed to the interests of the oligarchy—which is capable of unleashing a military coup at will—that, in fact, they are indirectly controlled by it.

This oligarchy that controls the government is no abstraction. Informed people know the families of which it is composed—owners of great stretches of land, who look down on the Indians and *mestizos*, frequently reside abroad, and meet socially at Lima's Union Club. It does not control the government directly in any crude fashion—as, for instance, by having members in it. On the contrary, its control is subtle: the politicians know that the oligarchy is able to incite a military coup and always take its interests into account when making decisions. The oligarchy thus exercises a kind of veto power, not only because of its wealth, but because it has always been accepted that the government should never do anything opposed to the oligarchy's interests, under pain of being overthrown. Nowadays, there are two branches of the oligarchy: that of the Sierra—owners of vast haciendas, traditionalists who form a closed society and send their profits abroad or reinvest them in land (although they have now virtually ceased to do so); and the oligarchy of the coast—politically more liberal and more modern, a group of owners of plantations (some mechanized) who put their money into industry and banking. So, today, we have a banking-landholding oligarchy.

The principal pressure group, since it has force at its disposal, is the army. Traditionally, it has been in the service of the oligarchy—defending it, arbitrating its internal rivalries, and preventing the rise of its adversaries. But the army does not view its function in this light. It regards itself as the defender of law and order, of "Christian civilization," and identifies the latter with the social status quo. Of late, however, anti-oligarchic tendencies have arisen in the army; they played some part in the 1968 military coup. The army does not have elements of the oligarchy in its ranks; its leaders and officers come, in general, from the middle class. Many are *mestizos*, and the oligarchy "seduces" them by a kind of social snobbery. But it does not take them to its bosom. For example, the dictator General Manuel Odría, a *mestizo*, never succeeded in being admitted to the Union Club, even when he occupied the presidential palace. Deeply rooted in the army is the sense of hierarchy and promotional rank, and military coups can almost always be carried out without violence, since those who order them are men in military position to do so—the minister of defense, the chief of staff, and so forth.

The church is also a pressure group—less important than in other Latin American countries, to be sure, but less divided today than in many of them. The Peruvian church has always been on the side of the oligarchy, refusing to support liberal reforms that might deprive it of its property; yet it has retained a considerable hold over the masses, particularly the Indians of the Sierra, who practice a syncretic Catholicism with holdovers from Inca beliefs. Although there are progressives among the young priests, and although some bishops have given away lands and have been critical of the reigning social system, most of the Peruvian church is still very traditionalist. But, in general, it keeps aloof from active politics, although this also means that it does not condemn military coups.

The bankers complete the picture of the pressure groups that we may call favorable to the status quo—that is, those that do not put any pressure on the oligarchy—but collaborate with it to resist pressure by other groups. Peruvian banking had its origins in foreign banks, especially British. But, at the end of the last century, and especially in the last fifty years, native banking has developed, closely linked to the landholders of the coast, strongly supported by the state, and exercising considerable influence upon economic and political life. These banks control a large part of the exportation of raw materials. They do not take part openly in politics, but there is no politician who ignores their influence or slights their counsel.

In recent years, younger elements calling for change and modernization have caused a split in the pressure groups. To some degree, they have done this under pressure from other groups. The latter, who may be classified as opposed to the status quo, include the industrialists (especially young ones) grouped in professional societies; engineers and technicians, usually unorganized but with a strong and quite common elitist and technocratic outlook; and professional men, organized in official, professional colleges. Besides protecting its special interests, each of these groups exerts pressure for moderate structural reforms in such fields as the administration or education. Irritated by the presence of North American competitors, the members of these pressure groups have become anti-American, which, generally speaking, they were not some years ago (many of the technicians and industrialists, after all, have been trained in the United States).

The workers cannot organize as much pressure as the above groups. Relatively few, scarcely half of those in the important cities, are organized. The labor union movement is organized in three federations. The most powerful is the Confederación de Trabajadores del Perú (Confederation of Peruvian Workers), or CTP; until World War II it was Communist-controlled, but today it is firmly in the hands of leaders affiliated with the ORIT (Organización Regional Interamericana de Trabajadores—Regional Inter-American Organization of Workers). A branch of the International Confederation of Free Union Organizations, its secretary-general for fifteen years was Peruvian. The other two federations are smaller: one, organized in 1968 by the Communists, is supported sub rosa (as we have said) by the military regime; the other, organized by the CLAT (Confederación Latino-Americana de Trabajadores—Latin American Confederation of Workers), takes a very radical stand but has little strength. Unlike those of many Latin American countries, Peru's labor federations have undertaken to organize the peasants and farm workers; each, for instance, has its own peasant federation, although the only one of real influence is that which adheres to the CTP. The labor union movement, though strongly politicized, usually keeps aloof on fundamental political questions, especially during a military coup, in the hope that it thus will gain the respect of the military establishment (although experience has shown that, in the long run, the latter respects only Communist-controlled unions). The principal pressure exerted by the labor union movement is confined to questions that directly affect the workers—wage policy, social security, working conditions, and the like.

The peasants exert double pressure, although it is somewhat weak. On the one hand, there is the pressure of the labor federations, in conjunction with the peasant federations; on the other, there is the pressure of the agrarian communes, or *comunidades* (the old colonial *ayllus* somewhat modernized and, in some Andean regions, organized into cooperatives), thanks to the activity of Aprista elements. Pressure by these groups is confined to matters that affect them most directly and is rarely extended to those of more general interest.

There is one more pressure group that, as in all Latin American countries, seems strong, because of its activity and spectacular methods, but is actually weak—the students. Students organize into sections of the different parties and compete among themselves for positions in student associations, and thus in the administration of the university, where they have a voice; they are remarkably energetic in their protest activities. The guerilla activities of the recent past were spurred on chiefly by students, and what little active opposition the military government of 1968 encountered came largely from the student population. The latter also feeds the New Left group.

Finally, there are the intellectuals. In Latin America, the term "intellectual" is applied to writers and artists, to actors and journalists, outstanding professional men and professors. Little organized and politically splintered, the intellectuals are generally leftist, in a widely varied degree, and very energetic in their protests, although those hardly ever go beyond the manifesto and declaration stage. But, because of the respect accorded them in a society where culture is still a privilege, the intellectuals are able to exert some influence, especially during constitutional regimes, which must depend on public opinion; dictatorships usually despise the intellectuals and crack down on them if they get too troublesome. The students and the intellectuals are profoundly anti-American (anti-imperialist, they say), and, in this, they agree both with the pressure groups within the reformist bourgeoisie and with the oligarchic traditionalists.

Except for the peasant and labor movements, these pressure groups have an elitist concept of their role; they see themselves called on due to their economic strength or their knowledge; and they feel that it is they who must decide for the great mass of the public. But these elites have little contact with the mass public and only a superficial acquaintance with it, and the public does not know much about them or pay much attention to them. The masses can exert pressure only through political parties, chiefly the APRA; but their influence diminishes every day because of the aging of the parties, which have been steadily losing their power to attract younger people.

Each of these parties and pressure groups claims to represent the public or a part of it, but none of them (except the APRA in the past and still, to a degree, today) bothers to go to the public and organize it. The absence of the public from the political process is the result of the Peruvian political system, which, although it has assumed different forms through the centuries, has remained unshakable: until 1968, actually, it has been a system constantly controlled by the oligarchy regardless of who was in office. An examination of the social structure of the country will make this easier to understand.

5

The Pyramid
above the Rectangle

The Peruvian social structure is not very different from
that of most Latin American countries, although it presents
certain individual traits. Given that, in Latin America, and
perhaps more so in Peru than in other places on the continent, this structure is very closely related to power and
wealth, it is not possible, and would not be very informative,
to try to describe it in exclusively sociological terms. Rather,
we should—to make the description a faithful reflection of
reality—call for help upon politics and economics.

The Social Structure

If a diagram were to be made of Peruvian society, we might
draw a rectangle as the base, with a pyramid on top of it—
somewhat like this:

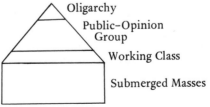

Oligarchy

Public-Opinion
Group

Working Class

Submerged Masses

Obviously the names given to the different social groups are
not those a sociologist would accept, but I think they nevertheless describe the Peruvian situation well.

In the pyramid, we find the groups between which there is
a degree of social mobility that lessens as we descend the pyramid. In the rectangle are groups within which there is a
certain mobility, of course, but which never escape from the
rectangle—that is, never (or only rarely) pass up into the
pyramid.

At the apex of the pyramid is the oligarchic group, composed of the great landholders—some hundreds of families—
the higher echelons of the army, and the upper church hierarchy, which, one might say, belong to this group ex officio.
There are also the bankers and some "traditional" industrialists—owners of family enterprises of a certain economic
strength. To some extent, it would be possible to include in
this group—at least in an economic sense today and in a political sense in the past—the great foreign mining firms and
others.

In the group I call "public-opinion"—because it is the one
that really represents this; the only one that, in normal periods, is taken into account by the government and the oligarchy—are the industrialists as a whole, the professional men,
the merchants, the technical men, the intellectuals and students, and, in its lowest stratum, the bureaucracy, including
the officers of the armed forces and the clergy. These people
read newspapers (a practice not very widespread in Peru outside the great cities), take an interest in politics, form a large
part of the political parties, vote regularly, and have opinions
that carry some weight with those in power. They represent,
also, the majority of the consumers of industrial products.

Below this group, but still within the pyramid, are the
owners of medium-sized farms and the organized working
class (or, in the provinces, the part of that class with the most
awareness). Although the government takes their state of
mind into account, the components of these two groups are
among the politically less active group, except for militants in
the APRA, a good part of whose effective membership comes
from among them. Although they are also consumers of

industrial products, the proportion of the latter they absorb is small in comparison with that absorbed by the groups in the public-opinion stratum.

Among the submerged masses, whence ascent to any of the groups in the pyramid is rare—at best, to the two lowest groups, those of the owners of medium-sized farms and of the politically aware organized workers—we find the dwellers in shantytowns, the unorganized workers (and, in the provinces, a part of those who are organized but have no political awareness). Then, there are the owners of little farms and the tenant farmers and, farther down, the peasants of the indigenous communes; finally, there are the peasants of the haciendas, who are genuine serfs. Proceeding across the dividing line between the pyramid and the rectangle, we may place the petty merchants of the villages and the farm workers on the coastal plantations.

A color line runs more or less parallel to the line of these social divisions. The oligarchy is white. The members of the public-opinion group darken in skin color as they descend the pyramid, and the people in the rectangle of the submerged masses are darker still, most of them Indians or *mestizos*.

It is very difficult to determine the numerical proportions of these different groups. The official statistics, of course, do not take them into account. But some sociologists have come to the conclusion that not more than 5 percent of the total population of Peru should be put in the oligarchic, or higher, group; that 25, or perhaps 30, percent of the population should be placed in the public-opinion, or intermediate, group, and 65–70 percent in the submerged mass, or inferior, group. If this evaluation is refined still further, it may be considered that, within the intermediate group, 10 percent of the country's population belong to the working class, 6 percent make up the bureaucracy (including the armed forces), and another 6 percent consist of professional men, intellectuals, and so forth. The rest of this group would consist of industrialists, and merchants. Similarly, the submerged mass breaks down as follows: 12 percent of the total population living in organized Indian communities—that is, recognized by law and having a certain juridical status; 20 percent living in shantytowns; 5 percent forming a group of industrial peons; and 10 percent made up of farm workers; with the remainder scattered in haciendas or in very small individual properties.

When the standard of living is discussed, it will be seen that there is an enormous difference both among the components of the three main groups and among those of the subgroups. This difference is one not only of economic income but of lifestyle, culture, color, political participation, and degree of organization, as well.

As one ascends from the coast to the Sierra, social differences become more marked, in the same way that, as Haya de la Torre pointed out in formulating his theory of historical space-time, there is a historical retrogression; the coast is modern, the Sierra is medieval, and the forest and jungle are prehistoric.

Tenancy of the Land

The life of Peru is based on land. The greatest part of its population is dependent, in one way or another, on the land, and a great part of its income is derived from the exportation of the products of the land (and, for some years now, of the sea, too). Many of the country's social tensions arise from problems concerning land. Finally, nearly the entire submerged mass—the people who exist within the rectangle of poverty—live on the land, or have lived on it until very recently, and preserve typically rural habits and values. It is necessary, then, to speak, first of all, of the system of tenancy if we are to understand anything about Peru. All we are about to say antedates 1968, since it is still too early to evaluate the results of the 1969 agrarian reform law—although what is explained here also explains why one of the principal acts of the military government of 1968 was to pass just such a law.

In the country, there are 878,667 farm and cattle units, with a total area of 46.5 million acres. Of this area, 31.75 million acres are privately owned, 5.5 million are the property of Indian communes, 6 million are cultivated on a partnership basis, and 550,000 are worked on a sharecropping or other partnership basis.

Of the nearly 900,000 farm and cattle-raising units, 34 percent are smaller than 2.5 acres; 49 percent are from 2.5 to 12.5 acres; 12 percent are from 12.5 to 50 acres; 2.9 percent are from 50 to 250 acres; .9 percent are from 250 to 1,250 acres; and the rest are larger than 1,250 acres. The .4 percent of the haciendas that are bigger than 1,250 acres include almost 35 million out of the 46.5 million registered.

In order to calibrate these figures, we must consider that, on the coast, a property is considered insufficient to support a family if it contains fewer than 7.5 acres; enough to sustain a family if it includes between 7.5 and 25 acres; and medium-sized if it includes 125 acres. Any property more extensive than this is classified as large. But, in the Sierra, a medium-sized property is one that contains up to 250 acres, if it is irrigated, and up to 6,250 acres, if it is pasture. Two hundred fifty acres of pasture is considered subfamily; 250 to 1,250 acres are needed to sustain a family.

Still more figures: 10,000 large, cultivated units contain 75 percent of the land, with an average of 3,250 acres apiece; but 100,000 units of family size occupy 4.7 percent of the land and average 25 acres; 720,000 subsidized units include 6 percent of the land, with an average of 4 acres. Fourteen hundred Indian communes include 8.6 percent of the land, with an average of 4,500 acres per commune—a commune often being composed of hundreds of families. Only the owners of medium-sized properties (20,000 units, which include 5.4 percent of the land, with an average of 108.5 acres) have enough land to support themselves and produce for the market—without getting into the latifundista class.

These figures are enough to give an idea of the degree of concentration landowning has attained. This concentration is not a thing of today; it was already in existence in the colonial period, during which, when its royal lands were exhausted by parceling them out to Spanish subjects, the crown seized the *ayllus*—the Indian communes that had survived the conquest. At the end of the eighteenth century, however, there had been some distribution of property to Creoles and *mestizos,* who had begun to buy land from their former owners.

With independence, the tendency toward concentration was emphasized. Bolívar ordered the division of commune lands among the members of the communes; for it was one of the liberal dogmas that property should be individual. The result was contrary to what the legislator had intended: it allowed the great landowners to extend their latifundia at the cost of the Indians, who had never owned land individually, and who allowed themselves to be despoiled of it or sold it at shamefully low prices. Moreover, the lands of the royalists were confiscated and turned over to Creole owners. This process lasted throughout the nineteenth century. To the Peruvian latifundistas were added, especially in this century, foreign ones, as well as some domestic firms that bought land to use for plantations.

Some examples will illustrate the importance of this phenomenon.[3] The Chicama Valley is one of the most important on the coast. It contains about 300,000 acres, of which 87,500 are cultivated. Forty-five percent of the Peruvian production of sugar cane comes from this valley. Four latifundistas own 90 percent of the cultivated land, and one of them owns 51 percent. Many medium-sized and small farms have been absorbed by these great enterprises, chiefly because of the pressure they can exert by refusing water for irrigation, for the latifundia control the sources of the valley's rivers. The valley enterprises are Peruvian; the greatest of them, before World War II, was German. One of these haciendas produces almost half of the country's sugar. There are others on which as many as 20,000 people live.

Another example is the Cerro de Pasco Company—an American firm that owns mines and smelters, primarily of copper. In 1922, the company established a smelter in La Oroya, in the department of Junín. The fumes, extremely toxic, affected the health of the inhabitants of the valley and their cattle and crops. The effect of the fumes was spread over 1.75 million acres. Finally, the company received a court order to install a system for purifying the fumes, but it did this only twenty years after the court order; meanwhile, the firm had bought, at low prices, 875,000 of the acres affected by the smoke. Peruvians are convinced that the smoke had two objects: first, to drive down the price of the land and, second, to make available a proletarianized population that would provide manual labor cheaply.

In the *selva,* concessions were awarded that soon developed into latifundia. For instance, in 1890, 5 million acres were ceded to a committee of foreign debt bondholders, who, in turn, ceded them to a British firm. The latter, however, did not carry out the stipulations of the concession, and, before the agreement could be annulled, sold most of the land to several of its own directors, affiliated firms, and various individuals. For this reason, the concession was not annulled until 1965.

In 1909, a law was passed which ceded land in the mountainous *selva* at the rate of 2.5 soles an acre, with a tax of 2.5 centavos a year per uncultivated acre. This paid for public works, political favors, and so forth. It also resulted in a monopoly of 12.5 million acres, so that 9 percent of the proprietors of the *selva* now own 97 percent of the land awarded under this arrangement.

Not all the concessions, however, are of many years' standing. In 1952, Gen. Odría's government awarded important concessions to two foreign groups—among them, one of 1 million acres to the American firm of Le Tourneau de Peru, Inc., in exchange for the construction of an 80-mile road over a term of four years. When this term expired, however, the road still had not been built, and the firm was allowed another five years.

These are a few examples—the most dramatic. But the concentration of lands—always the best lands—at the cost of the communities and the owners of middle-sized and small farms, is a phenomenon that has been in existence for three centuries. It has not always been accepted without protest.

The Agrarian Question

This system of landholding, which in Latin America is called "latifundism," could not fail to pose a problem, as much from the desire of communities to conserve their land, or to recover it when lost, as from the growth of population, which aroused in country folk the desire to own more land. Yet, it was in urban rather than rural areas that the problem was posed on the political level. This, in turn, led to the inclusion of agrarian reform in the programs of nearly all the modern parties that did not openly declare themselves partisans of the status quo.

It could be said that the Incas instituted the first agrarian reform, since, when they conquered other peoples, they established communal-type landholding systems known as *ayllus*. The *ayllu* was subjected to a centralized administration. Each member of the *ayllu* was allotted the yield of a parcel of land, which he cultivated and utilized on a family basis. Finally, the Incas made frequent distributions of the population, transferring people from places where the land was oversettled to regions where uncultivated land was plentiful and irrigating it by means of canals.

The colonial system brought a new reform. The *ayllus* survived, but the colonizers added to them *ejidos* (parcels of woodland, pasture, and cultivated land), which were recognized as the common property of a village and were intended to assure its subsistence. The indigenous communes of today are derived from this colonial system, which began to take form after 1575. There were also lands for the religious brotherhoods which belonged, in fact, to the Indians. And, finally, there were distributions of land to individual Indians in order to turn them into taxpayers.

All these arrangements, however, were complied with only when a viceroy and his subordinates were disposed to apply the law—and that was infrequent. Many in authority tolerated the gradual acquisition of the Indians' land by colonists and Creoles. Madrid's attempts at administrative reform in the second half of the eighteenth century did not stop the process, although it did encourage some redistribution of land among the Creoles and some protection of the lands still held by the communes.

We have seen that, shortly after the winning of independence, Bolívar effected another agrarian reform—without calling it such, of course—that gave the Indians individual ownership of the communal lands, which, as it developed, however, was tantamount to leaving the great landholders free to despoil them. The allotments of land ordered by Bolívar—especially of land seized from Spaniards who had returned to their native country—did not benefit the Indians greatly, since those who administered the laws tended to give the properties to Creoles and *mestizos.* In an attempt to protect the Indians, it was decreed that the lands they received could not be sold until after 1850; however, then this limit was revoked in favor of a decree that they might be sold only by those able to read and write—a requirement easily falsified when the authorities so desired.

The communities that survived often brought lawsuits against the hacienda owners, who were trying to take away their land. The Ministry of Indian Affairs—theoretically created to protect the Indians—devoted itself to mediation between them and the great landholders, with the result that the latter, in the end, became the beneficiaries. Some suits lasted for three generations. Many local functionaries became landowners, and the local churches received the lands of the ancient brotherhoods, which the priests then sold. This resulted in the Peruvian church's being less rich than those in the majority of Latin American countries. Finally, the hacienda owners took over by purchase cession, or simply by illegal absorption, many State or municipal lands—an easy matter for them, since the legal authorities, who should have prevented it, were submissive to them in everything.

The question of land could not cease to be basic in a country with the structure we have described and with the majority of the population dependent upon agriculture. But public discussion of the agrarian question came only in the twentieth century. At the beginning of the century, González Prado said that the so-called Indian problem was, fundamentally, a problem of land; years later Mariátegui said the same thing. Haya de la Torre not only condemned latifundism but advocated the donation of land to communities by the state, as well as the modernization of agriculture by governmental activity. Since 1930, there has been no electoral campaign in which the question of land has not been discussed; since then, too, dozens of books and hundreds of articles have been published on agrarian reform.

But it took a long time for the government to recognize the existence of the agrarian problem. Until 1919, the most that it did was to grant land to foreign firms or immigrants and to try to encourage cultivation of the *selva,* without, however, any aid on the state's part. President Leguía promoted irrigation along the coast, but without modifying the system of landholding and by favoring concentration of ownership in the irrigated zones. President Benavides maintained this policy but restricted land grants to persons who did not already own land. But instead of increasing the number of properties of small and medium-sized acreage, this enabled many wealthy city people to become absentee landowners, thus aggravating the problem. It is important to point this out, for it shows that, in a society based on latifundism, any measure that does not explicitly seek the disappearance of the latifundism ends up increasing it—although, indeed, its intention may be the exact opposite.

Not until 1945, when the APRA took part in the government, were there modest new agrarian measures to improve the condition of the tenants and sharecroppers. When a parliamentary debate on projected agrarian reform occurred, a military coup took place, sealing all further discussion of the subject until Manuel Prado's administration, which, in 1960, created a commission to draw up an agrarian reform law and establish an institute of agrarian reform and colonization. The Congress, however, did not discuss the project. In 1964, under Belaúnde's government, the Congress did pass an agrarian reform law, proposed by the APRA, that favored the communes, advocated mechanized plantations and development, and called for the expropriation, with compensation, and distribution of uncultivated or poorly cultivated land. The government, however, did little to apply a law that had originated in the opposition party.

During this period, there were numerous invasions of the land by the peasants, sometimes suppressed by the authorities, sometimes tolerated by the proprietors. These invasions, in general, involved lands of which the communes had been despoiled in the past, and which they were trying to recover. There was also invasion of lands that had regular, defined boundaries, by groups carrying flags bearing the motto Land or Death. These invasions were not caused solely by the peasants' impatience; they were influenced, also, by groups of the New Left (especially by the Trotskyites and APRA dissidents) and by the Castro mythology. The army, however, broke up these occupations, even after some of them had evolved into minor guerrilla wars. In areas where the invasions occurred, the authorities speeded up application of the agrarian reform law; even so, up to 1968, land had been distributed to only 20,000 families—about 1.5 million acres being expropriated. Finally, in 1969, the military government decreed a new law of agrarian reform, but more will be said about this later.

Rural Life

Today, 52 percent of the population live in the rural areas (as compared to 65 percent in 1940). A third of this group live in population centers; the rest are distributed among villages, or scattered houses, and solitary shanties. It is an odd fact that the same figure—52 percent—holds for the part of the economically active population engaged in agriculture and fishing.

Although statistics are lacking, it is possible to state that unemployment is rising in rural areas, primarily because of the increase of the families of small-scale farmers; there is not enough land for cultivation by the sons, who remain idle, going either to the city or, at harvest time, off to the coastal plantations, especially in the cotton-picking season. This emigration is particularly marked in the 1,400 farming communes that have survived, and whose holdings have remained the same while their population has increased. When peasants are employed as farm workers, their wages are scarcely one-third of the average pay of urban workers: 56 cents to $1.20 a day. While 80 percent of the population in the cities can read and write, and hence vote, only 40 percent of those in rural areas are literate. In reality, it may be supposed that nearly all the country people who live in scattered areas are illiterate, since they have no schools of any kind. Illiteracy is much greater among women than men; even where there are schools, the tendency is to send only boys to them, since the people do not want the girls to mingle with boys.

The peasants' standard of living varies considerably. In the smaller settlements, they have adobe or stone houses; in the open country, the homes are much more flimsy; in all cases, the dwellings are unhealthy, without running water or sewerage systems, and with electricity only in the larger towns. One can fly over Peru at night for long distances without seeing a single light on the ground.

Medical care is minimal. Many villages have no doctors, and fewer still have hospitals or clinics. Since roads between the country and the cities are bad, it is very difficult to get a doctor in an emergency. Most country women give birth with only neighbors to aid them, and many go through their entire pregnancies without visiting a physician. In the department of Puno, there is one physician to each 25,000 inhabitants and one nurse for each 148,000.

This makes for a rural infant mortality nearly four times that of the cities. Another result is that country women almost never have fewer than five children and often have ten, although only one-third live to maturity. In recent years, however, sanitary conditions have been improving. Malaria and yellow fever have been eradicated, and the incidence of gastrointestinal illness has been fairly well reduced.

Production on family farms is very low, rising to median on the big ones (although greater on the coast than in the Sierra, since there is greater mechanization in the former). The existence of communes poses special problems; for, if it is true that those organized as cooperatives have achieved an acceptable yield, the production of many hardly reaches the subsistence level, because of the population explosion and antiquated cultivation methods. It is not surprising, then, that, under such conditions, a large part of the agricultural population has an inadequate and unbalanced diet (those who eat meat once a week are the fortunate ones), and that their consumption of industrial products is extremely low— which, in turn, keeps many urban industries working below their capacity.

The chance to save is minimal, and any surplus takes the

form of work the peasant does on his land and house. In the Sierra, the peasants usually spin and weave the wool of their animals to make their own clothes and tan leather for their shoes. But they often go barefoot, even in the high, cold regions, where it is common to find peasants with the soles of their feet as tough as those of shoes. They have little furniture in their houses, and they usually sleep on woven straw mats spread on the floor or over planks.

There have been many theories and some attempts to modernize the life of Peru's farm population and integrate it into the national society. At times, the life of a community has been transformed by the building of a road or a small dam that enabled it to make contact with the outer world. Also, from time to time it has been thought that, if a great deal of effort were expended on a community or a series of communities, their neighbors would imitate them and progress, too. Cornell University undertook an experiment of this kind in the Vicos Valley in the *altiplano*. With the backing of Cornell's Department of Sociology and the Instituto Indigenista of Peru, the experiment was begun in 1951. After the anthropological characteristics of the valley's inhabitants had been studied, the university began the project of managed change on a 30,000-acre hacienda with about 2,000 Indians. The Indians trained for leadership in development, education, and hygiene. In 1957, the administration of the hacienda was turned over to a group of elected leaders. The Peruvian government could do no less than begin five similar pilot projects, which, however, were finally abandoned. Allan R. Holmberg, the anthropologist who was the soul of the project, was himself not sure about its success at the end of his life. The existence of the commune was partly democratized, and its economic level was raised, but the attempt to have other communes follow its example on their own initiative was not successful. Given all this, it is no longer certain that the experiment will continue when the anthropologists leave Vicos. There is a saying in the valley that an Indian family consists of a father, a mother, six children, two daughters-in-law—and an anthropologist. In any event, it is practically impossible to devote to each community the amount of effort, money, personnel, and time that has been devoted to Vicos.

During centuries, there have been hundreds of local peasant uprisings, but they were invariably crushed by the local authorities, sometimes with the aid of the army. Except in some sections of the coast, the central authority never extended into the provinces, not only because of the distances and lack of communications but because of the fragmentation of power among the plantation owners, each of whom had his own private police. The rivalries between the *hacendados* were frequent and often led to violence. For the peasants, who took part in these conflicts in support of their bosses, violence was thus a normal element of life.

In recent years, native rebellions have broken out in the Cuzco region, taking the form of seizure of land that once belonged to the communes—before the *hacendados* took it away—or of distribution of poorly cultivated land. In 1965, the Communists tried to capitalize on one of these uprisings (Cuzco is the strongest base of the weak Peruvian Communist movement), and afterward, as we have explained, the Trotskyite Hugo Blanco and the dissident Apristas organized guerrilla activity, with little success, in regions where there had been peasant agitation. But the Indians, it seems, preferred their own movements to those led by men from the city. The chief cause of these rebellions has not been simply hunger for land or protest against local authorities, but the social condition of the peasants.

The Condition of the Peasants

Some peasants are small landholders, others rent land, paying for it in crops or money, and still others are salaried workers on plantations or haciendas. But a considerable number, particularly in the Sierra, are still virtually serfs, who pay rent for their land in different forms of labor. In such a situation, the peasant receives from the boss, or *hacendado*, a piece of land, with a right to its produce and the right to pasture his cattle on the owner's land. While working for the owner, he is also entitled to a handful of coca to chew, the equivalent of the cost of a glass of fermented corn liquor (*chicha*), and, in recent times, food. The owner has to furnish him with the implements to work the land; they are usually very primitive, in some regions being entirely of wood. Finally, the tenant has the unwritten right to protection by the owner, especially when he is held by the police or taken before a judge. On the other hand, the tenant has to cultivate, not only his bit of land, but the owner's as well. This is done by turns, sometimes a week for the owner and a week for himself, sometimes on alternate days, sometimes the first three for the hacienda and the fourth for himself. The tenant's family and relatives also work on the owner's land, as shepherds or as house servants, sometimes in the country, sometimes in the city. Every year, they must turn over to the owner a certain number of cattle in exchange for pasture rights. Finally, it is not unusual for a patron to take a tenant or his children to the city for a time, to work for him without pay (in exchange for lodging and maintenance) in his house or in some other person's business. By renting a part of their land to tenants, the *hacendados* obtain a work force for their industries, or "sell" the labor to mines or to firms engaged in public works. When that happens, the *hacendado* pockets the pay he has fixed for his tenants, without giving them any of it or, only a small part of it as a gesture of generosity.

During the last decades, however, this form of serfdom has diminished, and it has become more customary to pay the rent partly in work and partly with a percentage of the crop. At other times, the value of the work the tenant should do for the *hacendado* is figured in soles, and this is considered the rent of the land, which must then be paid in money. In this case, the *hacendado* keeps only a small part of the land for his own use and rents out the rest.

More Sierra peasants live in communes that have survived from colonial times. The communes may be of three types: the traditional commune, in which land is divided every year among the members, and in which the commune, or its directing group, decides what crops are to be raised and admits or expels members; the mixed commune, in which the collective has lost the right to expel a member; and the formal hereditary commune, in which each parcel is worked at the pleasure of its "owner," who may also employ day workers from outside the commune. The first form—the oldest—is found only in places remote from cities; the closer one comes to the cities, the more one finds mixed and formal communes. The communes, which were firmly established for a long time—and some of which attained a degree of prosperity upon organizing themselves into cooperatives for the marketing of their produce and for the procurement of consumer goods—are today in a period of crisis because of the population explosion, which has caused them to have too many members for a normally fixed amount of land. Some communes have managed to acquire more land; others, however, are compelled to see their youngest and most dynamic elements move away to the cities because of a lack of land to cultivate or because of the constant reduction in the size of the lots assigned to the members in an attempt to satisfy everyone.

Not all rural workers have been resigned to these conditions. In certain periods, intense efforts have been made to organize unions among the farm workers. The first to organize were the farm workers of the coastal plantations. There is the fairly powerful Federation of Workers in the Sugar Industry, affiliated with the Confederation of Peruvian Workers, which though scarcely thirty years old, has done much to improve the sugar workers' working conditions and standard of living.

Among the peasants of the haciendas, organization has been more difficult, not only because of their isolation and lack of education, but also because of opposition from the government and the *hacendados*. Nevertheless, after 1920, some peasants managed to establish societies for mutual aid and savings which, in time, became militant organizations. The Apristas, in their first period of activity, made notable contributions to the organization of the peasants. They were also a deciding factor in the extension of the cooperative movement into rural areas.

The small landholders and tenant farmers—whom we shall call "modern," because they do not pay their rent in labor—are organized, in part, into the FENCAP (Federación Nacional de Campesinos del Peru—National Federation of Peruvian Peasants), which is affiliated with the Confederation of Peruvian Workers. The FENCAP has been powerful enough to obtain representation in all the agrarian reform organizations established before 1968 but has lacked this representation since that date, perhaps because the majority of its leaders are Apristas. In the region of Cuzco, there exists a Confederación Campesina de Perú (Peruvian Peasant Confederation), Communist-led and of lesser importance, which, since 1968, has received discreet support from the military junta.

In the *selva*, unionization is far more difficult, because there the local authorities are subject to little control and are more inclined to defend openly the interests of the local landowners than to enforce the law. Nevertheless, there are some unions in these regions.

The tenants of the Sierra are also organized, not in unions but in associations. Under the pretext that their relationship to the owner of the land is not the typical relationship of worker and employer, the law does not permit them to unionize. But the tenant farmers have discovered that the strike is a very powerful source of pressure; for, if they are not prompt about working the hacienda lands, the latter will become unproductive, whereas they can go on working their own and thus maintain their families during a strike. Since they are not dependent on wages but only upon their own crops for subsistence, they are, in a way, in a better position to strike than the industrial workers, whose only income is wages. Consequently, the tenants who have organized into peasant federations have won appreciable improvements, although, so far, they have not succeeded in abolishing the system of paying rent by their labor.

Unionization was also forbidden among the sharecroppers (called *yanaconas*) since here, too, the law held that their relation with the owners was not the typical relationship of employer and worker. Sharecropping is especially prevalent in certain parts of the coast where the sharecropper works a parcel of irrigated land not larger than 37.5 acres and pays his rent with part of the crop, or, at times, with money and work together. The contract is made in writing, and, since the sharecropper is usually an illiterate, it is not difficult to get him to sign a contract that generally cedes to the owner, without cost, any improvements the sharecropper has made. There have been cases, by no means rare, where the proprietors succeeded, under various pretexts, in evicting sharecroppers who had learned to read, considering them potentially more rebellious and likely to organize associations to demand better contracts.

Agricultural workers' claims and disputes are submitted to labor tribunals; tenant farmers and sharecroppers remain within the jurisdiction of the local civil courts, on which the owners and their managers exert an undeniable influence.

The great landholders have their own powerful local and national organizations. The principal one is the Sociedad Nacional Agraria (National Agrarian Society). In addition, there are associations of sugar producers, of cattlemen, and of wool raisers. The members of the National Agrarian Society dispose of a number of votes proportionate to the extent of their lands, so that the median owners and small landholders have no influence. The society always defends the interests of the latifundistas, and until now, it has done so very effectively. Since it does not often have recourse to public opinion, it prefers to bring pressure on the government through personal relationships, banks, and so forth. The most astonishing fact is that there is an official tax on *guano*, which reverts entirely to the National Agrarian Society. They do not have to give any accounting of what they do with this official subsidy, which the military junta of 1968 has respected. Hence, it may be said that the state and the great mass of Peruvians finance the great latifundistas.

The Committee of Sugar Producers comprises the proprietors of the country's fourteen mills, of which three are foreign-owned and control 50 percent of the national production of sugar. This committee fixes the price of sugar on the national market at its own discretion, arranges for exportation of the surplus, and tends to initiate violent press campaigns when it thinks its interests are threatened.

The Asociación de Criadores Lanares (Association of Wool Raisers) has, on its board of directors, the proprietors of 3.75 million acres of pasture lands, or 17 percent of the pasture area of the country. For its part, the Association of Cattlemen unites the cattle raisers of the coast and particularly the owners of milk herds; it fixes, de facto, the price of milk. It is less reactionary than the other landholders' associations, but is also less influential.

Urban Life

In 1940, 35 percent of the population of Peru was urban. In 1961, this proportion had risen to 47 percent. Today, it may be confidently set at 52 percent. The most urbanized parts are the north and south. The eastern *selva* is urbanized to the extent that, except for Indian tribes and some extensive rural exploitations, life is possible only in urban areas, but these are small.

Peru is not a country of big cities. Outside of Lima, not one has a quarter of a million inhabitants. But there are many cities of fewer than 50,000 persons. The only two cities that can be considered modern are Lima and Arequipa (Callao is, in fact, a part of Lima because of its proximity).

Lima, the capital, has perhaps 2 or 2.5 million inhabitants. No one knows precisely how many, for there is an enormous fluctuating population in the migrant quarters. In Lima is concentrated not only the political life of the country but also its cultural life. The growth of the other cities—particularly those of the north, which, in fewer than thirty years, have doubled in population—is attributable to the establishment of industries (in Trujillo, Chiclayo, Paita, Talara), to the presence of the country's only blast furnaces (in Chimbote), to the opening of oil wells (in Piura), and, in several cases, to the development of mining. Fishing, which, in the last ten years, has developed greatly, has encouraged the growth of a series of small coastal cities to the north of Lima.

The cities of the Sierra are growing much more slowly. Arequipa, however, which, as the manufacturing center of the south, has attracted a large number of migrants, has experienced a rapid growth rate. Iquitos and Pucallpa, situated in the Amazon region, have undergone a similarly rapid growth. For, as shipments of goods abroad have become both cheaper and faster via the Amazon than through the Andes to Callao, these two cities are developing into major ports of arrivals of supplies for the entire forest region of the country.

Peru's urban growth, from 1940 to 1969, exceeded 200

percent. (It rose 174 percent in 1961 alone.) In some cases, urban growth has been as much as 1,000 percent—in Chimbote, which has grown from 4,000 to 66,000 inhabitants, and in Pucallpa, which has grown from 2,000 to 27,000. Lima, which, in 1940, had fewer than half a million inhabitants, has roughly quadrupled this figure, according to the census, and and has sextupled it in actual population.

The enormous growth of some cities is due, of course, to internal migration; for, in Peru, immigration is statistically negligible, although it is important from the standpoint of quality, since it has brought into Peru businessmen, engineers, and skilled workers. As in the rest of Latin America, this internal migration has two concomitant causes: the population explosion in the rural areas, and the lack of enough cultivated land to give work to the new hands. Moreover, modernization of the rural areas is very slow—when there is any—in contrast to the speedy modernization of urban life. Consequently, many young people go from the villages to the cities. The young of provincial cities rush off to Lima, while the youth of the villages and haciendas flock to the provincial cities. But this is not confined to peasants. Except for sharecroppers and children of prosperous merchants, inhabitants of all social classes tend to migrate.

In a survey carried out by Lima's University of San Marcos, for example, it was shown that economic motives accounted for 61 percent of the cases of migration to the cities; social motivation (harassment or the desire for improved status), for 22 percent; education, for 9 percent; and reasons of health, for almost 3 percent.

Such migration has caused serious problems. Lima's growth alone poses a national problem; for nearly a fifth of all Peruvians are in the capital. Urban planning has been conspicuous by its absence; the cities have grown spontaneously, with enormous speculation in real estate. Actually, all that the municipalities do is try to preserve and improve conditions in the well-to-do neighborhoods, to regulate transit (inefficiently), and to isolate the marginal districts. The problems of housing, health, and the like are even more dramatic. In Lima, as in some other cities, there are entire quarters of shanties, on unpaved (often unnamed and unnumbered) streets, without electricity, running water, or sewerage. There are also quarters of tents made of matting that the Indians bring with them. Poverty, discomfort, and delinquency are general. Frequently, conflicts arise between the owners of the land occupied by these shanties and the residents. Exploitation of the migrants by small storekeepers, often their own people, is common, as is exploitation by greedy landlords, corrupt police, and even the petty politicians and *caciques* of the quarters. There are no schools or any other cultural or educational means that would help to make these displaced people aware of their own interests. In Lima, about a quarter of the population lives under such conditions, and the number keeps growing. It has been estimated that, in the entire country, there are 271 shantytowns (half of them in Lima) with 850,000 people in them. To these must be added the persons who live in the slums in the center of the city and those who, after living for a time in the capital, go off to other cities to look for work. Among those living in these quarters total or partial unemployment is rampant. When they do find work it is for the very low wages of unspecialized workers. Since vocational education is scarce, it is rare for a migrant to become a skilled worker.

Of course, the general conditions of life in the cities are different from those of the migrants. Lima has old mansions and aristocratic palaces that are true museums; it has modern hotels and middle-class houses in residential areas, with gardens, swimming pools, and well-lighted streets. There are also modest but relatively comfortable dwellings. There are many modern diversions and plenty of sports and night clubs, all making for an intense cultural life. There are well-stocked libraries, art galleries, gymnasiums, clubs and casinos, restaurants, and all the other elements of Western urban life. There is an added allurement—Lima probably is one of the cities with the greatest density of pretty women in the world.

It is, above all, the middle class that gives the city its tone, for the very rich spend most of the year abroad or ensconced in their own circle in the Lima section of Miraflores. The middle class includes the bureaucracy and the various professions. Peru, as of 1975, has 8,000 physicians, more than 2,000 pharmacists, and nearly 15,000 lawyers. The last are found everywhere, particularly in the bureaucracy, but also in the little provincial localities; on the other hand, physicians, architects, engineers, chemists, and the like tend to be concentrated in the big cities and obstinately refuse to lend their services outside the important urban centers. There are also about 40,000 public schools teachers, 10,000 high school teachers and university professors, and about 5,000 private school teachers. Although a segment of this educational personnel lives in small localities, the majority are in the cities.

All these groups—and obviously those of industrialists and merchants—have grown in the last decades, and their standard of living has greatly improved. In 1945, there were 15,000 pleasure cars in Lima; by 1961, the number had grown to 85,000; and today there are certainly more than 140,000. Lima has more than 200,000 television receivers. These figures indicate the increased prosperity of the middle class. Although the working class and the migrants compose the majority of the urban population, there is no denying that Peruvian cities are, first and foremost, middle-class centers.

Despite the urban style of life in Lima and some other cities, the traveler constantly encounters rustic touches that the Limeños themselves do not notice because they are used to them. For example, it frequently happens that, when a taxi driver is told an address that is not a very well-known avenue, he will reply: "Where is that? How do you get there?" And the modest middle-class families have servants, which would be impossible without constant migration from the country. Obviously, in the houses of the very rich, there are many servants of both sexes—chauffeurs, grooms, gardeners, and so forth.

Thus, the life of the cities holds a mixture of quasi-colonial customs and modern lifestyles characteristic of industrial societies. Household electric appliances are plentiful and so are modern, abstract works of art—but there are also street sweepers, child bootblacks, and news vendors, as well as beggars—with their conspicuously displayed sores—and witch doctors in the slums. Even among the laboring class, we find different lifestyles side by side.

The Condition of the Workers

The active population that makes up 32 percent of the total includes one-half who are employed in rural areas. Fifteen percent are employed as domestic servants; 13 percent are in industry, 9 percent in trade, and 2 percent in mining; the remaining 11 percent are engaged in other work, especially transport and skilled trades.

Although there are no statistics on total or partial unemployment, it is estimated that 5-10 percent of the working force have no jobs and that a much higher percentage are employed only part time. Furthermore, Peruvian industry works at only 50 percent of capacity. The most dense centers of unemployment are the coastal cities, where as might be expected, the migrant quarters are found. Industrial productivity is low, but there are not sufficient means for training specialized skilled workers. Apprenticeship in shops and factories, during adolescence, is still the common method of training workers. The CENIP (Centro Nacional de Acción para el Incremento de la Productividad—National Action Center for Increasing Productivity), formed some years ago by the unions and management organizations, tried without much success to change this, as did the SENATI (Servicio Nacional de Aprendizaje y Trabajo Industrial—National Service for Apprenticeship and Industrial Work), which was created by law in 1962. But progress here is slow, since Peru has no industrial tradition nor anything that might be called an industrial climate. At heart, Peru is still rural, and this is reflected in the people's attitude toward the machine, in the way work is organized and regulated. The majority of workers are first- or second-generation city dwellers; only a negligible minority had grandfathers employed in industry.

Labor legislation is not codified but consists of several fundamental laws and thousands of often contradictory supplementary laws and decrees. There is a complex social-security system, with illness, retirement, and accident benefits that are very complete on paper but, in practice, are translated into slow and inadequate medical attention and insufficient pensions. Furthermore, the system is not unified, and each branch has its own procedures. The workers, however, through the unions, do have representation on the directorial units of the social-security system.

Enforcement of labor legislation is the charge of the Ministry of Labor and Indian Affairs, which has ample authority not only to inspect places of work but also to intervene in union matters. The minister of labor is in charge of arbitrating labor disputes or attempting conciliation. In view of the complexity and prolixity of the legislation in this field, the help of many lawyers is required, and each union has to rely on the counsel of specialized lawyers in order to find its way around the legislative thicket.

Some general features, however, may be pointed out: the average pay in industry, as of 1975, is $3.50 a day, and the monthly salary of white-collar workers is $250. Outside Lima (except in the mines) the laborers' wages are lower. We must add cost-of-living bonuses, family allowances, and profit sharing (in some firms). There is no unemployment insurance; but discharged workers, unless the dismissal is for incompetence or negligence, receive an indemnity from management in proportion to their years of service.

More important for the worker than legislation is the contract signed by his union. Many contracts provide for maternity subsidies, days off with pay before and after delivery, and transportation to work. In actual worth, the fringe benefits are equal to a 60 percent addition to regular wages for industrial workers and to a 50 percent addition for white-collar workers.

The eight-hour day is recognized by law, as are forty-eight hours for a working week—forty-five hours for women and minors. This was established in 1919, after a long general strike in Lima. White-collar workers usually have a seven-hour day. Overtime may not be more than seven hours on one day and is paid at the rate of time and a quarter. There are thirty days of paid vacation a year.

The government periodically fixes the minimum wage, which actually applies only to peons. But, in this, as in the rest of social legislation, the law is observed only when there are unions strong enough to put up a fight with owners who ignore it. When there is no union, social laws are to all intents and purposes nonexistent.

The cost of living has been rising for years, nearly 6 percent annually and sometimes more. The raises won by the workers when they have a union usually exceed this increase, but, when there is no union, the workers' income decreases in relation to the cost of living. This is clearly shown by the statistics on per capita income. Yearly pay among workers in Lima is estimated at $244; in the rest of the country, at $123; and in the Sierra and the *selva*—both areas in which the labor movement is weak—at $76 and $48, respectively.

Living conditions for the working class are inferior to those of the middle class. The white-collar employees try to live like the latter, but they must make a great effort to do so because of their low income. For this group, the most important item in the family budget, after food, is shelter; whereas, for industrial workers, this item is only in fourth place. Workers' dwellings are inadequate, and their clothing is usually different from that of the middle class; they do not own cars or houses (except when their union organizes residential cooperatives, in which case only qualified workers with higher salaries are able to benefit). The education of their children is left to the public schools, which are usually in poor condition. Alcoholism is not rare in the working class, and many peons have the coca-chewing habit.

On the whole, the working class is a privileged group compared to the great mass of peasants and migrants. They have succeeded in attaining this status not only because it would have been impossible to create industry without their labor, but also thanks to the labor movement, which, in Peru, has a very intense and interesting history.

Around 1884, a group of anarchists took over the leadership of an artisans' society, the Unión Universal, and converted it into the original nucleus of the Peruvian labor movement. In 1904, the first general strike took place in Lima. The anarchists had spread to several cities, founding workers' libraries in spite of government harassment. In 1911, the first textile unions were founded (the first mill had been established in 1901). Strikes were frequent: there was one by stevedores in Callao, and another by sugar workers in the Chicama Valley. The latter was harshly suppressed in 1912, with about 500 workers killed by police. In 1919, workers in a Lima textile mill struck for an eight-hour day, which they won. Another outcome of the strike was the Federación Textil, which, with the sugar workers' union, has become the strongest union in the country. In 1923, when Leguía put Haya de la Torre and other students in jail and closed the people's universities, a general strike broke out in protest. Since then, the Peruvian labor movement has been inspired and led by Aprista elements, except during dictatorships, when the Communists, taking advantage of the harassment of Apristas, tried to assume leadership of the unions.

In 1926, the Confederación General de Trabajo (General Labor Confederation), or CGT, was founded. Subsequent dictators sought to divide the confederation by allowing freedom of action to the Communists while harassing the Aprista-led unions. Marshal Benavides and Manuel Prado (whom the Communists nicknamed the "Creole Stalin") did the same. Profiting by the outlawed status of the Apristas, the Communists, in 1944, created, with Prado's support, the Confederación de Trabajadores de Perú (Peruvian Workers' Confederation), or CTP; but, when the Apristas' legal status was restored in 1948, the latter took over the leadership of all the unions, one after another, and contributed to the creation of an inter-American federation of unions—the CIT,[4] later to become the ORIT,[5] which eliminated the Communist-controlled CTAL.[6] History repeated itself under the dictatorship of General Odría; while, on the one hand, the Communists remained free to pursue their activites among the unions, Odría, on the other, began harassing the Apristas, accusing them of being—Communists! But, when Odría fell, the Apristas regained control of the unions.

The CTP has become increasingly bureaucratic since then and has extended its radius of action into the rural areas. The peasant organizations, supported by the CTP, have grown, and many rural cooperatives have been founded, as well as some urban ones, particularly in housing. In 1962, when there was a military coup, the CTP called a general strike. Against the military junta of 1968, however, the CTP has proceeded very cautiously; without ceasing to demand a return to constitutional government, it has managed to protect its union locals against persecution. But it has not been able to prevent the military, who are fearful of the CTP's Aprista leadership, from favoring establishment of a federation led by Communists, with the intention of weakening the democratic one. At the moment, this scheme does not appear to have had much success.

The CTP is still the Latin American federation that does the most to keep alive the traditions of the labor movement in its heroic period. The leaders, for example, do not receive a salary from the union; rather, by means of collective contracts, the majority of the unions succeeded in getting the employers to pay this salary to whoever is elected secretary-general of a union, while, at the same time, giving him all the free time he needs for his labor duties. Furthermore, in view of the scarcity of trained leaders, the CTP is in the position of having several of its leaders represent it in different groups where there is union representation (thanks to the pressure of the CTP and such elements of it as were senators or deputies). To prevent the accumulation of the fees paid to these representatives, they had a clause inserted in the law that puts a ceiling on such fees; but, conversely, these fees go into the union treasuries and not into the pockets of the union representatives. Finally, it must be emphasized that the CTP has numerous schools of union training, both in the provinces and in the capital. The number of young members in the leadership groups of the CTP and its affiliates is much greater than that in the majority of the federations of other countries, since, thanks to these union schools, there is a constant turnover of leaders, from the locals up to the national levels. Although the CTP's relations with the management organizations are merely correct, they tend to be more cordial with certain units of industrialists, such as the Sociedad Nacional de Industrias (National Society of Industries), which has a more modern and progressive outlook.

Even if it had available better-trained teams, and even if, instead of having only about a million members, it could rely upon the adherence of all workers, the Peruvian labor movement could still not accomplish much more than it does, given the economy and the social structure of the country.

All that has been said in this chapter can be summed up in a few facts: forty-four families actually control the agrarian economy of the Sierra. Recent studies show that many of them, as we have pointed out, have extended their activities into industry and banking. They form, therefore, a real economic empire, grouped into about ten clans, that directs the economic life of the country and monopolizes the profits derived from it.

Emphasizing the already-cited coincidence between color and social position, Edgardo Seoane, a former vice-president of the republic, says that a group of whites, not constituting more than .1 percent of the total population of the country, receives 19.9 percent of the total national income; the 20.4 percent who form the *mestizo* class—middle class and specialized skilled workers—receive 53 percent; the 22.8 percent who form the group of *cholos* (unskilled workers, migrants, etc.) receive 14.2 percent; and the 56.7 percent who constitute the Indian and Indianized *mestizo* group (peasants, farm workers, etc.) receive 12.9 percent.[7]

6

An Unbalanced Economy

The Peruvian economy is an economy unbalanced in every respect: there is an imbalance between the inferior standard of living of the great masses and the provocatively superior standard of the minority; between rural production, which absorbs a disproportionate share of effort, and urban production, which finds no market in which to expand; between the comparatively rapid development of the coastal region and the backwardness of the Sierra and the *selva*; and, finally, between the minimum economic influence of domestic investment and the decisive economic influence of foreign capital.

The economy, moreover, is in a state of transition, the duration of which is impossible to predict, but which undoubtedly will be long; a transition between the economy of a semifeudal, oligarchic society and a capitalistic, industrial economy; between an economy that is semicolonial and one that is national; between an economy giving absolute freedom to business enterprise—an economy of exclusive private investment—and a mixed economy of public and private investment under government control.

The Various Factors

Although the agricultural population is slowly shrinking, Peru's economy is still based fundamentally on agriculture. Agricultural products, particularly cotton and sugar, make up 24 percent of the national income and a third of the country's exports. The rest of the exportation consists chiefly of minerals and fish products.

Nevertheless, mining is important, since, although it employs only 2 percent of the active population, it produces 15 percent of the national income and a considerable percentage of the national exports. On it depends, for the present, the import of capital goods necessary for development and also the purchase of not a few luxury articles consumed by the oligarchic groups and the middle classes.

To a great extent, mining sustains the cost of development, although, in recent years, a powerful contribution has been made by the fishing industry, which has seen enormous progress. Such new industries as foundries, blast furnaces, and chemical, electrical, and cement plants have sprung up. But this increase has been confined chiefly to the coastal fringe of the center and north and has occurred without obeying any overall plan, only the questionable judgment of the investors.

The urban markets have been growing in the last forty years, but they give the impression of not being capable of much further growth—which means that, in consequence, industrialization will not be able to progress, either, unless the rural areas become a market for industrial products. Many firms have never worked at 100 percent of capacity, and it is common, in most of them, for the machinery to operate only eight hours a day.

The distribution of income is extremely unbalanced, between different social groups and between different geographical regions. On the coast, the income per capita is triple that of the Sierra and five times that of the *selva;* it is almost twice the national average. This imbalance has been increasing, thus encouraging emigration from the country to the city—largely from the Sierra— and, at the same time, lessening the possibility of increasing income and accelerating progress in the regions distant from the coast. This, in turn, has produced a marked rise in unemployment along the coast. The economists point out, however, that this imbalance is a bearable one, thanks to the fact that many inhabitants of the Sierra and of the forest regions produce for themselves a great part of what they consume, which never enters the market, and which, therefore, does not show in estimates of national income.

. We must take into account, when we discuss the economy of Peru, that the country presents large obstacles to development and modernization—the enormous distances to be traveled over hostile deserts and rough mountain terrain, which add enormously to the expense of transport and slow it down. Not only economic progress, but the simple survival of the economy involves a constant struggle with nature—which modern technology, while making it less difficult, to be sure, though still very costly, has not abolished.

Under the Incas, there was a type of economy that, unintentionally, made up in organization what it lacked in technology. The use of terraces and paths in the valleys facilitated agricultural production, but these terraces could not be built without a centralized control that would impose a strict working discipline. To a certain degree, it may be said that the lack of wheels, beasts of burden, and machinery facilitated progress, given the geographical background. At a time when no other means existed, transportation by pack was normal and possible in the intricate mountain terrain, which explains the Incas' excellent communications network. But, in an age of trucks, railways, and airplanes, transport on the human back is unthinkable (except for short distances, in traversing which it is still seen); now, roadways, highways, and airports are needed. All these are much more costly and complicated in Peru than they are in other countries of less rugged topography; even natural disasters are less dangerous in other countries. Earthquakes, for example, which are frequent and violent, usually have their epicenters in the Andean region, where, owing to the abundance of valleys, they destroy extensive areas. In 1898, an earthquake caused 25,000 deaths in the north; in 1940, a third of Lima was

damaged; and only recently, in June, 1970, an earthquake
wrought havoc in the Chimbote region and in the Huaylas
(precisely where the Cornell University anthropologists had
made the experiment in accelerated acculturation). Tidal
waves and floods, because of the geographical configuration,
are also more severe in this region than elsewhere.

Under the Incas, the economy of what is now Peru was
a closed one. Except for some contact with traders from
the north, there was no intercourse whatever with other
societies. The colonial era, at the same time that it destroyed
the Inca organization and permitted the formation of the
antieconomic latifundia, gave Peru entry into the world economy. Since then, the Peruvian economy has been tied to
external needs—first, those of Spain and, then, those of the
world market, particularly Great Britain and the United
States. In precolonial times, production had in mind the consumer, and, during the colonial era, it took into account both
domestic consumption and the exporting of minerals to
Spain. But, after independence, the first thought was for exportation, and home consumption took second place, which
resulted in the present economic disparities and poverty of
the great mass of Peruvians.

Economic Attitudes

Industry in Peru is comparatively recent. All the problems of
the past were related to agriculture. The two chief sources of
income in the past century—*guano* and *niter*, or saltpeter—
depended on agriculture, though not the native agriculture,
which has hardly ever used those fertilizers. The use of *guano*
as a plant food was known before the advent of the Spaniards, but exportation of the fertilizer did not become economically important until 1840. The country was in debt,
and, to guarantee the loans it asked for, it offered the exploitation of *guano* and *niter*. This led to the introduction of
British capital, which also paid for laying out the main railway lines, which the governing latifundistas would never have
financed of their own accord. The exploitation of *guano* and
niter, finally, served to give the coastal areas, whence both
substances came, preponderance in the economy.

At the beginning of this century, attempts at economic renovation centered upon agriculture. During World War I, the demand for sugar became so great that the plantations were extended from the coast into some of the Andean valleys. But, after the war and with the crisis of 1929, demand fell sharply, and many plantations were abandoned. Only the most modern mills survived, and they eventually absorbed the others. This gave rise to the sugar latifundism of the coast, which is still predominant there.

As cheaper artificial fertilizers became popular and the exportation of *guano* and *niter* fell off, the exportation of sugar and cotton increased. Cotton is probably the industrial crop that has attracted the least investment of foreign capital; so that there are many small and medium-sized plantations in Peru, side by side with the great landowners, that find a market for their product in the textile industry. This should be enough to show that, if foreign capital is dangerous, it is dangerous in areas where the great latifundistas have not ventured to invest their money; it offers no risk when there are average-sized and small holdings.

Toward the end of the nineteenth century, rubber caused the Amazon region—until then virtually forgotten—to integrate itself with the national economy. The raw material brought high prices, and trade converted the river port of Iquitos into a sort of capital for jungle adventurers. But Asian rubber soon came to be cheaper than South American, and the industry disappeared from Peru almost before it had really made a start.

Peruvian mining, on the other hand, has had a more fortunate history. A flourishing industry from the start, it overcame a period of sluggishness, following independence, with the infusion of foreign capital at the beginning of this century. The Incas used oil as fuel, and, more than a century ago, a private citizen opened the first well of a "tar mine." But prosperity from oil had to wait (especially until after World War II) for systematic prospecting and exploitation of the country's oil riches—producing dollars and headaches simultaneously. The foreign firms that came into Peru adopted from the beginning an intransigent attitude toward the government, demanding (and receiving) privileged treatment, avoiding paying taxes in full, and, in general, functioning without scrupulous regard to local laws.

No less fraught with problems was the exploitation of copper, which began as soon as the trans-Andean railway made possible the transportation of copper at a reasonable cost. In 1902, as we have noted, the American Cerro de Pasco Company was formed, with its principal mines in a part of the central Sierra where they had been worked in colonial times. Later, copper was discovered in the south.

Obviously, Peru has always depended on products obtained far from the cities and sold outside the country. These two characteristics explain, in great measure, the economic habits that still prevail in the commercial and industrial life of the Peruvians.

Above all, Peruvians have not completely overcome the aristocratic prejudice against manual work and commercial activity in general. To be a producer, even if it were on the directorial level, was, so to speak, to be lacking in distinction—a capital sin in an oligarchic society. So, there was no opposition to foreign investments, since these served to fulfill a function looked down upon by the ruling Peruvian groups. Hence, also, the tendency of the sons of middle class families to dedicate themselves, as far as possible, to nonproductive activities—the law, politics, literature, diplomacy—and not take any interest in technical problems or careers. Up to a few years ago, Peru's shortage of technologists and of skilled labor was one of her chief obstacles to progress.

The outlook of the latifundista—who sees his hacienda almost in the light of an autarchy of artisans—was transferred to the economy in general, putting a brake on its modernization. Until a few decades ago, there was no central reserve bank, and, until the second half of the nineteenth century, there were no government budgets. Only after World War I were direct taxes levied, and, only in the second half of this century were there taxes on uncultivated land. Even today, only business firms make use of bankers' services. Private persons pay their bills in cash, unless they are for very large amounts.

Of course, there are young entrepreneurs and technical men who are trying to modernize not only the methods of production and administration but also the very outlook of businessmen. But this is a slow and long-term effort; although, under the influence of American investors, there has been rapid adoption of some of the more dramatic techniques, such as the use of computers and market studies.

All in all, however, Peru's economy is anachronistic. Its procedures are slow and oppressed by the double weight of the official and private bureaucracy. There are more family firms than corporations, and above all of them hovers the shadow of the banks, which in Peru are extremely powerful, linked as they are to the coastal oligarchy, with more interest in international trade than in domestic development.

Agriculture

Thirty percent of the cultivated land is in the coastal region, 60 percent in the Sierra, and the remaining 10 percent in the *selva*. Most of the coastal land is irrigated. The land of the overpopulated meridional region is badly eroded and wasted by drought. As a rule, the farming techniques of the Sierra are very primitive, and erosion is advancing (as already noted) because of postconquest abandonment of the system of terraces and steps on mountainsides used by the Incas. Deforestation has further aggravated the process of erosion.

About one-fourth of the cultivated land is given over to potatoes and corn—the staples of the Peruvian diet. Cotton and sugar account for only 15 percent of the cultivated acreage, although these are two of the country's chief exports. Also cultivated, for domestic consumption, are barley, rice, wheat, and *quinoa*, a native cereal. Still produced, although in smaller amounts, are kidney beans, coffee, yucca, fruits, and coca. Yet, despite the progress that has been made in agriculture, Peru must still import more than 40 percent of her food. Some years ago this figure was as high as 50 percent.

Lumber is a possible source of wealth; but, although more than half of the nation's territory is covered with forest (especially in the east), the difficulties of transportation are an obstacle to deriving the best advantage from this resource. What lumbering there is, is uncontrolled and thus contributes to deforestation, which has already stripped the Andean region. To give an idea of the costliness of transportation: pine for ordinary woodworking is imported from the United States; for it would be more expensive if it were carried to the cities from the mountains where it grows. The woods yield, for exportation and domestic use, a bit of rubber; essence of rosewood; and caspi milk, which is used for chewing gum.

More than half of the population live in rural areas, but the rural areas produce only a third of the gross national product. The total cultivable area contains about 75 million acres—one-fourth of the national territory. But only a fifth of this arable land is profitably cultivated; the remainder is untilled and given over to cattle. Since the population is growing more and more rapidly, it will be necessary to increase the production of the land, either by modernizing the methods of cultivation or by extending the areas under cultivation. Both are being done, but on a scale the technologists consider inadequate, with the result that importation of food products continues to increase. Plans for irrigation have been made by fits and starts and, on the coast, have produced a significant increase in agricultural production—above all, in production for export.

Apart from the crops that are used to nourish the Peruvians, the agricultural economy is based, as we have said, on three exports—cotton, sugar, and tobacco. Cotton is produced in the valleys along the coast (Ica, Lima, Piura). More is exported to Europe than to the United States; Chile, also, buys a good amount for its textile industry.

Sugar is harvested in the valleys near Trujillo and Chiclayo. Since 1946, the land given over to this crop has increased 12 percent, and the production of sugar has risen 60 percent, indicating efficient modernization of the industry's methods. Of the 800,000 tons produced yearly, 600,000 are exported, mostly to the United States, which allows Peru a favorable quota.

In recent decades, coffee has also begun to take its place

as an export, and brings in about $20 million a year. More-over, the coffee plantations, along the edge of the *selva*, can act as a bridgehead for the modernization of this extensive eastern region. The production of wine is also increasing—not for export, but to compete with imported Chilean and Argen-tine wines, which previously had enjoyed a quasi monopoly.

Tobacco, the curing and manufacturing of which is a state monopoly, is cultivated in Tumbes and is sufficient for do-mestic use (but not a match for the caprices of fashion, which make it necessary to import large quantities of American tobacco products).

Cattle raising has made rather good progress in recent years, but not enough to satisfy the demand. The urban population eats chiefly imported meat. The demand for milk in urban areas has caused a reduction in consumption of this essential food in rural areas. For that matter, the consump-tion of milk and meat are both low in the cities and still lower in the country.

Sheep and other wool-bearing flocks are pastured chiefly in the high part of the Sierra, and the milk and beef cattle in the low parts. Fifteen million head of sheep produce scarcely enough wool for the needs of the textile industry. On the con-trary, the wool of the llama—the herds of which number about 4 million—the alpaca, and the vicuña—which are found in the higher levels—is exported almost entirely, since it is much sought abroad. There are also 5 million head of beef and milk cattle, 4 million goats, and 2 million deer. Poultry raising on a large scale is localized in the vicinity of Lima; in the rest of the country, their rearing is a part of the domestic activity of the peasants.

The consumption of fish has traditionally been low and confined to the cities on the banks of Lake Titicaca. In re-cent years, however, Peru seems to have discovered the sea as a source of wealth. After 1955, in fact, a very special fishing industry developed. Around 1963, its volume had risen 60 percent. Since then, it has undergone another increase, this time about 30 percent above the 1963 level. Ninety-seven percent of the fish are anchovies, which live in the plankton-rich waters near the coast and are used entirely for making fishmeal; only the remaining 3 percent, which include several varieties, are for domestic consumption. There is also some whale fishing in the regions rich in these creatures, near the coast, but the meal and frozen meat derived from the whale amount to only 1 percent of the national fishing production and have not increased for many years.

Fishing, on the industrial scale, has two bases—Callao, and, principally, Chimbote, 250 miles north of Lima. Today, the catch of anchovies is beyond the limit considered permissible by biologists if this source of wealth is not to be destroyed. But protective measures appear to be obeyed only occasionally.

Fishing is carried on chiefly by Spaniards who have immigrated in recent years. With growing international demand for fishmeal since 1955, the Peruvian fishing industry has absorbed a great deal of foreign capital. Now, however, with the demand stabilized, this industry appears to be stagnating. The meal derived from Peruvian fishing—70 percent of the world's supply—brought in foreign currency at a time when the country's economy was feeling the pinch and permitted it to continue its development. About 300,000 persons depend indirectly on this industry, which pays the highest wages in the country. But it is feared that advances in the technique of cattle feeding, for which fishmeal is chiefly used, may bring about a crisis for the fishing industry. To halt the approaching crisis, an investigation has begun into the possibility of using fishmeal as a food for human beings. At present, the industry accounts for 6 percent of the gross national income and nearly a third of the value of the country's exports.

Peru is now the world's leading fishing country, producing 10.5 million tons a year, which puts her ahead of Japan and the Soviet Union. But it is American fishermen who present problems for Peru. Incidents are not rare: seizure of American boats in waters that Peruvians consider their own; claims; fines; and diplomatic protest. In 1968, Peru, together with Ecuador and Chile, adopted a 200-mile fishing limit, which Washington refuses to recognize. The Peruvian argument is that the fish taken near the coast come from the inner waters, and that, if boats of other countries, using better techniques, are allowed to fish up to the normal three-mile limit, the Peruvian waters will be entirely depleted.

Mining

Before and after the colonial era, mining in Peru was basically for gold and silver. Today, it has turned to copper, lead, and zinc, which account for nearly half of the exports.

In addition to half a dozen great mining centers, there are eighty-five of medium size and nearly 4,000 small ones. Peruvian mines are among the most difficult to work, since they are in the Sierra (except the phosphate mines, which are in the coastal region). Since the altitude makes the work extremely fatiguing, the miners must be replaced after a few years of work. Only the Indians, who are inured to the height, can endure this work; even so, they suffer a considerable loss of vitality. Moreover, the undulated mountain terrain makes it expensive to transport the minerals to the place of use or shipment. Since all this requires a great deal of capital, the government has encouraged foreign investment in the mines, giving exemptions and privileges without troubling itself about what this might eventually mean to the economy. Ninety-seven percent of this foreign investment is by American firms. In recent years, they have modernized the Toquepala copper mines in the south to such an extent that now more is produced there than in Cerro de Pasco in the north, once considered the richest copper mine in Peru.

Finally, despite the fears that had arisen in the United States, several agreements were signed with American mining companies. In one of them, the Andes Exploration Company bound itself to invest $106 million for development of the Cerro Verde copper mines in the department of Arequipa. This firm is a subsidiary of the Anaconda Copper Mining Company. It is estimated that within a few years, 20,000 tons a day will be taken out of these mines. In another agreement, the Southern Peru Copper Company pledged the investment of $355 million for development of the Cuajone copper mines, near the Chilean frontier, which contain deposits of 450 million tons of ore with a copper content of 1 percent. An agreement was also signed with the Japanese

Marubeni firm for exploitation of the copper, lead, and zinc deposits of Madrigal and the installation of a concentrator plant. Another Japanese firm has agreed to take over the entire production for a period of three years.

In 1970, Peru, which along with Chile, Zambia, and Kinshasa, is a member of the Council of Copper Exporting Countries, passed a new series of laws pertaining to mining (and directed especially toward copper mining) by which the state receives the right to refine and market all metals. This law is to be applied within a term of eighteen months. Existing agreements with foreign firms, however, are to be respected. Fiscal exemptions and other benefits are offered to firms that increase production by 20 percent or more, and also to those firms whose profits have been affected by the fall of prices on the world market. Firms in which the state owns 25 percent or more of the stock will enjoy certain additional benefits. To carry out these laws, a decentralized government department, the Empresa Minera del Perú (Peruvian Mining Enterprise), was established.

The annual production of copper is valued at slightly less than $100 million—much less than it could be, according to engineers, if all the mines were exploited with modern methods for full yield. New deposits have been found near Arequipa, and, when developed, they will double the production of copper and allow Peru to move up from her present seventh place among the world's copper-producing countries.

Lead and zinc are also metals of economic importance for the country. Most of the mines are in the central part of the Sierra and are owned by the Cerro de Pasco Company, an American firm. Although American limits on the importation of these minerals have restricted production, it still is worth about $40 million a year. The principal copper, zinc, and lead smelting plant is in La Oroya, in the central Andes.

Iron mining began in 1953. There are deposits in Marcona and Acar (the latter Peruvian-owned; the former, American) in the south, near the coast. In 1958, the first blast furnace went into operation at Chimbote, about 500 miles north of the mines, making it possible to smelt the ore in Peru. (This blast furnace was partially destroyed by the earthquake of

1970.) The annual extraction of 3.5 million tons has made Peru the second-largest exporter of iron in Latin America. Peruvian industry uses only 60,000 tons of steel a year, which indicates what a small beginning it still constitutes.

Although gold and silver have lost the attraction they used to have, $24 million worth of bar silver is exported annually. And these minerals do not exhaust the mineral wealth of Peru. Altogether, about forty different minerals are extracted—tungsten in Ancash, magnesium in Junín and Puno, antimony, arsenic, bismuth, mercury, molybdenum, tin, cadmium, and others elsewhere. Many of these minerals are by-products of the smelting of major minerals. There are also radium deposits, which, however, are not being mined. The reserves of manganese are considered very important as well; but they are not operated, because the world market is already sufficiently supplied by other countries.

The deposits of phosphates in the north, which extend over 800,000 hectares in the desert of Sechura, near the coast, appear to be among the world's largest, but small amounts are being extracted. The mining of salt, calcium-oxide stone and the quarrying of marble (all found in various parts of the country) are sufficient to serve only local needs. The same may be said of the deposits of sulphur and of bituminous coal, whch are plentiful. The greater part of the anthracite that is mined, in the Ancash department, is exported to Argentina.

All told, Peru's potential mineral wealth is great, but the difficulties of transportation, the height at which most mines are situated, and the lack of capital have conspired to prevent greater development. Foreign control has been the cause of frequent friction with the government, of continuous anti-American propaganda, and of many campaigns for nationalization of the mines. This has been particularly the case with oil.

Oil

In 1896, Peru became the first Latin American country to produce petroleum on a commercial scale. But the deposits are so few that the country remains fourth among the producers in Latin America. Exportation has diminished with the increase in domestic consumption.

The chief oil fields are in the Talara region, in the coastal north; but others are being prospected for in the forest areas, where, some years ago, natural-gas deposits were found in the Pucallpa zone. The ocean floor is also being explored, thus far with little success. Recently, new concessions were granted to American firms for prospecting in the forest area.

Peru uses 17 million barrels of oil a year—which means that, however little industrialization and mechanization increase, domestic production will be inadequate, and it will therefore be necessary to resort to importation. Since 1962, there has been a refinery for domestic crude oils, which also processes some from Venezuela for reexportation.

The chief oil firm was the International Petroleum Company (IPC), an affiliate of the Standard Oil Company of New Jersey. Other foreign firms have been interested in Peruvian oil, and there was an official-type national company, the Empresa Petrolera Fiscal (Fiscal Petroleum Enterprise), which was replaced in 1968 by Petroperú.

In recent years, friction with the United States has been mainly over oil. In 1965, the American government tried to bring pressure on the Peruvian government by radically reducing its aid to the country. Later, when it became clear that this merely exacerbated nationalist sentiment in Peru, the United States reversed its policy. But by then, the International Petroleum Company had already become a first-class domestic issue.

According to the preceding as well as the present Peruvian government, IPC's possession of the oil-bearing territories in 1924 had been illegal, and the firm had extracted petroleum valued at $690 million without paying all the taxes due under law. The government demanded payment of the back taxes, and three months before the military coup of July, 1968, IPC agreed to the nationalization of its fields in exchange for cancellation of the government's demands. But the military junta nullified this agreement and expropriated IPC's property. Since then, the military government has signed agreements with several other American firms for the exploration of regions believed to contain oil. The agreements do not entail concessions, but establish rules of exploitation, taxes, and so forth, in the event that prospecting is successful.

Transportation

Transportation is expensive. To send merchandise from the capital to the *selva* costs more, and takes more time, than to send it there from New York. To reach certain mines in the Andes takes longer than to go to any other point on the globe, because they cannot be reached by railroads or airplanes. This difficulty is a very costly obstacle to progress. As has been explained, there are only two main highways: the Pan-American, along the coast—a two-lane asphalt road; and the central highway, from Lima to Pucallpa. The latter, which joins the coast and the *selva,* cannot be used in periods of flood rains.[8]

Railway transport consists of a few local lines and two lines from the mining centers in the Sierra. None of these lines, however, serve regions with prosperous markets or have any relation to local economic needs other than those of the mines themselves.[9]

On the other hand, water and air transportation have made satisfactory progress. There are about fifty airports, which serve four Peruvian companies (one international and the others domestic) and about ten foreign lines whose planes land at Lima. This system is administered by the Empresa Peruana de Aeropuertos y Aviación Comercial, a decentralized government department. In recent years, private aviation has grown greatly, especially on the coast, where many plantations are thus linked by air to nearby cities.[10]

The rivers are a considerable aid in the development of the *selva.* Several companies share the burden of joining villages and cities on the Oriente by riverboat. Ships of medium displacement come up the Amazon from the Atlantic to Iquitos. When the water is high, they can go as far as Pucallpa and, thus, join the central highway.

The commercial shipping fleet, however, is small. It consists of about 50 vessels, with a scant 250,000 tons of displacement. Most of the international shipping goes in foreign bottoms. But the fishing fleet, as we have said, has grown rapidly.[11]

One of the chief objectives of much international credit (from U.S. aid, the World Bank, and the Inter-American Development Bank) is to foster and modernize transportation, which had hardly begun to operate in earnest a decade ago. Today, several highways that were usable only at certain times are now practicable year round.

Sources of Energy

The sources of energy are not better than the transportation. Except for oil and coal—the first much used and hardly adequate for domestic use; the second little used—the chief source of energy is electricity in some parts of Oriente, and, of late, natural gas, exploitation of which is still in its beginnings.

But electrical power is not very widespread. Fifty-three percent of the electric power produced by the country is destined for use by the firms that produce it; sometimes, they sell the surplus to the villages in which they are situated, but very often they produce only what they need. Every mine, every important industry, every plantation has its own power plant. Only 47 percent of the electricity generated in Peru is used for public service: 40 percent, produced by a commercial company, serves Lima and Arequipa; the remaining 7 percent is intended for the other cities and villages. Outside of the two cities mentioned, no urban center enjoys even moderately satisfactory electric service.

A French cartel, under government auspices, studied the country's electrical situation and concluded that it would have to be increased 500 percent to begin to satisfy the needs of development. This would not be impossible if capital were available and profitable rates established, since Peru, with her abundance of waterfalls and rapid rivers, has a hydroelectrical potential of nearly 6 million kilowatts, whereas her output today is scarcely more than a million. Since the passage of an electrical power law in 1955, production of electricity has increased 8 percent a year in Lima and Callao, but much less in the rest of the country. There are plans for rural electrification; but, until now, they have come up against the lack of funds.

This scarcity of sources of energy has serious collateral consequences: wherever (as in the highest parts of the Andes) the droppings of cattle, which are dry but combustible, are not used, charcoal, or wood itself, is used—and this accelerates deforestation. As a result, erosion is increased, and the already small agricultural production is diminished.

Communication

Telegraph lines join the cities, but rarely reach the small settlements. In recent years, electronic communication has been extended by a network of short-wave radio stations. Mail service, although theoretically extending throughout the entire territory, leaves many villages on the fringe, and, outside of the big cities, is very slow.

Telephone service is largely confined to the urban centers, and one needs money and influence to get a new phone. A mere connection is also often difficult to obtain, especially in the cities, because the lines are worn out and overloaded. In Lima, one can buy a phone already installed, for about 2,000 soles (or $46). This is illegal but it is tolerated.[12]

In October of 1969, the military junta reached an agreement with ITT to purchase, at a price of 17.9 million soles (or $500,000), a block of stocks sufficient for the control of the telephone service in Lima, which meant that the junta would thereafter be responsible for improving telephone service.

Manufacturing

The two world wars and the Korean war have been great incentives for the industrialization of Peru—the world wars by limiting the importation of manufactured goods, and the Korean War by raising the price of raw materials to such a height that the country had a surplus of dollars available for the importation of capital goods. For all that, industrialization has hardly gone beyond its beginnings (except the textile industry, created in the middle of the past century), and the country has to acquire from abroad not only machinery and other capital goods but many consumer goods. Existing industry is designed chiefly to satisfy the demands of the domestic market; this means, in essence, only the cities–and, even in these, only that part of the population which has urban ways.

The Industrial Bank was created after World War II to encourage new industry with credit. But governmental investment has been necessary for the development of heavy industry. Production costs are high because of Peru's shrinking market, and industry could not compete with foreign firms without the support of the protectionist policy that has been in force since 1946.

Although limited, the increase in sources of power, especially electrical, has encouraged the rapid development of certain industries. In the last decade, the construction industry has grown by 15 percent a year, and nonmetallic industries have grown by 12 percent. The beverage industry (alcoholic and nonalcoholic), the rubber industry, and production of foods and metallurgy have grown at an annual rate of 7–10 percent. Altogether, Peru's industrial output increased by 63 percent in the decade from 1950 to 1960 and at a slightly lower rate in the past ten years.

The most rapid development is seen in the construction industry which has shown a remarkable increase in the production of cement. The textile industry is growing less rapidly, but continues to be the leading industry of the country after mining. It is localized in the Lima-Callao area, with some wool-weaving shops in Arequipa, Cuzco, Puno, and Huancayo. But the costs are high, due to antiquated machinery that the owners are not replacing. If it were not for the protective tariff, this industry could not compete with that abroad; indeed, it barely suffices for the demands of the home market, which often has to import European fabrics.

The chemical industry was begun by an American firm, the Grace Company. This company had a virtual monopoly for a while, but, with World War II, the industry was diversified and grew. There are centers for the production of fertilizers, caustic soda, and sulphuric acid, and a petrochemical center is projected. The pharmaceutical industry depends heavily on imports.

Shipbuilding (the vessels are only of the fishing type) has increased of late, thanks to the availability of the iron goods produced at Chimbote and the demands of the fishing industry. Obviously, for its industrial development, the country needs a larger iron and steel industry. The present one is limited to the Chimbote complex, which is financed by the government and produces 68,000 tons a year of semifinished articles, a quantity just adequate for present domestic needs. This production is 1 percent of that of all Latin America.

The other industries—leather, rubber, and their by-products; linseed meal cake, and so forth—are growing, but each is still at the stage where a single firm, practically speaking, has a monopoly.

Following a general tendency in Latin America, the government has recently begun to foster a domestic automobile industry. According to law, a constantly larger percentage of the motor vehicles sold in Peru must be assembled in that country, and a given number of the parts used must be Peruvian-made, with the ratio increasing in proportion to the increase in the production of iron and steel goods. As a result, some firms have joined to establish common assembly plants. Thus, Diesel Motors and the International Harvester Company produce trucks together. General Motors and Ford have their own plants, each of which turns out about 7,000 units a year. Chrysler produces 4,500 vehicles and the Industrial Automotriz Peruana (American Motors and Renault) will turn out 3,000. Nevertheless, every year since 1966, 25,000 units assembled abroad have been imported. By a 1970 decree, the use of parts produced domestically will be increased, and 1974 was fixed as the last year in which engines were to be imported, but the deadline has been extended indefinitely. Also prohibited is the importation of new models more than once every four years. This will reduce the habitual change of models every year, which had been growing common in the well-to-do middle class, and will permit American companies to send their surplus of outdated models to Peru.

Many small shops must compete with imports and with some modern industries; and since their owners are not powerful enough to obtain tariff protection, they protect themselves by working under conditions that hardly maintain them. At times, these shops achieve a certain amount of development by producing for new industries in their regions—as is the case, for instance, with electromechanical shops, tire factories, and even furniture makers. Much of the production of consumer goods, however, particularly in the provinces, continues to be on the craftsman-artisan level.

Commerce

Outside of Lima and some other cities, distribution of merchandise is done by small local stores. There are no chain outlets and only a few supermarkets. The storekeeper is always an economic force in the villages, since he gives credit to the peasants in anticipation of their crops. Sometimes, this leads to activities that might be called monopolistic. It is not unusual for a storekeeper to buy a standing crop and to go on allowing credit on it. After the harvest, the peasant finds that he has very little money and realizes that he has paid very high prices for the food and goods he has bought, whereas he is receiving for the crop prices fixed earlier by the storekeeper. The storekeepers sell, in turn, to monopolistic buyers and intermediaries of the region—the ones who carry out the big deals.

This tends to disappear along the coast and near the cities, but still prevails in the Sierra. On the great haciendas, the peasants are sold what they need on credit, generally at outrageous prices; so that the peasants cannot leave the hacienda without first paying what they owe, which is virtually impossible. At other times, the hacienda has its overseer give a kind of monopoly concession to a merchant, who then takes over the binding of the peasant by means of the debt system.

The modernization of commerce, however, especially in the cities, is more rapid than the modernization and development of industry. The merchants exert a constant pressure, in opposition to the industrialists, against protectionism.

In the distribution of certain pharmaceutical and automotive products and the like, it is not exceptional for a firm to enjoy a de facto monopoly in a region or in a small town, and for the local authorities to help them prevent the establishment of competitors.

Strolling vendors, tiny arcade shops, and very small bars and restaurants are plentiful, as are itinerant market vendors, who go from one village fiesta to another with their merchandise. Finally, it should be pointed out that selling on the installment plan is very common in the poor quarters, and that this is usually carried on by Peruvians of Syrian-Lebanese origin (called "Turks" by the people because they had begun this activity when their ancestral homeland was still part of the Ottoman Empire).

Banking and Finance

Peru's financial structure is an anachronism. Computerized accounting in banks has barely begun; in the majority, accounting by hand is still the rule.

Interest is generally high. Eleven percent annually is legal, but 20-25 percent is common and is tolerated. Usury, particularly in the provinces, is frequent. Only the cooperatives, which have developed a good deal in the past years, thanks to union support, are a counterforce to the high cost of credit.

Many Peruvians feel today that the banks—established primarily for elements of the coastal oligarchy, which, unlike those of the Sierra, have diversified their investments—are more powerful than the great landholders; that the country, therefore, has been changed, de facto, into a dominion of the national banks, operating in close relationship with international bankers (particularly with British banks, in the past, and now with American ones).

The Banco Emisor, or Central Reserve Bank, was established in 1922. It not only issues money but controls the other banks, rediscounts their paper, and keeps watch over gold and other hard money, which, in 1959, amounted to $34.1 million and had risen, by 1969, to $166 million, and, by 1976, to $400 million.

There are twenty-six major national and foreign banks (of the latter, one is British, one Canadian, one American, and one Japanese). But, in many national banks, there are important foreign interests. By a decree of the military junta in

December, 1968, 75 percent of the capital of every bank was to be in Peruvian hands, and no new bank not integrally Peruvian was to be established; also, four-fifths of the directors had to be Peruvian. All banks are under the control of a superintendent of banks.

Before the military coup of 1968, the government had commenced negotiations aimed at refinancing the foreign debt, in the face of the impossibility of countering the obligations contracted during a long period in which foreign credit and aid were received. The military junta concluded these negotiations; the creditor countries (especially the United States, West Germany, France, and Great Britain, in that order) agreed that 75 percent of the debts reimbursable in 1970 and 1971 should be paid in 1976 and 1977, respectively, with interest at 9 percent (except in the case of West Germany, which would collect 8.5 percent). Altogether, debts amounting to nearly $1.35 billion were repaid, $1.12 billion being owed to the United States alone.

The credits opened by the banks rose from $16.4 billion in 1967 to $18.7 billion in 1969. The money supply rose from $18.3 billion to $21.7 billion in the same period. Although Peru suffers from an inflation problem, it is not as serious as in other countries of Latin America. The cost of living has risen from the index of 100 in 1958 to 190 in 1965, to 230 in 1970, and to 270 in 1975.

The national unit of money, the sol, divided into one hundred centavos, has been periodically devalued since World War II. In 1950, a dollar was worth 14.95 soles; in 1960, it was worth 26.76; and, in 1965, it was worth 26.82. There was a devaluation in 1967 (39.70 soles to the dollar), and, in January, 1970, the dollar was quoted in the free market at 43.48, and, in 1976, at 65.00.

In 1970, the military junta established very rigid controls on exchange; it ordered all Peruvians who owned foreign money to deposit it in the banks and all those who owned it outside the country to make a declaration. The banks were obliged to open their vaults for examination to see whether they contained foreign currency. In May of the same year, the junta ordered the repatriation of all the capital of Peruvians who were abroad, but this order and the others we have just mentioned were practically ignored.

In short, the Peruvian banking and financial system is in a period of change—no one knows in which direction. An indication of this, perhaps, is the decision of the military junta, in June, 1970, to nationalize the Banco Popular, owned by one of the "great" families of the country (the Prados, from which, in the past, came several ministers, many prominent figures of business, and a president). The Prados supported the military—before and after the coup of 1968—but from the moment the latter decreed agrarian reform, the family began to withdraw from the Banco Popular the accounts of the businesses that were controlled by them. This put the bank in a difficult situation, and negotiations were begun with a view toward merging it with the Continental Bank (controlled by the Chase Manhattan Bank in the United States). In view of that, the junta decided to nationalize the bank and its 140 branches and, indirectly, to take control of the complex of industrial and agricultural firms still dependent upon it. The Banco Popular, founded in 1899, was the second largest in the country, immediately after the Banco de Crédito del Perú (Peruvian Credit Bank), controlled by Italian interests; thus, it was the most powerful strictly Peruvian bank in the country.

Public Finance

The national budget has been deficit-based for a decade and has adjusted to this by the emission of bonds, with, chiefly, advances from the Central Reserve Bank. In 1956, the budget rose to $69 million in income and $80.5 million in expenses. In 1960, the expenditures were $180 million and the income equaled the expenditures. The distribution of the different expenses is approximately as follows: military expenses, 20 percent; the interior, including police, 12 percent; education, 17 percent; public works, 12 percent; and health, 15 percent. In 1970, the military junta expended $1 billion, and the autonomous departments $575 million. Public investment rose to $214 million—one-fifth of the total national investment. In 1970, the junta issued bonds for a total of $69 million at 10 percent interest. Of this, $58 million was used to pay the treasury's debts to the Central Reserve Bank, and $9 million to pay the government's debt to the social-security system.

The financial system is superannuated. It is based on in-direct taxes—a system that, as is well known, most heavily affects the least economically favored groups—and on taxa-tion of imports. Direct taxes are relatively low, and their progressive character is negligible; land taxes barely exist. In 1970, however, the military junta effected fiscal reforms which obliged business firms to pay an income tax ranging from 20 percent on profits of less than $2,300 to 55 percent on profits of more than $23 million. Foreign mining com-panies pay up to 65 percent of their profits, except for those that have won the exemption provided by the mining code.

The government's income is derived from the following sources: 47 percent from direct taxes; 22.5 percent from in-direct taxes; 21.1 percent from customs; and 5.1 percent from state monopolies, with the balance provided by various minor sources.

Foreign Trade

Peru has always been an exporter of raw materials. Until World War II, she exported chiefly agricultural products. Since then, this trade has moved down to third place, first and second places being occupied by mining (especially of copper) and fish (fish meal).

In the last five years, the balance of foreign trade has been unfavorable, because of the considerable increase in imports and because, while the price of consumer goods and capital goods bought by Peru was rapidly rising, that of the raw materials sold by Peru was rising only slowly or, at times, even falling. To the unfavorable character of the balance of payments should be added—on the debit side of income—credits and investments (which have been falling) and—on the credit side—interest and repayments. The balance of pay-ments problem also emphasizes the exportation of the profits made by foreign firms, which has been increasing.

In 1965, there was already a deficit of $52 million. In

1966, exports rose but there was also a sharp rise in imports, which produced a deficit of $100 million. By 1970, the situation had improved somewhat and there was a surplus of $42 million. This was the result of measures taken by the military junta which included a drastic reduction in imports, an increase in the fees for services performed abroad (visas, consular services, and the like), and a decree that a given percentage of freight should go on Peruvian vessels. The volume and value of exports, however, both failed to rise. The chief cause of the fluctuation in exports lies in the uncertainty of the catch of fish and the oscillation of the demand for fish meal in the world market. By 1975, the deficit was $1.113 million.

Nevertheless, Peru's position as an exporter has constantly improved. In 1950, the country exported goods worth $190 million; the 1965 figure was $667 million, and that of 1969 was $865 million—an increase of 400 percent in twenty years. Today, Peru is sixth among Latin American exporting countries, after Venezuela, Brazil, Argentina, Mexico, and Chile.

The United States is Peru's chief customer (36 percent) and chief supplier. Peru has been able to increase the range of countries from whom she buys as well as the variety of nations who make purchases from her, but with only relative success. The country has an active interchange with Switzerland and the United Kingdom (which is increasing), on the one hand, and with Belgium, Canada, Italy, Japan, and West Germany (which is declining), on the other. In 1969, the military junta reestablished diplomatic and commercial relations with the Soviet Union and several of its satellites (broken off for political reasons twenty years earlier); but, for the moment, commercial interchange with them is small.

One of the aspirations of Peru—as of all Latin American countries—is to export manufactured and semifinished products, especially since the mining and fishing industries—which provide the bulk of the exports—use only a limited percentage of the labor force. It is hoped that this will be accomplished through interchange with other Latin American countries, joined in the LAFTA (Latin American Free Trade Association) and in the Andean Pact, signed in 1969 under the aegis of the LAFTA by Peru, Bolivia, Colombia, Ecuador, and Chile. Peru figures in the LAFTA within the group of "countries with inadequate markets." So far Peruvian industry has been unable to compete with the industries of Argentina, Brazil, and Mexico; its commerce with these countries, therefore, is limited, but it has been moderately successful in penetrating the Ecuadorean market and has hopes, through the Andean pact, of doing the same with the Chilean and Colombian markets, profiting since its labor force is cheaper than theirs. Bolivia, on the other hand, has always been a moderate-sized but steady market for several Peruvian manufactured products, such as textiles and electrical supplies.

Traditionally, Peru's foreign trade has developed with full freedom of enterprise; controls have been established only in moments of economic crisis or of alarm over the balance of payments. But, on May 15, 1970, the military junta created a system that virtually converted foreign trade into a state monopoly, or at least subjected it to strict government control.

Planning and Development

In Latin America, Peru has been a paradise for the supporters of free trade. Until the middle of the last century, there was no budget, and, until 1962, there was no mechanism for economic planning. In that year, the military junta then in office set up a planning system, with regional and local councils in the various ministries. It also created the National Planning Institute, the National Council for Economic Development, and the Consultative Planning Council. The National Planning Institute, the axis of this system, absorbed the National Statistical and Census Council, but, to date, has not elaborated any plan for development. The National Development Council advises the president of the republic and is composed of various ministers and chiefs of government branches. The Consultative Planning Council is the channel through which private interests—unions, chambers of commerce, industry, etc.—explain their points of view to the executive branch.

There are some planned activities in relationship with international organizations. The most important is the Andean

Program of the FAO, UNESCO, WHO, and ILO, which takes in not only part of Peru but also parts of Bolivia, Ecuador, Colombia, and Paraguay and the north of Argentina; its purpose is to encourage integration of the Indian population into modern life.

Obviously, the planning of development is itself little developed. The present military junta has announced that it proposes to set up a development plan, but so far has done nothing in that direction. The only planning apparatus with any degree of efficiency is the budget—and that is rarely used.

It is not strange, therefore, that, in spite of Peru's favorable economic elements—diversity of production, relatively diversified exports (as much in the matter of products as of the markets themselves)—her rate of economic growth has been low compared with that of some other Latin American countries. The rate of economic growth has averaged 3.7 percent in the last twenty years, but the population growth has absorbed most of it. For 1969, the military junta calculated that the rate of increase would be 5 percent (compared to 1.3 percent for 1968), but the actual rate reached was only 1.7 percent, and has not been consistently higher than that.

To understand what the term development really means, some figures will suffice: in Peru, the per capita annual income is $338. But .1 percent of the population absorbs 19.9 percent of the national income. On the other hand, if we take the year 1965—which was an exceptionally good one, with the rate of increase of the gross national product then being 5 percent and the rate of population growth 3.3 percent—it becomes obvious that the real growth was only 1.7 percent. Therefore, it would be necessary to maintain this increase for forty-four years in order to Peru to double its per capita income—which would then be equal to that of Argentina today. Some Peruvians attribute this situation to the fact that their society is oligarchic; others, to the influence of foreign investment.

Foreign Investment

Although in recent years foreign investments have attained a

rate that could be easily assimilated, there was a mass of earlier invested foreign capital that, in comparison to capital of
domestic origin, was considerable and, in some industries—
for example, mining and petroleum—was in the majority.
British capital was dominant in the country before World
War I, and American investment began to increase after 1919
until it itself became dominant after World War II. In 1924,
American firms had invested $124 million in Peru; but, in
1936, the figure fell to $96 million. This gradually grew,
however, until it reached $295 million in 1950, $502 million
in 1960, and $605 million in 1967. Today, American invest-
ment in Peru represents 5.2 percent of all American investment abroad. In the last three years, the figure has been falling, although the agreements that the military junta signed
with various American firms predicate greater investment
than ever in the years to come, especially in mining. Agreements have also been signed with firms from other countries
in connection with their investments in Peruvian enterprises.
Thus, Japan has interests in the bauxite deposits; Belgium, in
building a telephone equipment factory. The junta offers
inducements such as no other government has dared to suggest: reduction of taxes on profits; authorization to increase
the yearly depreciation rate; guarantees to foreign firms of
the availability of dollars to cover the capital invested; interest, benefits, and services; the right to deduct from profits
losses undergone previously; a guarantee in foreign money
to companies interested in developing the mines.

The total American investment in Peru has risen to $645
million, but its sale value exceeds $1 billion (because the first
figure is based on book value after subtracting depreciation
of plant and machinery). The convenience and danger of foreign investments have been the subject of heated debate for
almost half a century in Peru as in the rest of Latin America.
Those who favor them assert that foreign firms pay better
salaries (not always a certainty); that they create industries for
which domestic capital is insufficient; and that they contribute generally to the modernization of the country. Opponents point out that they entail discrimination in treatment
and salaries between Peruvians and foreigners (particularly in

the field of raw materials); that they are concerned with the interests of the investing country and not with those of Peru; that they cause intervention in national politics (which was formerly more true than it is now); and that they export great quantities of foreign currency to repatriate interest, profits, and so forth. For example, it is noted that, in 1950, $295 million invested by American firms, $15 million went out of the country; these figures were, respectively, $605 million and $101 million in 1967. In all, from 1950 to 1967, out of a total of $605 million invested, profits amounted to $712 million, of which $628 million were sent out of the country.[13] Of these, $340 million are invested in mining, $38 million in oil, $98 million in manufacturing, $54 million in public services, $22 million in commerce, and the rest in various other activities.

American investment represents 67.5 percent of the total foreign investments in Peru; the rest can be broken down as follows:
- British—$86 million (in transportation, manufacturing, and commerce)
- Swiss—$50 million (in electricity, manufacturing, commerce, and public services)
- Dutch—$18 million (in electricity and commerce)
- Canadian—$14 million (in manufacturing and commerce)
- French—$10 million (in public services)
- Swedish—$9 million (in manufacturing and commerce)
- West German—$5 million (in manufacturing and commerce)
- Japanese—$5 million (in mining and manufacturing)
- Italian—$5 million (in electricity)
- Other—in smaller amounts

Perhaps the most harmful feature of foreign investment is that it has constituted an obstacle (more powerful than national interest) to the formation of developmental plans and thus has done more to retard such plans than to encourage them by technical contributions and capital. In any case, the existence of foreign investment has aroused major passions for many decades, and these have led, on one side and the other, to irrational attitudes and behavior. Examples are the practice of labeling as "Communist" all who oppose concessions to foreign firms, and the charge that American business is solely responsible for the country's backwardness.

7

A Fragmented Population

What sort of people are the Peruvians? The question is a very difficult one to answer, because there is not one type of Peruvian, but several. Peru is an archipelago of peoples, a society of microsocieties, and the course of history with its diverse influences: pre-Inca peoples, Incas, Spaniards; the contributions, before and after independence, of Europeans, Orientals, and Negroes—has only increased the country's complexity.

Haya de la Torre used to say that, in Peru, it was possible to retrace all the stages of history: there was the primitivism of the *selva*, the feudalism of the Sierra, the capitalism of the coastal cities. How could elements so diverse be culturally and politically equal? To answer that, we must repeat that the history of Peru is that of a struggle to form a nationality out of all these elements, to unite the islands of this archipelago of peoples into one compact nation. Without the techniques of our time, this could not even be hoped for. Even with them, it is still far from accomplished.

Ethnic Make-up

In the nineteenth century, it was customary to speak of *castas*, or "castes" (Indians); *pardos*, or "browns" (Negroes and mulattoes); *criollos,* or Creoles (whites), and *cholos* (mestizos). The process of mixing these ingredients has not gone very far. There are still many "pure-blooded" Indians and many "pure" whites, although the number of *mestizos* is increasing.

In speaking of Peru's ethnic makeup, Indians are mentioned first, but who is an Indian? Should the *mestizo*, who lives like an Indian, who has the physical features and the culture of an Indian—although his mother may have been a *mestizo* or, less frequently, a white—be considered an Indian? On the other hand, should an Indian who dresses, speaks, and lives like an urban *mestizo* or white person be considered an Indian?

Anthropologists have concluded that 47–51 percent of Peru's population should be considered Indians, because of their lifestyle and customs. More than 7 million Peruvians are Indians; 40 percent are *mestizos*; and the remainder are "pure" white, "pure" Negroes, or "pure" Orientals.

Thus, Indians form the basic population of Peru. Almost half the Indians (or "indigenes," as they are called by Latin Americans to whom the term "Indian" is offensive) in all of South America are found in Peru. This is not so obvious in the cities as in the rural areas, and still much less so in business offices, hotels, government offices, or the cafés where the intellectuals meet. For, the Indian is at the bottom of society; whereas the *mestizo* is in the middle class and the whites are in the upper class. One cannot emphasize this too strongly, since, without understanding it, one cannot understand Peru's politics, culture, or economy.

The indigenes have scarcely any influence on the culture or way of life of the non-Indians, except a certain degree on speech (many Peruvians of the well-to-do class had Indian nurses when they were just learning to talk) and on physical characteristics, in the measure in which *mestizáje* is slowly increasing. On the contrary, the culture of the whites—which is, fundamentally, that also adopted by the *mestizos*—has a considerable influence upon the Indians, mostly in the major cities but also in the smaller provincial cities and even in the villages. It determines changes in their methods of work, in their clothing, in their language, and in their relations with the government (although these are, for the most part, limited).

Sometimes the Indian adopts; at other times, he turns in upon himself in his little communes. Often, he gives way in external matters but clings to ancestral customs in the concept of family, of sexual relations, and of religion.

Where the Indians are being most rapidly integrated is in language. There are still 2 million Indians who do not speak Spanish—the official language; 3 million who speak Quechua and Spanish; and nearly a half million in the region around Lake Titicaca who speak Aymará. Since only Castilian Spanish is taught in the public schools, the Indian school children have to study a language that is strange to them, a fact which is an obstacle to their cultural progress, which is also hindered by the persistence of ancestral custom and the social status of the majority of Indians.

For the Indian, society has always meant the *encomendero* and the *corregidor* of the colony, or the hacienda owner and *cacique* of the republic. For this reason, he views the outer world with distrust and lives on the defensive. He does not realize that, in doing so, he isolates himself from economic progress. But he does know that external influences are destroying his way of life—a very old and very solid collective identity.

There are various bodies charged with protecting the Indian and integrating him into modern society. The general direction of indigenist policy—so far as there is any—is in the hands of the Ministry of Labor and Indian Affairs. The Instituto Indigenista Peruano, affiliated with the Inter-American Indigenist Institute, a branch of the Organization of American States, is in charge of cultural matters—encouraging the use of Spanish among the Indians, studying their customs and the problems of acculturation, suggesting protective legislation, and even seeking a market for their handicrafts. It is also in charge of the instruction of Indians in the *selva*, which begins in their own language and later passes into Spanish.

The Directory of Indigenous Affairs is a liaison between the government branches and the Indians. Various university schools and some academic societies are also interested in the Indians, and collaborate especially on sociological and anthropological projects, with foreign universities. Some Catholic orders—such as Maryknoll, the Franciscans, the Dominicans, and the Jesuits—have Indian missions or centers of social action; and various Protestant denominations maintain missions, especially in the eastern *selva*.

None of this has much influence on the Indians' condition; for they are handicapped not only by poverty and by the isolation of the communities many of them live in, but also by the fact that, when they do receive an education, they are taught in Spanish—a strange language—which lessens scholastic progress and discourages many.

In reality, the country is faced with the difficult choice between, on the one hand, destroying the personality of the Indian majority in order to integrate it with the personality of the non-Indian minority, and, on the other, finding a way to make material progress compatible with the Indian personality. Until now, the urban minority has silently chosen the first solution and allowed the mechanism of economic development itself to compel the Indian to cease being an Indian and live like the *mestizo* or the white man. Few studies have been made to find a formula for compatibility.

The Indians may be in the majority, but the most dynamic part of the population, the one that is interested in politics and active in middle-sized and small businesses, and from which come many professionals and intellectuals and many soldiers, is the *mestizo* group. The *cholos*, as they are called, are privileged in the Sierra (at least those who live like whites are), subject only to the white administrators and *hacendados*. But, on the coast and in the cities, they compose the frustrated, ambitious middle class, which feels superior to the Indian and yet is attracted to him—a class that imitates but distrusts the whites, who everywhere in Peru compose the upper class.

On the coast one finds Peru's 50,000 Negroes, 15,000 Chinese, and 30,000 Japanese, as well as the "foreign colonies," of which the largest is the Spanish, now augmented by the fishermen around Chimbote. They are followed, in order, by the Americans, who live in real ghettos, virtually isolated residential quarters, and by the *mestizos* and Indians who have come down from the Sierra.

All these groups are undergoing change. What was not accomplished by centuries of rural existence is being imposed by urban life: the mingling of all groups into one nationality. This mingling is increasingly biological. The whites (especially those who do not belong to the upper classes) marry *mestizos* or Indians; the *mestizos* marry Indians as well as whites. But much more frequent is the nonbiological mingling, what we may call the blending of lifestyles. Little by little, very slowly, Peruvians are tending to live in a more uniform way, a way that does not correspond to their ethnic origin but to the social class to which they belong. And this is a big step toward the formation of nationhood.

The Population

The process of forming nationhood is also abetted by the geographical and economic evolution of the population. As the mineral wealth of the south is exploited and the riches of the *selva* are explored, the exclusively agricultural population of these areas is increased by the addition of industrial workers, miners, and engineers; and around the new centers develop commercial activity and small industry, which change, if only a little, the character of each region. At the same time, the death rate, which is very high in the strictly agricultural areas, is lowered, and the birth rate is raised. Life expectancy has risen from thirty-two to forty-three years in the last two decades. The total population has grown by 63 percent in a period of twenty years; and the urban population has risen 130 percent.

Furthermore, the work force in general is evolving. The increase of engineers and administrators is not the only growth—the number of skilled workers also is rising. But the most profound changes are in the distribution of the labor force. If 50 percent of it is devoted to agriculture, this is a considerable drop in the figures for the period just before World War II, when 70 percent of labor was employed in agriculture. Thirteen percent is engaged in manufacturing, 15 percent in services, 9 percent in trade, 2 percent in mining, 3.2 percent in building, and 3 percent in transportation; the rest is composed of directive groups, small tradesmen, artisans, and so forth.

The tendency is still toward a very slow decline in agricultural labor, a slow growth in manufacturing labor, and a relatively rapid increase in the portion devoted to services. The last is increasing most rapidly. This may represent a danger to the economy, since the level of industrialization does not yet require such a large bureaucracy; on the other hand, it helps promote urban habits and a middle-class way of life among a steadily larger percentage of the population.

A fifth of the labor force is composed of women, especially in the services, in which one-third of the employees is female. Women comprise one-third of those who till the soil, and the percentage of women employed in industry and trade (17 and 11 percent, respectively) is greater than that of men. The number of children employed in agriculture (which does not figure in the statistics) is extremely high, and, in industry and services, there are many apprentices younger than sixteen. In reality, the working child begins to work when he is ten to twelve years old, and many slum children begin, at six to eight years, selling newspapers, shining shoes, running errands, even working as servants. There are still many female servants in the country as well as in the cities; and, if all middle-class families have one maidservant, it is not unusual for those who are more prosperous to have several, even one or two couples.

All the effects of demographic evolution are being counteracted by population growth. The population has grown in the last twenty years at the rate of 2.4–2.6 percent a year (3.3 percent in the last six years), not so much because of a fall in the death rate (although it has declined) as because of a rise in births. In 1950, Peru had 8.5 million inhabitants; in 1960, 10.8 million; and, in 1975, 13.5 million; it is estimated that the population will reach 19 million within ten years. The gross birth rate is 42–48 per thousand and the death rate is 15–22 per thousand. Forty-four percent of the population is less than fifteen years old; only 40 percent is between twenty and sixty. This population explosion entails important social and economic consequences. For one thing, it absorbs almost all of the increase in income, so that the bulk of the population does not improve its standard of living. Moreover, the higher percentage of youth means that the work force is small in proportion to the population.

In spite of the population explosion, Peru is thinly populated and has always been so. The pre-Hispanic cultures were concentrated in pockets, in which were gathered the work forces; these were separated by extensive desert zones, or by regions with a very scattered population. That has continued to be the case, and it has been emphasized in urbanization.

The aspect of the cities is changing, for skyscrapers and shantytowns or slums are rising in them simultaneously. The rural landscape is being modified, since villages are being abandoned and little towns are springing up in the mining centers. But are the Peruvian and his way of life changing so much?

The Family

The family is the most solid base of Peruvian life, despite the failure of half of the sexual unions to be legalized. Yet, many of these unformalized unions are as stable as legal ones. One-third of all Peruvians found a family before they are twenty. In the rural areas, many couples continue to live in the house of the husband's father, at least until they have children. Scarcely 15 percent of marriages end in divorce, and nearly all the divorces occur in the cities.

Another solid institution, in the Sierra, is the indigenous community, understood here not in the economic sense of a communal ownership of land, but in the sense of a people, a clan who have lived all their lives in the same place, and who know all their neighbors and are joined to them by ties of kinship. The sense of kinship is much broader than it is in industrialized countries; it extends, for example, to those who are witnesses at a wedding, to godmothers and godfathers of new-born children, even to the brothers and sisters-in-law of the different family branches of the individual person. Servants, in rich families, are part of the kinsfolk, although a marginal and dependent part.

Paternal authority is very strong (but less so in the cities, especially among Lima's middle class). Even the old customs prevail: a man must still ask permission of a girl's parents to go regularly with her, for example, and must ask for the hand of a girl; virginity is still ranked high by men, even if it is considered normal (but every day less so) for servant girls and those in haciendas to lose theirs to white men. An Indian lover would not reproach a girl for this, but, on the other hand, he would not forgive her for losing her virginity to another Indian—in other words, without the virtual coercion represented by the insistence of the white man.

The woman is the axis around which the practical life of the family turns. The father may be the authority but the mother is the force that keeps the family running. She is the permanent element; the father and the children come and go, are sometimes absent in search of work or adventure, while the mother stands guard over the family.

Children are another matter. They are not usually stable in any way. For them, the family is a refuge when they are out of work, or when they, in turn, have too many children. This, of course, is the case among the lower classes. Middle-class children do not, as a rule, leave the family to study or to work. The wages paid young people are low, making it difficult to find a place to live within one's means, and there is the matter of "what people will say," especially with regard to women. A young woman who lives alone is still considered, by most people, a person of easy virtue, as though she were inviting masculine aggression. And masculine aggression nearly always turns up.

Single mothers are not rare, for contraceptive methods are little known and there are few clinics or centers to explain their use. Sex education in the schools is nil, and the girl who becomes pregnant has nowhere to turn. Half a million single mothers have been counted in the country—one out of every twelve women, and probably one out of every six mothers. And it is not unusual to find fathers who, when their daughters tell them that they are going to have a child, throw them out of the house and pronounce the phrase consecrated by custom: "You are no longer my daughter!" sometimes adding: "You would corrupt your sisters."

It is not rare for these same fathers to maintain not one, but two, or—if their means and physical capacity permit— even three families. The result of this and of the frequency of illegitimate unions is that there is a high percentage (40 percent) of children born out of wedlock, with all the expected consequences for their psychology and even for their education. Another consequence is the high incidence of abortions. In Lima alone, there are 16,000 a year, most of them performed by women with no medical training. Despite all this, the family is still the institution that most Peruvians regard with the greatest respect.

The poverty of many peasant families—especially in times of drought or famine—is taken advantage of by dealers in human flesh. In 1968, it was revealed that, in a period of drought in the Cuzco region, there were people who offered to take peasant children from eight to fifteen years old, who were dying of hunger, to work in the city; actually, they took them to the *selva,* where they virtually "sold" them to planters short of cheap labor. It is not unusual for parents unable to feed their children, because of drought and the slowness of government aid, to sell them to well-to-do families in the cities as servants.[14]

Religion

In Peru, 1.6 percent of the people are protestants, .3 percent call themselves agnostics, and the rest are Catholics. Country Indians and *mestizos,* though Catholics, practice a syncretic type of religion, in which pre-Hispanic and Catholic beliefs and rituals are mingled. The clergy has great influence in the villages and haciendas and, up to a few years ago, exercised considerable political pressure. Today, thanks especially to the activity of the APRA, the Indians no longer listen to the *padrecito* at voting time.

Among Peru's most famous saints, are Ste. Rose of Lima (1586–1617), and San Martín de Porres (1579–1639), a Negro. The former, a Creole of the Dominican order, was the first resident of the New World to be canonized; the latter, also a Dominican, dedicated himself to working with the poor and is the patron saint of those struggling for social justice. Other Peruvian saints are San Francisco Solana

(1549–1610), a Franciscan missionary, and Santo Toribio de Mogrovejo (1530–1606), archbishop of Lima.

Among the middle class, religious life is losing importance; whereas, in the upper classes, it is maintained with all the ritual observances but without much theological consistency. Among the workers, Catholicism is still very influential; progressive priests are rejected and thus find themselves confined to working in the migrant slums and among the middle class, which they are trying, through preaching of a "social" type, to attract anew to the church. It is also interesting to note that the various Protestant denominations—supported primarily by American churches—have found a response only among the poor of the cities, particularly the provincial ones.

We must emphasize the importance of religion in the life of the masses. In the Sierra, the fiesta system is still common. Families take turns, year after year, in paying for the fiesta of the patron saint of the village or community, a custom that ruins them and, though less so than in the past, enriches the local priests. Pilgrimages to famous sanctuaries in certain regions unite thousands of the faithful, who go many miles on foot to press their foreheads, hands, and lips to the relic of some saint. Women in a state of religious trance are quite common and are revered by the people, and in the Sierra there are witches and faith healers who claim powers bestowed on them by the local saint. The church tries to struggle against these superstitions but not formally, for it is by no means certain that, if the people had to choose, they would choose the church.

The first book printed in Peru was a catechism in Quechua for the use of priests in teaching. The Indians were not taught theology, but ritual and a few simple rules of faith. To make these more acceptable, pre-Hispanic rites were used and silently modified into Catholic rites. Even today, in village processions, it is customary to find *disciplinarios*—Indians who carry whips in remembrance of the flagellations administered to Indians who did not worship their Lord's image. The procession ends with a benediction, which all receive kneeling, after which the faithful give themselves over to feasting, drinking, dancing, and fireworks.

In March, the Indians always held a feast to honor the harvest; the missionaries replaced it, in the same month, by a feast in adoration of the cross, called la Santa Cruz. Crosses are fastened to the houses and raised on the mountains and hills, and on the day of the fiesta, they are borne in procession to the nearest parish—sometimes a long way off. Animals are taken to church to be blessed, and flowers and fruits are left for the parish priest. Afterward, the bearers set about drinking, chewing coca, and dancing.

The Feast of the Sun was changed into that of Corpus Christi, during which each section of the town or *barrio* celebrates its religious feast. Corpus Christi is often marked by quarrels between the devotees of the saints of the different quarters. Of course, everything ends with *chicha* and coca. Drinking, perhaps a remembrance of ceremonial libations in the time of the Incas, is so closely associated with religious festivals that some sociologists have attributed the alcoholism of the Indians to the fiestas.

In these and other feasts, mass is the central ceremony. Every year, it is paid for by a different person, and he, in turn, is responsible for finding someone to pay for it the following year. Not unusually, when the parish priest asks who will be responsible for the next mass, the sponsor of the present one will rise and name a neighbor he has not consulted; the person thus honored accepts, for it would shame his family if he refused the distinction. During the entire year, the family will save, sometimes even at the expense of their diet, to pay for the mass for which they have been made responsible—as well as for the serenade given to the saint the night before, the fireworks that precede and follow the mass, and the orchestra of violins and harps that gives it an agreeable accompaniment. At the mass, the white sit in the front pews, the *mestizos* behind them, and the Indians kneel at the back. The money brought in by these masses is the priest's chief support, for his salary is very small.

Respect for the clergy is limited. In earlier years, parishioners knew and accepted the children of many priests, but this did not enhance the clergy's prestige. The fact that, until a very short time ago, the church systematically took the side of the oligarchic groups and gave its blessing to military coups also contributed to skepticism with regard to the clergy. The divisions that characterize the church in the rest of the world are less marked in Peru. There are, of course, progressive and disputatious young priests and lay people, but their influence upon the masses is not as great as it is, for example, in Colombia or Chile. What the intellectuals and the middle class criticize is not so much religion as the conventional way of living that takes advantage of it to keep customs fixed and rigid.

There are about 1,600 priests in Peru, and the number is diminishing. There are about 400 Catholic schools, with about 100,000 pupils, 60 percent of them girls. Since 1929, only Catholic religious education has been permitted in public or private schools. There are four archbishops, twelve bishops, four vicars-general, 6,000 nuns in convents, and 3,000 male members of religious orders. The hierarchies today try simultaneously both to reflect traditional attitudes—for instance, the archbishop of Lima, Juán Cardinal Landázuri (1913–   ), blessed the jet planes bought to appease the air force when the country was going through a severe economic crisis in 1967—and to keep themselves in tune with post-Vatican II demands. For example, the same Cardinal Landázuri announced that he would abandon the luxurious archiepiscopal palace and take up residence in a modest house in the working-class quarter of Lima.

Apparently, none of this has much effect on the relationship between the church and the people, who proceed on a basis of tradition and superstition rather than on one of symbolic gestures, as may be seen in the matter of the population explosion. In 1968, thirty-five priests in Lima declared themselves in opposition to the papal encyclical *Popularum Progressio* against birth control. The Peruvian cardinal lauded their declaration, but maintained his support of the Pope's position.

The church cannot get the majority of Peruvians to marry sacramentally, no matter how many of those couples are faithful Catholics. Logically, the blame for the public's failure to practice birth control should not be laid at the door of the church. If children were not at once an investment, a kind of security for their parents' old age and a prestige symbol, what the church said would have little influence on the behavior of the faithful. This is actually the case with the middle class.

Lifestyle

In the United States, a farmer's wife, a worker's wife, and the wife of a university professor do not live in fundamentally different ways. Whatever difference there is in their income is reflected in other things (travel, cultural media, or investments, for example). In Peru, however, even when their incomes are comparable, the wives of professors, of peasants, and workers live, dress, work, and think in completely different ways. This difference is manifested not merely in exterior forms of life—lodging, food, clothing—but even in concepts of religion, in family feeling, and in lovemaking.

Another detail that should be heavily emphasized is the degree of submission that characterizes the entire life of great segments of the population—such as peasants, migrants, industrial laborers—and even infiltrates more prosperous levels. The Peruvian, like many Latin Americans, is always subject to somebody and striving to dominate someone else. The husband dominates the wife, the father his children, the military man the civilians, the bureaucrat the citizen who asks something of him, the man in authority those he orders. The hacienda overseer dominates the peasants, the policeman the passerby, the skilled worker the laborer, the old migrant bosses the newcomer, the *mestizo* the Indian, the white the *metizo*, the mulatto the Negro. The urban man is superior to the countryman, the political student to the nonpolitical one. This submission shows itself at times in very subtle ways: for example, in language (the *mestizo* is called *cholo,* in a depreciatory and paternalistic tone),—or in forms of politeness, which become more and more ceremonious as one goes lower in the social scale; even in delinquency, for the Indians are less aggressive toward whites than toward *mestizos* and, similarly, less so toward the latter than toward other Indians. All this is a mixture of concealed racism, with a disinclination to admit that it is such, and of caste spirit derived in great part from this very racism.

In rural areas, life is still rather patriarchal; but, in the city, with its abundant night life, modern amusements, meetings, conferences, and banquets, life is much more modern, and patriarchalism is gradually diminishing.

Also tending to disappear, though slowly, are those inevitable concomitants of poverty that are so enchanting to the tourist: folklore, native cooking, peasant costumes. In reality, the folk dances and songs are the result of the convergence of pre-Hispanic survivals with Spanish ceremonial and religious influence. The diet—consisting basically of corn for the masses (and potatoes in the Sierra)—is slowly becoming universalized in the cities, especially among the middle class, which has already begun to drink wine and whiskey with great enthusiasm at all social functions, while the masses remain faithful to the rums known as *pizco* and *chicha*.

Dress, too, is becoming uniform in the cities. Only in the Sierra is there still some survival, and that steadily lessening, of the native garments—ponchos for the men and bowler hats for the women. To dress like city people is, in rural areas, a sign of social status, and the native garb (again, a mixture of pre-Hispanic and Spanish colonial) is a sign of poverty. Popular arts would have disappeared entirely by now had it not been for tourism and the stimulus provided by official cultural organizations. There are hand-woven fabrics, pottery, sun-baked clay articles, and silverwork of great beauty and individuality; but Peruvians, as a rule, do not buy these, preferring imported ones. Except for collectors and merchants, there is not even much interest in archaeological objects, which the Indians are highly skilled at imitating, burying them for long periods before putting them on sale.

Like all peoples whose political life is agitated, and whose social structure is almost immobile, Peruvians tend to be violent in moments of emotional stress. This is seen in the large number of crimes of passion, which greatly exceeds that of crimes committed for profit—as well as by the squabbles among villages chiefly about the use of land and of water, and in the frequency with which fights occur during sports events.

Sports form a large part of Peruvians' diversion. Soccer, baseball, and cockfighting are favorites. Neither television nor the movies have been able to supplant them.

Women

If the Peruvian is always dominated by somebody, the most-dominated figure in the country is the woman. She is subject to her husband, to her children, to her family, to local society, to the church, to the very mediocre education she has received, to the colonial inheritance, to pre-Hispanic survivals, and now, in some degree, to the rage for modernization.

It is difficult to speak of "the" Peruvian woman. There are several. The Indian woman of the communes has status and conventions that are not basically different from those of the middle-class provincial woman. The migrant Indian woman, and the *mestizo* woman of the proletariat, are much more free, since they work with men not of their families and have to protect themselves and earn their living. They are, in a way, modern women. And then there is the woman of the upper classes—they type called by writers the *limeña*—who gives the capital its tone and is a very special sort, indeed.

A proverb says, "Lima, paradise of women, purgatory of men, and hell for husbands." That was the rich Lima, now oligarchic, of the colonial administration of the eighteenth century. Lima has been the scene of many singular tales of love, which inspired Thornton Wilder's *The Bridge of San Luis Rey* and the *Tradiciones peruanas* of Ricardo Palma (1833-1919), and which inspired, too, many men in their daily lives, beginning with the viceroy Manuel de Amat, who fell in love with an actress, Micaela Villegas, "La Perichole" (1748-1819). Ladies went about wearing an ample cape, with whose mantle they covered their faces, leaving only their eyes visible. These were the *Limeñas tapadas* ("covered Limeñas") famous in legend. So strong is the memory of these coy and provocative ladies that, instead of selecting misses' sizes, it is customary in Lima to select *tapadas*, no matter how short the miniskirts may be. In 1561, the viceroy forbade the use of feminine mantles, but the women protested in the streets, and, despite husbandly pressure, the viceroy withdrew the ban.

Once, everything about the *limeña* was small—her stature, her feet, her waist. Today, the girls are taller and more svelte than their grandmothers. But Lima is not Peru. Peruvian women, outside the capital, continue to resemble those of a century ago, although they, too, wear miniskirts (though, to be sure, not very mini outside of Lima).

Peruvian society is a society of men; theirs, fundamentally, are the social activities, the fiestas, the meetings. Women are either at home or in nightclubs. But, in Lima, and a few other cities, and particularly among the well-to-do, women are beginning to infiltrate men's meetings, their fiestas, and even their politics. Women have had the vote since 1956; some have been elected to public posts; and first the APRA, and then the Christian Democrats, have made efforts to organize and mobilize them. In the unions, they are not only members, but militants and leaders. There are fewer business women than women union executives, but, on the other hand, the number of professional and university women is growing. Nearly a fourth of all students are female.

There is some sexual liberation of women. According to a questionnaire, half the women of Lima had their first sexual experience before they were twenty—that is to say, nearly always when they were single. Nevertheless, women must still pay lip service to certain prejudices, which cause the flourishing of clinics for the restoration of virginity, on the eve of marriage. In Lima, also, 62 percent of the upper-class women under forty use contraceptive methods; 46 percent of the middle class use them, and 32 percent of the lower class.

Change is most evident among the daughters of rich or well-to-do families. Today, there is no prejudice against their going to the university, being secretaries, or dedicating themselves to a profession. To go to work, for a woman of the well-to-do group, does not mean that she needs money—the only reason, earlier, for working—but that she is going "modern." But she manages to make it plain that she is working for pleasure and not out of necessity; for, to work because you need to continues to be degrading. Not to be rich, is, so to speak, immoral.

Also a sign of change is the rise in the number of neurotic women among the middle class, where the pressure for change is strongest, and the resistance also stronger. Some find personal solutions like the one who said: "My husband does not understand me, that's certain, but I understand him very well. At breakfast, I play my part, which is to be dumb and not to know anything of politics, literature, or sports, or of anything that hasn't to do with the church, the kitchen, and the bed. When he is not at home, I read or go to the movies. I am not happy, naturally, but things could be worse."[15] Others resign themselves to the obsessive urge to be married young and submit to the bourgeois *huachafería*, the vulgarity, bad taste, and snobbism of the middle class.

There is not yet a "new Peruvian woman," but the matriarchal figure of the woman of the people is disappearing, and so is the image of the doll-woman of the middle class and the *tapada* of the upper class.

Attitudes

Many other things in Peru are undergoing change. Certain attitudes, however, seem immutable; the names given to them are changed, but not their essence. Among these attitudes, the most readily recognizable is paternalism. In Peruvian society the powerful exploit the weak but, at the same time, look out for them. The state is paternalistic, leaving no place for local initiative or participation by the people in making decisions; the state knows best what is good for the citizens. On other political levels, this is expressed as personalism, the custom of forming parties around a personality; not even the APRA has been able to shake this attitude. In economics, paternalism is expressed by the "friendliness" between the owner and his workers; in smaller firms, by the custom of regarding the boss as the person to whom one appeals in the case of family problems or when money runs short. The same owners, diehard advocates of free enterprise, turn to the paternal state when they have problems. Of course, the supreme image of the *paterfamilias* is the army, which arbitrates disputes and keeps order.

If everyone in Peru is subject to someone, this someone is

paternalistic with respect to those subject to him. This excludes neither the occasional rebellions nor the systematic exploitation of the subjects. But, at the same time, all who are subject to the same person, institution, or group of persons, and all those who have subject to them the same social group, feel united in a group or community that they possess in common. From this comes the elitist sentiment. From skilled workers up, all Peruvians belong to some elite or other (and it might almost be said that the old migrants to the slums are an elite as compared to the recent arrivals). The students form an elite, just as the intellectuals and teachers do. The military form an elite, and, naturally, the oligarchy considers itself the supreme elite. Politics is, really, the struggle among these elites for shares of power, under the control of the armed forces, which, paternalistically, will prevent these struggles from endangering the system.

From this elitist attitude is derived the tendency toward monopoly, which manifests itself whenever there is occasion. Every elite would like to have a monopoly of power, of course, or, if it cannot succeed in obtaining it, at least the monopoly of some source of wealth. It defends this monopoly vigorously. The intellectuals form a closed circle; the students do not bother about making entrance to the university available to the sons of the poor; the men of business look distrustfully at competitors, particularly if they are foreigners. The owners of taxis oppose the granting of more licenses, in spite of the growth of the cities, because they want the monopoly of taxicab transport. The church, for many years, was opposed to public education, which broke its monopoly of the schools, and to the admission to the country of ministers of other sects.

Another attitude very closely linked to paternalism is nationalism. Although, in his personal relations, the Peruvian is not in the least chauvinistic, in his collective nationalism he is. But it is a nationalism divided against itself; since, while it wants to affirm the superiority of all things Peruvian and to defend them against foreign assault, it feels, at the same time, the desire to imitate foreigners—particularly Americans.

In the United States, there is an erroneous belief that the

anti-American elements of Peruvian nationalism are of popular and leftist origin. Nothing could be further from the truth. Historically, the first and most aggressive anti-Americans have been members of the oligarchy, in spite of the fact that it was they who invited foreign capital into the country. To the aristocratic oligarchy, Americans have always been contemptible for their democratic spirit, their "materialism," and their directness. The mere existence of the United States is seen as a threat; and, when John F. Kennedy attempted to practice politics of a populist type, the oligarchy felt completely justified in being anti-American.

The anti-Americanism of the middle class—which has come to replace its anti-Hispanism of the past century—is of another kind. The United States is at once a model and an obstacle. The United States is reproached for having always supported military governments, for having developed the wealth of the country in accordance with the needs of the American economy instead of Peru's, and for intervening diplomatically whenever foreign firms have felt threatened. Among the masses, there is no anti-Americanism. If Washington's policy were really directed toward the people, it would find support among the submerged masses.

It might seem that all this paternalism and nationalism would make the Peruvian an inhospitable person. Nothing could be further from the truth, for these attitudes are never transferred to the personal plane. The Peruvian is cordial, affable, and friendly. At the same time, he is inscrutable to the visitor; depending on the conditions and his mood, he will tell the visitor what he thinks he would like to hear, or what he thinks would annoy him. But he rarely speaks frankly about himself, even among other Peruvians. Long centuries of pressure have accustomed him to living on the defensive, and the best way to defend himself is to wear a mask. This can be perceived even in Peruvian cultural expressions.

8

A Protective Culture

It is not really possible to speak of a Peruvian culture. We must speak of several: the urban, on the one hand, the rural, on the other; and it is even possible to differentiate between a culture of *señores* and one of those subject to them. But these different cultures are not apparent to the eyes of visitors, nor are they studied in the university courses.

What is generally taken for Peruvian culture and most frequently discussed in books is urban culture, a protective culture, of and for the elite, in which the immense majority of Peruvians take no part.

Languages

There are three principal languages in Peru: Castilian Spanish, Quechua, and Aymará. Castilian, the official language, is spoken by 80 percent of all Peruvians. Quechua or Aymará-speaking Indians who migrate to the cities have to learn Spanish; as a result, native languages are losing ground.

Thus, we have Peruvians who speak Spanish, others who speak only a native language, and a growing number who are bilingual. Although they are few in number, mention should also be made of the Indians of the *selva,* who speak local languages, each one used only by a tribe: Aguarana, Bora, Cocama, Chama, Huanca, Murato, Ocaina, Piro, Shapra, Ticuna, Witoto, and others. In the *selva,* the Instituto Lingüístico de Verano (Summer Linguistic Institute) is trying to teach in the native tongues. Psychologists and anthropologists engage in passionate discussion of whether the results of this experiment are favorable or unfavorable to the development of the personality of the Indians.

Hispanization is more marked among smaller Indian children and adolescents than among adults. In the latter, it is more marked among men than among women, women being, because of the sort of life they lead, less subject to pressures outside the family. In some regions, especially in the south, native languages are in the majority, as in the departments of Apurimac, Ayacucho, Huancavelica, Cuzco—in all of which Quechua is dominant—and Puno—in which Aymará and Quechua are dominant. In the north, Spanish prevails, and, in the center, the two languages are about evenly matched, with Spanish tending to be more widely spoken.

In the transitional phase between the native languages and Spanish, which involves a considerable part of the population of the country, the most noticeable consequences of bilingualism are of a traumatic sort: loss of contact with tradition; and psychological incompatibility between the indigenous mental patterns and their expression in Spanish, to which must be added the also traumatizing effects of the acculturation caused by transference from country to city. It may be said, also, that at least a fifth of the population of Peru is suffering from the effects of tensions that provoke psychological maladjustments. But, in the by no means rare cases of a father who speaks Quechua or Aymará and of children who speak Castilian and know very little of their native language, tensions are aggravated by the inevitable lack of communication.

Education

In the last twenty years, education has made many advances—but, even so, 35 percent of the school-age children do not attend classes because of the lack of schools and teachers.

Progress has been much greater in cities than in rural areas, because many rural families do not send their children to school when there is one, but put them to work. Moreover, many teachers are reluctant to bury themselves in rural communities.

The Peruvian educational system has three grades: elementary (six years), theoretically free and compulsory; secondary, with two cycles, one basic for three years and the other, in preparation for higher education, of two years and more; and university and higher technical schools, from four to six years, depending on the specialty elected. There are also vocational training and middle-grade technical schools.

Eighty-five percent of the school population attend institutions maintained by the state. Private elementary schools (operated chiefly by religious orders, foreign colonies, and commercial firms) give better education but are expensive; the same is true of private secondary schools. Vocational training depends largely on private support, from management or religious institutions. International organizations and American aid groups have given special attention to the question of Peruvian education. The pilot program of school breakfasts maintained by the United States in Puno has raised attendance by 40 percent.

Higher education is entirely state supported, except for the Catholic University of Lima. University education is organized on the European model—that is, by rigid curricula—and the students have no freedom in the choice of courses. Most professors teach part time and combine their professional careers—as lawyers, physicians, and the like—with their professorial duties, which is prejudicial to the quality of instruction that they give. Examinations, as a rule, are not very rigorous, and memorizing facts is still a great part of education.

Although the government pays their expenses, the universities are autonomous. The professors elect the rector and the university authorities choose the professors and decide on the programs. The students, organized in associations for each university school, take part in university government.

The universities (and even some secondary schools in the

big cities) are heavily politicized. For more than half a century, students have been active in Peruvian politics and in the vanguard of protests against dictatorships. Every party struggles—sometimes with violence—to get its student members elected to the directorship of student associations. For years, Aprismo was predominant. Now the principal struggle is between members of APRA in one corner, Communists following the Soviet line in another, and the various groups of Castroites, Maoists, Christian Democrats, Trotskyites, and so on in the third.

The proportion of university students from working-class or peasant families is very low, probably lower than 5 percent, and scholarships are scarce and limited. The sons of the rich usually study at the Catholic University, which is private, and complete their studies in the United States or in Europe. Daughters of rich families often go to Catholic schools in Canada. The percentage of women university students has been growing and today must be about 25 percent in Lima. The percentage is smaller in the provinces.

In the last ten years, the number of students enrolled at all levels has outgrown the number of schools and teachers. Classes are crowded, and, in many primary schools, there are two daily sessions. School absenteeism is relatively low in Lima (10 percent) and very high in the Sierra (as much as 50 percent in the south).

Expenditure for education has been increasing and has risen from 12 percent of the national budget in 1950 to 20 percent in 1968. In the former year, 1.71 percent of the gross national product was devoted to education, and 3.6 percent in the latter year. In 1975, there were 120,000 teachers in 25,000 schools and 3.35 million students. Of these, 2.5 million attended primary schools, 540,000 attended secondary schools, 77,000 were in technical schools, 20,000 were in normal schools, 18,000 attended vocational schools, and 135,000 were in the universities. Of the thirty-five establishments for higher education in the country, nine are in Lima: the University of San Marcos, oldest on the continent, founded in 1551; the Villarreal University; the Catholic University; the schools of Agriculture, Engineering, Veterinary

Medicine, and Social Service; and the Polytechnic Institute. In recent years, several provincial universities, small and rather scantily financed, have been founded.

The educational composition of the public has changed greatly in the past thirty years. In 1940, 58 percent of Peruvians had no education of any kind; by 1970, this percentage had fallen to 28. But this does not mean that the number of illiterates has fallen to 28 percent. Many who have gone through primary school revert to illiteracy at the end of a number of years (especially in the Sierra and the *selva*) through lack of any need for reading and writing. Radio and television have made it unnecessary for a large percentage of Peruvians to read.

Information Media

Radio is the medium with the widest audience and transistors have enabled it to penetrate regions that have no electricity. Nevertheless, the majority of Peruvian families do not even have transistor receivers.

There are 152 commercial broadcasting stations, with much advertising, little news, and many dubbed foreign programs, especially of American origin. Nineteen stations are government-controlled, and there is a missionary station in Puno. There are also numerous private shortwave stations that are useful in maintaining contact between the haciendas or plantations and offices in the city.

Television has also been a factor in the unification of language. Some commercial broadcasting stations (five of these are in Lima) offer a fair number of public-service programs—news, discussion, and so forth. Advertising is superabundant. Censorship of radio and television is virtually limited to news affecting the public order and social questions. At least, this was the case up to the military coup of 1968. Since then, government pressure on the stations has been fortified and used sub rosa with comparative frequency.[16]

The majority of the films shown in Peru are in Spanish and produced in Mexico, Argentina, or Spain. Films produced in English or other foreign languages are dubbed. There have been attempts to produce Peruvian films, but isolated initiatives of this sort have not had much success. There is no national motion picture industry.

The media of information we have mentioned play a much more important role in Peru than in industrial countries. They exercise a unifying influence—completely unintentional, on the cultural level, especially on language—and even foster a state of mind more receptive to technical changes and the accompanying modifications in lifestyle. Some attempts have been made to use the radio, and to a lesser extent television, to educate migrants in Lima's slums, and help them adapt to urban life. But even though most of the stations are local or regional, very few programs, on radio or on television, have any direct relation to the life of the mass of people.

Newspapers and Books

The printed word still has enormous prestige in Peru. Intellectuals are greatly respected, and anyone who writes regularly for the newspapers quickly wins popularity—never equal to that of sports figures or pop singers, of course, but proportionally greater than is achieved by authors and journalists in industrial countries.

There are 40 dailies, in thirty different cities, and 168 other periodicals, most of them weekly. The number of copies per 100,000 of population is 76. All told, the dailies have a circulation of 800,000. Some are national in character, like *El Comercio,* (90,000 circulation), which, until 1948, was the only modern publication. It was owned by the Miró Quesada family and was rabidly anti-Aprista. After that year, several other important dailies were founded: *La Prensa,* with an 80,000 circulation, published by Pedro Beltrán, who was several times prime minister; *La Crónica,* belonging to the family of former president Prado; *El Correo,* the flagship of a fleet of provincial dailies; *La Tribuna,* organ of the APRA; and the *Espresso,* with a circulation of 120,000, belonging to friends of Belaúnde Terry.

The most popular magazines are those for women and some that model themselves on the American *Time.* In general, the influence of American publishing techniques is the prevailing one. There is also an abundance of literary and art magazines, usually short-lived, and periodicals devoted to economy, philosophy, medicine, and so forth.

The press in Peru has had a rather troubled existence. Under constitutional regimes, it has suffered the indirect pressure of politicians and the big interests; under dictatorships, it has often been censored, and it has not been unusual for dictators to close down newspapers. In 1970, the military junta promulgated a law that, under pretext of "Peruvianizing" the press—that is, eliminating foreign influences—made it completely subject to the government. Yet, there is a certain amount of critical freedom that the journalists themselves take care not to overstep. Furthermore, since Peru has to import most of its paper pulp, publications are de facto always at the mercy of the permits the junta grants, since the military have established governmental control of foreign trade. The fact that this situation is considered relatively tolerable should give some idea of the conditions under which the press existed during earlier dictatorships.

Another means of exerting pressure on the press is through government advertisements which provide an important percentage of the income of dailies and weeklies. Suppression of their advertisements can ruin a publication. Thus, the opposition is prevented almost entirely from overstepping the limits that the dictatorial government is disposed to tolerate.

Peru has no important book publishers. Those who exist, and those who are established only to disappear in a brief time, produce about 700 books a year, either of religious context—mostly for women—or textbooks. Few volumes are exported. On the contrary, considerable numbers are imported from Spain, Mexico, Chile, and Argentina, and the market for books from the United States is growing with the spread of English—the second language for the majority of Peruvians who study foreign language (a very small minority, however, even among students).

In this field, too, there is government activity. It is not unusual for the customs to confiscate and destroy books considered subversive or pornographic. Protests have never succeeded in preventing recurrence of such incidents.

The libraries are inadequate to supply the deficiencies of the publishing business. There are about 350 public libraries—170 of them in the universities—but none have any abundant endowment, although some possess incunabula and other old books of incalculable value. Funds for the purchase of books are so scarce that it is difficult for libraries to keep pace with world publication. Under these circumstances, scientific investigation is difficult, and it is remarkable that, despite this, Peru has produced outstanding scientists and authors who have done important scientific, sociological, and economic research.

Amusements

Films constitute the basic amusement of Peruvian villages. Lima has cinema houses that show European and art films, but most devote their programs to melodramatic Latin American films or American westerns and mysteries. Football and other sports, as we have noted, compete with films and bullfights for the attention of the great public.

The theater, the opera, and concerts—centers for upper-class social life in the past century—have lost their importance and can be enjoyed only occasionally. Although there are quite a few experimental theater groups—particularly in the universities—and cinema clubs, opportunities for keeping up with world production are sporadic, and opportunities for Peruvian authors to have their works produced are very rare. There is only one permanent orchestra. Ballet companies, formed now and then, meet with less success than the folkloric organizations.

Actually, a good many amusements, outside of films, are folkloric. Peruvian folklore is very rich, and contains pre-Hispanic, Spanish, African, and American elements. It has been commercialized by various modern organizations and singers, and as a result has lost some of its authenticity.

The Plastic Arts

In pre-Hispanic and colonial times, the art of Peru had a strong individuality; but it was lost after the coming of independence, no doubt because of the imitative and European-

izing spirit of the only patrons available to Peruvian artists—
the members of the oligarchy.

Excavations since the end of the last century have un-
covered buildings, temples, stone sculpture, pottery, textiles,
and gems of an enormous variety of styles as well as of strong
individuality. They may be recognized as being of Peruvian
origin by anyone, even though not an expert, who has seen
specimens of the same derivation.

Archaeologists distinguish various "cultures," each with its
own characteristics, but all having features in common. The
Chavín culture is known to us by the temple and the village
of the same name, in the department of Ancash, not far from
Lima; by the stela found there; by numerous monolithic
sculptures; and by the black ceramics of global shape and the
carved decorations with Amazonian motifs—for this culture
came from the *selva*. Ceramics, for the same reason, imitate
wooden utensils, wood being the material originally used in
the *selva*. The greatest concentration of the remains of this
culture, proceeding in great part from the necropolis of
Ancón, is in the Museo Antropológico of Magdalena.

The remains of the Tiahuanaco culture are more numerous. They were found chiefly in the neighborhood of Lake
Titicaca at an altitude of more than 12,000 feet. There are
enormous monuments fashioned of huge stones, with human
figures carved on the blocks. The effect is titanic, super-
human. The temples and fortresses have ramparts and moats
reminiscent of medieval European castles. Colors—black,
yellow, and red—were used in the decoration of the ceramics.

Metallurgy appears in Peruvian art with the Mochico-
Chimú culture in the north and along the coast. Adobe was
the basic material of its architecture in general and of its py-
ramidal temples. Some of the ceramics are true sculptures,
the portraits of chiefs having a very realistic expression. Many
of the utensils have the form of animals and plants and are
decorated in chestnut brown, red, and white. But the most
interesting finds are the golden jewel work and the vessels
and masks of that metal. The city of Chan-Chan (near Trujillo) and the fortress of Paramonga (in the department of
Ancash) are the two most important centers.

Outstanding relics of the Nazca culture (in the Ica region) are the aqueducts, some still in use. In their very fine ceramics, the people of this culture used as many as eight colors and all kinds of symbolic forms. Erotic sculpture is abundant.

To the south of Lima flourished the Paracas culture. In its cemeteries, there is evidence that they practiced trepanation of the skull and obturation with golden plates. The dryness of the atmosphere has made it possible to take from the tombs very beautiful and well-preserved textiles of linen and cotton with as many as sixteen different shades of color and decorated with apparently mythological figures of plants and animals.

The Incas' culture offers an enormous wealth of artifacts of all types. Its textiles, less perfect than those of the Paracas culture, have kept their colors to the present day. Their ceramics, nearly all utensils, are inferior to those of the earlier peoples. Their metallurgy was superior to that of the others, for the Incas knew smelting and rolling; but only a few pieces of their jewellry are known to us, most of it having been melted down by the conquistadors for its silver and gold. There are many monuments of Inca architecture, mostly in Cuzco, built of tremendous stones finely cut and fitted without mortar. We should single out for its majesty the citadel of Machu-Picchu in the highest part of the Andes, apparently built before the coming of the Spaniards.

Colonial art contrasts sharply with the grandiosity of pre-Hispanic art. Although there are buildings, convents, and cathedrals of noble proportions, its best examples are in palaces and temples of more human dimension. The plans were drawn by Spaniards, but native artisans executed them side by side with workmen from Spain. This produced a mingling of stylistic characteristics, traditional Catholic symbols side by side with others of pre-Hispanic origin. A fabulous ornamental richness known as Peruvian baroque is the prevailing feature of the colonial style, although examples of Renaissance style are to be found in the façade of the Lima cathedral, the Casa de Pilatos—also in Lima—and many buildings in Cuzco. Outstanding examples of baroque are the church of San Francisco, the palace that houses the Foreign Ministry, the Nazarene convent in Lima, and the Quinta de Presa—the house in which the viceroy Amat and his mistress, the actress Perricholi, used to meet.

Colonial painting, principally the work of *mestizos,* was religious and iconographic. Diego de Mora, a soldier of the conquest, made a portrait of Atahalupa in prison. But the most astonishing work of this period is the work of the so-called Cuzco school of the sixteenth and seventeenth centuries. With their gilded frames and backgrounds, and great weight of floral and zoological ornamentation, the saints painted by anonymous artisans of Cuzco are unmistakable.

After independence, art declined. The painters and sculptors generally confined themselves to imitating European fashions, and it was not unusual for oligarchic families to have paintings sent from Paris or London. The romantic realism of this period abounds in many picturesque touches—Indians in the marketplace, soldiers in battle, and so forth—but there is nothing of genuine interest. Not until the period following World War II do we find artists who, though following the artistic currents of Paris and New York, express their personality as Peruvians, not so much in subject matter as in color and form. Even in modern abstract Peruvian art, there are no elements of colonial baroque and pre-Hispanic monumentalism. This is less apparent in architecture, which is, in general, strictly utilitarian, and the most original examples of which are the tourist hotels in the *selva,* on the coast, or on the shores of Lake Titicaca.

Literature

The most outstanding figures in Peruvian literature are not novelists or poets, but essayists, historians, and political writers. The work of even the most prominent novelists and poets is rich in social content. This is not due to any ideological influence but to the simple fact that Peru is an unintegrated state and not yet a nation. It is natural, then, for intellectual Peruvians to be primarily concerned with problems relative to this integration.

As might be expected, the pre-Hispanic people had a

literature, but we are not yet certain whether it was "written"—by means of the *quipus*—or entirely oral. Thanks especially to the chroniclers who collected them, we know fragments of poems, proverbs, and myths. Perhaps the most important work of this period is the drama *Ollantay* in Quechua verse. Neither its author nor the date of its composition is known. Nowadays, it is performed from time to time in modern versions and has been the basis of six operas. It tells of the secret love of the general Ollantay, plebeian origin, and the princess Cusi Coyllar, daughter of the Inca Pachacutec; Pachacutec placed great trust in Ollantay, and, when he found out about the love affair with his daughter, he banished him instead of ordering his execution and shut his daughter up in a cave. The child of this illicit love, Ima Sumac, wandered around the garden that surrounded the cave and every day, all day long, heard the sound of lamentation, without knowing that it came from her mother. Ollantay, meanwhile, took up arms against his lord; after conquering the latter's forces, he was betrayed and seized. Meanwhile, Ima Sumac persuaded the new Inca to pardon the princess Cusi Coyllar, and the princess won a pardon for Ollantay and married him.

Obviously, here is a story that could have come out of the Viking sagas, the *Thousand and One Nights,* or a play by Shakespeare. But there is a social ingredient in it—the plebeian origin of Ollantay—that was never to be lacking in the later literature of Peru.

During the colonial period, this social aspect is very clearly evident in the chronicles of the conquistadors—for instance, in that of Francisco Xerez (1504-1539), Pizarro's secretary, who told of the conquest itself; or in those of Pedro Pizarro, and Cristóbal de Molina (1495-1578).

In the same period, many friars described the pagan beliefs of the Indians in great detail, thereby transmitting to us things that we should otherwise not have known. Perhaps the most interesting chronicle of this type is that of Guzman Poma de Ayala, who devoted a large part of his life to the search for dates, legends, relations, and so forth, and who wrote a true history. His manuscript, long lost, was found only a few years ago in the Swedish archives; how it got there is a mystery.

During the colonial period Peruvian literature, whether written by Spaniards or Creoles, followed Spanish fashions, and there were many clerics who cultivated political satire. One outstanding work of this period is a lyric poem, the *"Epístola de Amarilis"* (perhaps a nun, or the daughter of a conquistador, but at any rate from Huánaco), whose anonymous author sent it to the famous Spanish dramatist Lope de Vega, who in turn published it in one of his books. Within the classical form of the poem, there are touches of surrealism, eroticism, and multiple personality, which give it a special importance in the literature of the Spanish language.

But the great figure of the colonial period was the Inca Garcilaso de la Vega (1539-1616), who was born in Cuzco, the son of a Spanish captain and a daughter of the last Inca. He went to Spain, enlisted in the army, fought, became a priest, and retired to Córdoba, where he died without ever seeing Peru again. Basing his work on memory, an active correspondence, and nostalgia for Cuzco, Garcilaso wrote what may be considered the first "American" work—the *Comentarios Reales,* or *Royal Commentaries*—the complete title of which is *Commentaries That Treat of the Origin of the Incas, Who were Kings of Peru; of Their Idolatry and of Their Government in Peace and in War; of Their Lives and Their Conquests; and of All That Was That Empire and Republic.* Thanks to this work, which took twenty years to complete, much is known about pre-Columbian Peru that would not have been otherwise. The book, which is also the first affirmation of the Peruvian *mestizo* personality, is very classical in style and can be read today with pleasure.

It took two centuries for a similar affirmation to appear in the work of Mariano Melgar (1791-1815). Among many mediocre lyric poems, Melgar composed *yaravís,* or popular songs of Indian origin; love poems; political songs for the war of independence; and satirical verses that represented, in his own words, an attempt to free Peruvian letters from the Spanish mould. Captured in the struggle for independence, Melgar was shot by the royalist army, but his *yaravís*

were sung for many years by the people. More erudite—and
also less mordant—is the work of the scholars of the last half
of the eighteenth century, who were influenced by the
Encyclopedists. In their work as well, we find an affirmation
of what may be called a "national will."

More than a century was to pass before the appearance of
new affirmations of *mestizajé* and national will. The nineteenth century, was, above all, a period of imitation, of
importation of fashions and styles, during which writers in
Peru wrote as they would have written in Madrid or Paris.
Only in genre literature do we find anything peculiar to Peru.
Ricardo Palma (1833-1918) is the century's major representative with his *Tradiciones Peruanas* [Peruvian traditions]. A
liberal, Palma took part in plots, served both in the diplomatic service and on the field of battle, and reconstructed the
Biblioteca Nacional. He wrote extensively on philology and
history, but the *Tradiciones* are his masterpiece. Through
legends, relations, and fables, they draw a picture of society
under the viceregency.

Carlos Augusto Salaverry (1830-1891), a soldier without
vocation, son of a president who was executed, was Peru's
major romantic poet. Like all military men in Peru, he took
an active part in politics, but went off to Europe as a diplo-
mat when the woman he loved was obliged to marry—
precisely as in some romantic novel—one of her father's
creditors. His poetry had considerable influence, and, if it is
not highly valued today by the intellectuals, girls of "good"
families still learn his verses at school.

Like these two, other writers have mixed in politics. But
the majority have done so merely as participants in factional
struggles. Some, however, have gone further and denounced
the social situation. Paradoxically, this tendency was initiated by a writer who was only half-Peruvian. Flora Tristan
(1807-1844), who was born in Paris, went to Peru when she
was very young to seek recognition by her father, a merchant in Lima. Peru surprised and scandalized her. In her
Peregrinaciones de un Paria [Wanderings of a pariah], she
denounced the poverty and social inequalities, as well as the
racism and militarism, of Peruvian society. She devoted the

rest of her short life to the labor movement, becoming one of the first unionists and feminists of France.

Another woman, Clorinda Matto (1854-1909), followed the same path. In her realistic novels, particularly in *Aves sin Nido* [Birds without nests], she denounced the church's complicity in the exploitation of the Indians by the landholders. Her works made her many enemies, and, when she married an Englishman, she left Lima, where people of her class had completely cut her off.

But they could not isolate Manuel González Prada (1848-1918), the son of a *hacendado,* a soldier in the war with Chile, a founder of the Radical party and, later, of the Unión Nacional. He did not have great success in this field; but the denunciations he constantly expressed in severe prose, which was at once serene and impassioned, and in mediocre verse found echo, a generation later, among students and in the anarcho-syndicalist movement. The workers' schools founded in 1919 were named, in his honor, the González Prada People's Universities. His *Horas de Lucha* [Hours of struggle] and his *Páginas Libres* [Free pages] are still read by students and workers, and many an Indian hut in the Sierra displays behind its door, next to a picture of the Sacred Heart of Jesus, a portrait of González Prada, together with one of Víctor Raúl Haya de la Torre.

Haya, despite his high-pitched voice, is a great orator of formidable charisma. But, he writes in a tortured style that is difficult to read. Nevertheless, his numerous books on political philosophy, his ideological polemics, and his newspaper articles have exercised a transcendng influence in all of Latin America's populist Left.

Although his influence was not as wide as is that of Haya, José Carlos Mariátegui (1894-1930) was an excellent essayist. His travels in Italy led him to Marxism, through the critical writings of Benedetto Croce and Giovanni Gentile. He founded the Socialist party (later, the Communist party), but the Third International condemned his theories. He wrote numerous essays on international politics and on literature, and his opinions are summed up in his *Siete Ensayos de Interpretación de la Realidad Peruana* [Seven interpretative essays on

Peruvian realities], a work which still inspires many of the young. He died after several years of confinement to a wheelchair and is buried between the tombs of a bullfighter and a priest.

While the quasi-commercial production of poets and novelists who reflect European fashions continues, several figures, all of them passionate critics of Peruvian society, stand out in our century. In *Cuentos Andinos* [Andean tales] and the novel *Matalache,* Enrique López Albújar (1872-1965) exposed the exploitation of Indians and Negroes, and was severely criticized for depicting in the novel the love story of a Negro farm worker and the white daughter of a plantation owner.

José María de Arguedas (1911-1970) was a sociologist who spoke Quechua, lived among the peasants, and studied the survival of pre-colonial and colonial customs on the haciendas. In his novels *Los Ríos Profundos* [The deep rivers] and *Todas las Sangres* [All the bloods], he takes us into the Sierra and brings the process of *mestizajé* to life before our eyes. He also wrote poetry in Quechua.

This is also the period of some poets of international standing, who have been able to unite modern influences with the realities of Peru. Alberto Hidalgo (1897-   ), with his *Carta al Perú* [Letter to Peru], and José Santos Chocano (1875-1934) are precursors. Chocano was Pancho Villa's secretary during the Mexican Revolution, was crowned with laurel in the main plaza at Lima, and was assassinated in Santiago de Chile by a disappointed associate in an organization for the discovery of buried treasure. He believed in dictators in politics and modernism in poetry. He wanted to be an epic poet, but his best work is lyrical. He was buried in Lima, in 1965, with ministerial honors.

José María Eguren (1882-1942), an official of the Ministry of Education and a man without a biography, founded the review *Contemporáneos,* in which he published symbolist verse. This periodical revived Peruvian poetry and prepared the way for César Vallejo (1892-1938), one of the greatest of American poets and a truly international figure, though little known outside the Spanish-speaking world. Born of a poor provincial family, he had a troubled life of contretemps and poverty. After studying literature and law, he became a professor—a delight to his students but a frequent source of indignation to their parents for his radical teaching. In revenge, the latter accused him of incendiarism; he was put in prison and, upon his release, devoted himself entirely to poetry. In Vallejo's poetry, surrealism became the expression of what he called the new man—the ordinary Latin American. There were times when his friends had to support him, for he became discouraged and vascillating. From this period of near-starvation came his book *Trilce;* he wrote before his term in prison *Los Heraldos Negros* [The black heralds], which may be classified as within the Peruvian color tradition. When he managed to get together a little money, he went to Europe and there visited various countries; he finally settled in Paris, married a Frenchwoman, became, for a short time, a Communist, and visited the USSR. But it was the Spanish Civil War that awakened his passion and inspired his best poetry, and it was in *España, Aparte de Me Este Caliz* [Spain, take away this cup from me] and *Poemas Humanos* [Human poems] that he found his own personal utterance. The spontaneous metaphysics, daily preoccupations and collective problems of the Peruvian, and the need of faith converge in these poems, which are written in a language that is a mixture of the popular and the learned, and immediately find an echo in the heart. Today, Vallejo is one of the few Latin American poets who is known and admired in all Spanish-speaking countries.

Another Peruvian with an international audience is the novelist Ciro Alegría (1909-1967). Like many other writers, he was involved in politics; he passed his youth in prison and some years in exile (part of the time in the United States) and in hiding. Of his many novels, the most widely translated and undoubtedly the best is *El Mundo Es Ancho y Ajeno* [Broad and alien is the world], published in 1941. Its subject is the life and vicissitudes of a native commune.

Another prose writer we must mention is Abraham Valdelomar (1888-1910), who is important—less for his stories than as the founder and director of *Colónida,* a review which had great influence on the intellectual life of his time. He also brought the world of the coast into literature, which, until he came along, was occupied entirely with Lima and the Sierra.

Among the most important writers of the postwar generation are Sebastián Salazar Bondy (1924-1965), author of a fierce yet tender book about the capital, *Lima, la Horrible,* and Mario Vargas Llosa (1936-   ), who has emerged only recently; his novels *La Cuidad y los Perros* [The city and the dogs] and *Conversaciones en la Catedral* [Conversations in the cathedral] not only justify their translation into many languages but are indispensable—and this is especially true of the second book—for a thorough knowledge of modern Peru.

Only in recent years has the state given some support to cultural activities. Campaigns for teaching reading and writing have been undertaken, though with more statistical than real success; and art has been encouraged in the schools, through the Direción de Extensión Cultural, which also supervises the Conservatory of Music, the Institute of Dramatic Art, and the various schools of fine arts. It has also supported the National Association of Writers and Artists, founded in 1938. The Peruvian House of Culture, which has headquarters in an old palace in Lima and receives official aid, is in charge of the National Symphony Orchestra and public museums and fosters the encouragement of folklore; it also awards prizes for various cultural activities. There are no private cultural foundations of any importance, although charitable and religious ones are numerous.

9

What Is Peru's Future?

As this book has tried to show, all of Peru's problems center upon one fundamental problem—the need to convert a country into a nation. Will the military succeed in doing this? What alternatives are there for accomplishing it if the military fail, or if the cost of their experiment proves unsupportable?

No doubt the reader has been asking these questions. I shall try to answer them in the light of the preceding chapters. For that, it will be necessary to repeat, now in the context of the behavior of the military junta of 1968, some things already discussed in the context of history, economics, and politics. They are surely important enough to keep repetition from becoming boring.

First of all: What was the coup of 1968 like? What conditions had prepared the ground for it? What elements took part?

The 1968 Coup

President Fernando Belaúnde, elected in 1963 with the obvious sympathy of the army, made a very energetic start but soon stalled. Belaúnde was an architect, and he came to power armed with a series of plans: a highway that would open up the Amazon region and unite Lima with Río de Janeiro; a campaign to make the people pay for the development of their various communities. Actually, Belaúnde's policy would have maintained the social status quo by making it compatible with technical progress and the modernization of the upper strata of the country. The phraseology was revolutionary, but the policy was conservative. Belaúnde found himself facing Parliament with a majority in the opposition. The APRA had the biggest bloc of deputies and senators, but not the majority; its leadership, impelled by its members' dissatisfaction, decided upon a parliamentary alliance with the partisans of General Odría—the very man who, as dictator, had persecuted the APRA and accused it of being Communist. This coalition succeeded in ousting various ministers and imposed an agrarian reform law—moderate, but nevertheless reformist—that Belaúnde applied very gingerly. It approved a motion to expropriate the property of the International Petroleum Company, and, finally, it investigated a wholesale smuggling scandal in which friends of the president and military men of high rank were involved. Little by little, the regime, having lost its initial momentum, was faced with an economically weak country; it was obliged to devalue the currency twice and slowly slid into corruption. Everyone was certain that the next president would be one backed by the APRA, and everybody feared that this would lead to another coup. The Apristas were optimistic, for the minister of war had said, on one occasion, that the army had expunged the word "veto" from its vocabulary. In any case, there was no doubt that the disappointment with Belaúnde gave the APRA every chance of winning. There were no significant divisions in the APRA, for a group that had split off years before and started guerrilla warfare had been wiped out by the army. On the other hand, there were three factions in Belaúnde's Popular Action Party: the Belaúndists proper, a leftist Castroite group, and the adherents of vice-president Edgardo Seoane. In the Christian Socialist Party, which supported Belaúnde, there were also divisions: the mayor of Lima, who had presidential ambitions, withdrew from it and founded his own, more moderate party.

The older military men had two motives for wanting a coup: first, to forestall continued investigation of a smuggling scandal, which would expose corruption among the higher echelons; and, second, to keep the APRA from winning the July 1969 elections. But the traditional militarists no longer had the absolute control of the army. In the past decade, different elements had emerged; they were the product chiefly of the CAEM (Colegio de Altos Estudios Militares— College of Higher Military Studies), trained in American military colleges, where, however, they did not receive any democratic education. These elements saw in social change the only way of modernizing the army and making it more efficient. For they did not abandon dreams of expansion (let us not forget that Peru has frontier problems with Ecuador and an old account to settle with Chile, and these things, which the public tends to forget, are important to military men). At the same time, there had arisen, in the Peruvian bourgeoisie, a new generation: sons of industrialists who were educated in Europe or in the United States; and technologists trained abroad, now returned with modern notions acquired in societies very different from Peru's and with a desire to put these ideas into effect. They did not proscribe the use of force to bring conditions in Peru into line with their new models. They wanted a revolution from above, not to give power to the people but to use it themselves, in order to impose the reforms they desired. They were extremely nationalistic—i.e., anti-American—and this won them the sympathy of the New Left, which has very vague ideas about everything except its very real anti-Americanism.

The coup was prepared by the land forces, whose commander-in-chief was General Juan Velasco Alvarado. The navy and air force knew nothing of it until it had succeeded; whereupon, according to custom, they got into the picture. The older military men relied upon the support of the younger ones in the preparation of their coup.

Early in morning of October 3, 1968, soldiers occupied the presidential palace, seized Belaúnde (who later took a plane for Argentina and finally became a professor in the United States), and broadcast over the radio a manifesto that spoke of "revolution," gave assurance that the "definitive emancipation of Peru was beginning," and attacked plutocratic groups. At midday on the fourth, the country was offered the Revolutionary Statute, without revolutionary phraseology, which set some simple rules for the functioning of the new regime. No mention was made of elections.

What had happened to the coup in the meanwhile? The simple answer is that the more nationalistic and "progressive" elements, the harder ones, had taken power. But the old-timers did not resign themselves to this, and the threat of an armed struggle between the two factions of the army led to a compromise. The nationalist General Juan Velasco Alvarado remained chief of state; the traditionalist General Ernesto Montagne became head of the government.

The history of Peru since 1968 is the history of how the nationalists, supported by the New Left, the Communists, and the younger businessmen, imposed very moderate measures of social change from above; and of how the traditionalists, with the backing of the traditional conservative parties, the landholding oligarchy, and the ecclesiastical hierarchy, have tried to prevent the application of these measures —or, at least, to see that they were applied in a way that did not really injure the interests of oligarchic groups.

All, naturally, talked of "moralizing the administration; of putting an end to economic chaos; of ending the relinquishment of sources of wealth to foreigners and their exploitation for the benefit of privileged groups." They wanted to "transform the structure of the state, foster a higher standard of living, give a national meaning to the acts of the government, moralize the country, and assure the unity of all Peruvians." Who could disagree with such goals? What discord there might be, rather, would arise between the military government and the politically conscious mass when it became a question of how to achieve them. The government wanted a revolution from above (and a part of it wanted the smallest possible dose of that revolution); politically conscious citizens would like, in any case, a revolution with guarantees of freedom and democracy—a revolution to give more reality to the vacillating kind of democracy Peru has intermittently enjoyed.

The military government was composed of elements of diverse tendencies. General José Benavides, son of a former dictator and friend of the big landowners, became minister of agriculture. General Alberto Maldonado, the minister of public works, had commanded the forces detailed to end the guerrilla warfare three years earlier, which was done by physically eliminating the guerrillas. Upon being appointed, each minister was assigned a technical adviser, since it was taken for granted that, being a military man, he knew nothing of the matters with which he was going to be occupied. A good number of these technical advisers were respected experts of the New Left.

The APRA (Haya was in Europe) and the other parties condemned the coup. There was an abortive attempt at a general strike. The parliaments of various Latin American countries condemned the seizure of power by the Peruvian military. Prime Minister Indira Gandhi of India, who was in Chile, canceled her scheduled visit to Peru; and Belaúnde, believing that a part of the army would support him, tried to return from Buenos Aires; but the Argentine authorities prevented him from boarding the plane.

During the procession of Our Lord of Miracles, a few days after the coup, a crowd of one hundred thousand Limeños gave Velasco Alvarado an ovation when he appeared on a balcony. And the students, so radical and demanding, approved the general by marching with Peruvian flags and singing the national anthem. What opposition there was, was verbal; it did not take the form of overt action. It was, so to speak, isolated. The government did not adopt any terrorist measures and was satisfied with exiling a few journalists. No censorship was imposed, and the press was free to criticize within limits. Political parties continued to function, but without any real influence. After the first rush of emotion, the country went back to business as usual, with greater than customary indifference, more apathy among the submerged masses, and a moderate feeling of apprehension on the part of the oligarchy.

No one could say whether this was what the stagers of the coup had planned, or whether they had abandoned the idea of repression because it proved unnecessary. At any rate, they were able to profit by a situation they had done nothing to produce, but which offered them the opportunity of neutralizing possible adversaries of the dictatorship and disguising the dictatorial and militaristic character of the regime. This situation was the oil problem.

The Oil Issue

In the north, the deposits at La Brea and Pariñas were exploited by the International Petroleum Company (IPC), an affiliate of the Standard Oil Company of New Jersey. Many times, in the course of electoral campaigns, the nationalization of these deposits had been urged, and Belaúnde had promised, in his campaign, that he would accomplish this. Once in authority, he began by raising the companies' oil taxes and then, in the summer of 1968, negotiated a contract with IPC, according to which the holdings were returned to the nation via the Empresa Petrolera Fiscal (EPF), a government body. In exchange, the IPC obtained the right to refine the crude oil from these deposits and to distribute the refined product in the installations constructed by IPC and the EPF.

The president of the EPF resigned, for he felt that his company should be able to refine its own petroleum. Parliament agreed to revise the contract, but it was found that the last page of the contract—page eleven—had disappeared. This page contained clauses safeguarding EPF's interests. The prime minister was accused of being responsible for its disappearance. The government, however, denied the existence of the missing page. The Left accused Belaúnde of having sold out to foreign interests, and the Right—angry with him because he had raised the taxes and had appropriated, albeit with compensation, five million acres of land in accordance with the agrarian reform law sponsored by the APRA—accused him of selling out to the extremists. Even Belaúnde's own party, Acción Popular, as has been said, was split over this issue.

The dean of the Bar Association of Lima, Alberto Ruiz Eldredge, who had been a Castroite and had also been the Christian Progressive Party's candidate for the presidency, formed a group of nationalistic lawyers—the Petroleum Defense Front—who carried out a major campaign of agitation.

The problem of IPC was not new. Ownership of the surface and subsurface of the La Brea and Pariñas mines was conceded in 1922 by the government to a foreign firm that sold its rights to IPC. There has been a constant accusation that this concession was excessively favorable to IPC, and several successive governments had tried in vain to renegotiate it. Belaúnde introduced a new feature into pressure on IPC: the government demanded that the company pay $140 million in the form of taxes unpaid since it had taken possession of the deposits.

When a deputy of the extreme Left asked the army to give its opinion, Velasco, then chief of staff, announced that the three branches of the armed forces were considering the matter. The Apristas denounced this as preparation for a coup, which they attempted to obviate by demanding the resignation of the government. The government complied; Belaúnde then formed another government, presided over by an independent, which was installed on October 2, Velasco attended the ceremony and congratulated the new ministers. Fifteen hours later, he was in the presidential chair.

A week later, on October 9, Velasco appeared on television. He announced that the Talara Industrial Complex that was exploiting the La Brea and Pariñas mines (refineries built in 1926, electrical plants, transport systems, offices, and so on) had been expropriated, with compensation, and that the armed forces would occupy the holdings. The government set a value of $77 million on these properties and valued those of IPC at $120 million. By May, 1972, all the compensation payments to IPC had been completed, according to the junta's evaluation.

For this purpose, the new rulers used the text of a decree that Belaúnde had prepared but not signed expropriating the mines; the other installations were simply added to the original. Then it was discovered that IPC owed not $140 million but $690 million "for oil extracted illegally for twenty-four years." Three of Belaúnde's ministers were held and tried on a suspicion of negligence. In all this, the man who advised Velasco was the former candidate of the Christian Progressive Party, Ruiz Eldredge.

Upon taking power, the military dissolved Parliament. They did not have to account to anyone. Basically, they were using the oil problem to influence public opinion; they not only presented themselves as defenders of the national interest and saviors of the national honor, but put all those who opposed the dictatorship in the position of opposing ipso facto the country's recovery of the oil holdings. Opposers of the junta, the members of the revolutionary government were saying in so many words, were for IPC. Naturally, as nobody was for IPC, nobody was against the junta—at least, not in those terms.

Washington's reaction was immediate. Invoking the recently passed Hickenlooper amendment which requires that all aid be withdrawn from any country that expropriates American property without compensation, the United States suspended aid to Peru and withheld recognition of the junta pending resolution of the IPC matter. (The precedent for doing so had been set by President Kennedy in 1962.) But the junta held that IPC's tax debt was such that it exceeded what amount the company could claim as compensation. IPC then appealed to the courts; it was asked by the court, however, to deposit the $690 million in tax arrears, in accordance with Peruvian law, until a final decision could be made.

Meanwhile, the expectation grew in Peru that this conflict with the United States would induce the traditionalists among the military to stage a countercoup and return the country to constitutional government. But, in March, 1969, President Nixon suddenly dispatched a special negotiator to Lima, John M. Irwin, who succeeded in persuading the junta to allow IPC to appeal to the courts without depositing the $690 million in question. To Washington, the junta's concession, though partial, constituted, in effect, a first step toward final negotiation of IPC's compensation. Accordingly, the

new military government was officially recognized, and aid
to Peru was resumed, beginning with the shipment of arms.
In return, Lima also agreed to attend a conference, together
with Chile and Ecuador, to resolve the question of territorial
waters that the United States considered a source of friction.
(The reader will recall that these three Latin American
countries adopted a 200-mile limit from their coasts for
foreign fishing fleets, as opposed to the traditional three-
mile limit recognized by international law).

Washington had yielded, with a legal subterfuge, to pressure from Lima. The $120 million at which IPC's proper-
ties were valued had been lost, but many more millions in
other American investments, which undoubtedly would have
been expropriated if the Hickenlooper amendment had been
applied, were saved. Numerous American firms with interests
in Peru brought pressure on the U.S. State Department to
arrive at an arrangement with the junta, for they were afraid
of having to pay on the rebound for any tense situation that
might arise. On the other hand, the military junta, with no
publicity, was giving new concessions to American firms, as
has been said, and this increased the pressure in favor of an
adjustment, since such firms did not cease to pressure the
State Department in this direction.

When the situation was finally cleared, the military government created a new organization, the Compañía de Petroleos
de Perú (Petroperú), inspired by Pemex of Mexico and
Petrobras of Brazil. It will have a monopoly on the extraction, refining, and distribution of oil. Petroperú receives the
holdings of the Empresa Petrolera Fiscal (including the La
Brea and Pariñas mines and the property of IPC) and controls fifty thousand of the seventy thousand barrels of oil
produced daily in the country. Outside the jurisdiction of
Petroperú, for the present, are the Belco Petroleum Company, which takes oil from under the sea, the Compañía de
Ganso Azul, and the Compañía de Petróleo de Oriente,
which produce an aggregate of thirty thousand barrels a day.
To satisfy the domestic demand, twenty thousand barrels
more per day have to be imported. In time, Petroperú,
which has an initial capital of $115 million, will exercise a

government monopoly. At least, that is the stated intention, although, for the present, as we have said, new concessions for prospecting and extraction have been given to American firms.

The petroleum coup was very profitable for the military junta, for it not only permitted it to present itself in a revolutionary and nationalist light, but, at the same time, silenced the opposition and established new bases for relations with the United States. The prestige of the new regime rose rapidly in Latin America, where many people were coming to regard it as a model for the possible solution of problems that neither the democratic Left nor Castroism had been able to solve. The passing of an agrarian reform law added new luster to this image of the junta.

Agrarian Reform

During the first months of the junta's regime, all the talk was about oil. When this then was exhausted, the talk in official spheres returned to the subject of agrarian reform. Expropriations and distributions of land had virtually ceased since the coup, with the result that the landholding oligarchy felt confidence in the military men in spite of their revolutionary rhetoric. General Velasco had stated several times that there would be reform, but without any seizures of the Castro kind. On June 24, 1969, he announced a new agrarian reform law, one that would supersede that of 1964. The new law had been prepared by the Presidential Advisory Commission, composed of military men and advised, in its turn, by technologists, generally from the New Left. The minister of agriculture, Gen. José Benavides, a friend to the landholders, resigned when the plan of reform was first discussed in the council of ministers and was replaced by a colonel recently promoted to general, Jorge Barandarian, regarded as one of the abettors of the coup and one of the main figures of the president's advisory group.

The main characteristics of the government's agrarian reform may be sketched briefly. To begin with, all land is divided into five categories:

1. *Land arable but idle*. This is annexed (potentially expropriated) in toto.

2. *Land insufficiently exploited.* This is land whose yield is less than 80 percent of the average for the region and is annexed in toto also.

3. *Abandoned acreage.* Such land, if still found in that condition after three years, will be incorporated into the public domain.

4. *Land on rental.* The tenants of such land have an option to receive it when the government expropriates and then adjudicates it.

5. *Farmed land.* Whether farmed personally by the owner or through hired workers, such land remains unannexed if it does not exceed 375 acres on the coast, and 37.5 and 165 acres, respectively, in the Sierra and the *selva*; if it is in an irrigated zone; and if it does not exceed 3,750 acres on the coast and up to a variable limit in the Sierra and the *selva* (as much as will support 5,000 head of wool-bearing flocks, this being all in pasturelands and *nonirrigated* sections).

Corporations or silent partnerships are forbidden to own lands. They were given six months to convert to personal companies. The limits of nonannexable land (land that may not be expropriated) are enlarged when the holdings are operated with special efficiency, when the owners pay their taxes, and when they give proper wages to the workers (a provision that, as may be supposed, allows all kinds of exceptions, since it deals with immensurable requirements, capable of only subjective evaluation). The lands and their installations are considered a single unit, but not the plants that process the products of such lands, as, for example, the paper mills (in the future, this will force the new owners of expropriated lands to remain linked to the mills or factories that use their products). When the state carries out an expropriation (or an annexation, as the law has it), it will assume the assets and liabilities of the annexed enterprises. Expropriation will be made after a previous evaluation (one not based on the value declared in the tax assessment—which is equivalent to legalizing evasions, without penalty for the evasion of taxes in the past). The expropriated lands may be adjudicated—sold—by the state with a twenty-year mortgage for extended payments. These sales may be made to individual peasants and to cooperatives, peasant communes, or farming enterprises. Sales to individuals shall not be of an area greater than that necessary to maintain a family in the region involved. The beneficiaries of the reform will receive credit, technical assistance, insurance, and so forth. (There are no mechanisms or necessary capital today for this type of large-scale aid.) Properties of less than 7.5 acres will be integrated into units sufficient for the maintenance of a family. The law permits parceling out on private initiative, but under the supervision of the Dirección General de Reforma Agraria (which offers latifundistas the possibility of parceling out their lands among different members of their families, to trusted friends, and so forth—either by true sale or by means of fictitious sales that will permit the continuance of exploitation as before).

Expropriation will be compensated as follows: for lands directly farmed, 100,000 soles (about $2,000) in cash and the balance in 20-year agrarian debt bonds at 6 percent; for rented acreage, 50,000 soles (about $1,000) in cash and the remainder in 25-year, 5 percent bonds; for idle land, 25,000 soles (about $500) cash and the balance in 30-year, 4 percent bonds. Installations, machinery, and the like of expropriated properties will be paid for up to 1 million soles (about $20,000) in cash and the balance in 20-year, 6 percent bonds. The law also gives advantages to those who wish to offer their lands voluntarily for expropriation and to invest the compensation in industry.

The first comments upon this law pointed out that it was not radically different from the Aprista reform law of 1964 that it pretended to replace, although it was expressed in more radical language. Basically, it is a moderate law, which tends to convert landholders into industrial capitalists. The chief difference is that it does not allow the peasants any part in the mechanisms for enforcement of the law; rather, it grants to the state a function of supervision or intervention so strong that, in practice, the state will become the effective owner of all land and the peasants simply its serfs. Although the law provides for the formation of cooperatives, when expropriation began the lands were not turned over to cooperatives but

were put under the administration and jurisdiction of representatives of the state—always military officers; this provoked
immediate distrust among the peasants, who had already
shown a rather skeptical attitude. To the peasant, accustomed as he is to regarding the military as enemies who take
him to jail or support the land owners, the idea that these
same army officers were now going to give him land was incredible. Experience has confirmed his doubts; for instead of
giving him land, the military have kept it themselves, and the
captain or colonel has now come to replace the hacienda
owner or plantation administrator. This may not be so in economic terms, but that is how it looks to the peasants.

The landholders who thought that the junta would leave
them alone were taken by surprise by the agrarian reform
law. Reaction was weak and was confined to insisting that
agrarian reform should mean an increase of productivity—or,
translated, that the proper course was to give credit to the
latifundistas so that they might modernize their holdings and
open up new lands (those that were to be distributed) to cultivation. The moderate Christian Democrats considered the
proposed form of payment confiscatory; the Apristas, for
their part, pointed out that much that the law decreed had
already been contained in the law of 1964 that they had
proposed and added that enforcement of the new law would
not do any good, because it did not entail participation by
citizens, and because it substituted the owner-state for the
private owner instead of replacing him by democratic cooperatives. On the other hand, the technologists generally received the new law with approval, for it seemed to them to
create conditions favorable to increased production and to
promise distribution of the political power of the latifundistas. The Communists and some groups of the New Left
applauded the law, which the former called antifeudal, anti-
oligarchic, anti-imperialistic, and radical. But other groups—
Castroites and Maoists—pointed out that the law was of a
bourgeois type and tended to convert the "latifundist bourgeois into an industrial bourgeois," though admitting that it
was "an advanced bourgeois law, whose authors apparently
intended to enforce it promptly."[17]

Fidel Castro, in Havana, profited by the occasion to give his accolade to the Peruvian officers, whose "military movement had a character different from that of other military movements . . . [The agrarian reform law is] a measure that, enforced with firmness, could be characterized as a revolutionary measure."[18]

The peasant organizations approved of the law, of course, but complained that the peasants themselves had no part in its enforcement. The only group that did not demand participation was the Communists, whom the military junta had, since 1968, been discreetly supporting against their Aprista rivals. The sugar workers' union expressed a more hostile opinion of the law; for they were quick to see that, instead of turning the sugar industry over to them and thus giving them ownership status, the law granted de facto control of it to the state. It was, as far as they were concerned, only a simple change of management, nothing more. Several leaders of the Federation of Sugar Workers were arrested for this opposition. On the other hand, a small organization of sugar workers, founded after the coup by the Communists and helped to its feet by the military, gave the law its wholehearted approval. The law does not appear to have weakened the adherence of the farm workers and peasants to the APRA where that party was strong, but where the APRA was weak—in the south—the law seemed to favor the Communists, who agreed that only they, with their influence in Lima, could effect the distribution of land.

In the first year, 2.5 million acres were expropriated and distributed among 40,000 families. What is surprising is that the reform, instead of beginning with the appropriation of idle lands, as is traditional in Latin America, began with the expropriation of eight large haciendas owned by Peruvians, Europeans, and Americans. The military government announced that 1973 would bring the end of the emission of bonds for payments of indemnities, for a total value of 15 billion soles, or about $370 million. Among the enterprises taken over by the government are plantations and paper mills belonging to the Grace Company, as well as the Casagrande hacienda—property of a German family and the biggest sugarcane plantation in the world, bigger than Belgium and Switzerland both put together! So far, there have been no diplomatic repercussions.[19]

Of course, every true agrarian reform, if thoroughly enforced, produces profound changes in the social structure of a country and has repercussions on its political structure. It is still too soon to say in what measure the agrarian reform law passed by the Peruvian military will alter the social structure, although it seems likely that it will do away with latifundism; or to what extent it will affect the political structure, although, as of now, it seems that an attempt is being made to produce a reform from above without participation by the people. The case of Peru may clear up many ideas about the possibilities of success of agrarian reform from above, without the participation of the peasants—reform with paternalistic methods and intentions. These intentions were manifest, immediately after the coup, with regard to another area of concern—the country's youth.

The University Crisis

Peru, like all Latin American countries, for years has had a university crisis. In 1946, when the Aprista Luis Alberto Sánchez (1900–   ) was rector of San Marcos University, there were a restructuring plan and a plan for renovation, inspired, in part, by the American university system and, in part, by Aprista ideology. These plans intended to link the university to the people and to make it useful in the country's development. But, two years later, the Odría dictatorship annulled them. Since then, the university crisis has only grown worse throughout the country, aggravated by politicization and the students' fragmentation into minuscule political groups of the New Left, which, with their rivalries, have often succeeded in paralyzing university life. Dogmatic violence has become general in the universities throughout the country; and the students have become isolated, not only from the public, but even from the middle class from which the great majority of them came.

This student discontent, although manifested in political gestures as ineffective as they are dramatic, has profound causes. For one thing, the number of students in the humanities and in education has grown much more rapidly than the number of students in science, medicine, and technology. Furthermore, the number of job offers for graduates is only one-fourth the number of graduates in the humanities and in education—and jobs are declining in the sciences and in medicine, whereas they are doubling in economics. This means that many students know that, when their studies are finished, they will be without employment in the profession to which they have apprenticed their youth.

Such frustrating circumstances affect a constantly growing number of students. In 1900, there were 1,000 university students in Peru; in 1970, the number was 128,000. From five in 1954, the number of universities has increased to thirty-four in 1970. All these universities have schools in the humanities, but only half have scientific schools, and medical schools are in only a third. Thus, the student not only feels lost in a sea of other students, but must face the reality of a proportional diminution of the demand for his services—that is, the uselessness and seeming futility of his studies.

All this, we repeat, has led to a grave crisis among university youth—the only youth in the country who express themselves—and that has been aggravated by the general university crisis resulting from the excessive politicization of professors and students, from lack of economic means, and from a system of education that is irrelevant to the real problems of a country antiquated in methods and structures.

In 1969, the military junta sought to remedy this situation by creating the so-called System for the Peruvian University, which unified all the universities of the country, public and private. In this system, the National Council of the Peruvian University, with representatives from all of the universities, formulates the objectives of higher education and sees that they are carried out. The system is legally autonomous, but the universities that compose it are not. They must obey the decisions of the national council, which assigns to each university the sums that it may spend in accordance with the council's plans. The council, seated in Lima, can also permit or forbid the creation of new universities. So far it has shown a decided tendency to structure curricula on the American model, with elective courses, and has replaced the various university schools with separate departments.

Each university has an elected university assembly. The rector and the department heads form the executive council of the university, which makes decisions in accordance with the general directions of the assembly, which must, however, remain within the framework of the national council's plans. The students are represented in these bodies in every university, the proportion being one-third as many students as professors. But the majority of students, and many professors as well, say that the machinery established for choosing these representatives really is destroying student participation in the government of the universities. Moreover, the powers that the law gives to the rector of each university—always within the frame of the decisions of the national council—are sweeping; and there has not been any lack of voices to charge that the intention is to make the rector an academic dictator.

The law immediately aroused stubborn opposition among faculty and students. How much of this is clinging to tradition and acquired habits, and how much of it is legitimate fear of losing academic autonomy, freedom, and student participation, is something only the future will tell.

In 1971, the minister of education, a general surrounded by a group of young technicians, announced a general educational reform for 1971, to be in force until 1975. "Education," he said, "must be Peruvianized in its spirit in order to produce Peruvians with the requisite new revolutionary morale," and in order that education shall cease to be a matter of class and a privilege of the economically favored groups.[20]

This reform, however, has so far remained in the study stage. But a campaign has begun in the Ministry of Education against corruption and carelessness. "For the first time all the offices [of the ministry] were numbered and all the names of the personnel put on a list on the doors. The time clocks of the earlier era, which had been sabotaged, were repaired."[21] The same thing has been done in other ministries and government offices. It has been accomplished not only through bureaucratic discipline and publicity campaigns but, to some extent, through the limitation of civil liberties.

Civil Liberties

The military regime is undeniably dictatorial, since it does not owe its existence to elections and has not established any system of consulting the citizenry about its decisions. It calls itself the Revolutionary Government of the Armed Forces, and it is military in the sense that its power does not originate with the public but with the army.

But it is different from earlier military dictatorships in Peru. For one thing, it has not hastened to form its own political party, and it makes no attempt to exert systematic political pressure on its opponents. Nobody is arrested for holding opinions hostile to the regime; and opposition parties function freely, though they have little real influence since there is no constitutional legality. All this could change, of course, if the opposition grows strong enough to threaten the regime.

Labor organizations function normally; but, as has been noted, the government gives sub rosa support to Communist-led unions in order to play them off against independent and Aprista unions. Nevertheless, there has been no radical social legislation. The government also maintains good relations with private organizations of industrialists and merchants.

There is one thing, however, about which the military government has a very thin skin, indeed—the press. The Peruvian press, which is in the hands of a few economically powerful and socially conservative familites—the Prados, the Miró Quesadas, and so on—has a tradition of influence. People are accustomed to believe what they read in the newspapers. No doubt this was why, at the beginning of its operations in 1968, the military junta exiled some journalists—and decided, on December 30, 1969, to "Peruvianize" the press. The declared purpose of the Statute of Freedom of the Press, promulgated on that date, was to make sure that there would be no foreign influence on the information media. But its real purpose was to keep the press from continuing to criticize the government. In other words, a nationalist guise was used to give acceptability to a measure against freedom of expression.

This statute promises to guarantee freedom of the press, to the extent that the latter shows "respect for the law, the truth and morality, the exigencies of the integral safety of the state and the national defense." Obviously, these limitations are so vague that any published information could be considered as affecting one of these areas. It also stipulates that censorship may be imposed only in time of war. Furthermore, the newspapers, of whatever class, can be owned only by Peruvian-born residents of Peru; the capital of journalistic enterprise will have to be entirely Peruvian; and no stock can be transferred to foreigners.

There was an immediate reaction against the statute, as much on the part of the publishers, who feared loss of their property, as on the part of journalists, who feared the loss of their freedom of expression. The matter was brought before the Supreme Tribunal, but, as the military junta had already illegally replaced several members of that body, the tribunal threw out the suit against the government.[22]

The military government has a peculiar notion of what constitutes freedom of the press. For example, in February, 1970, it ordered all daily press to publish, free of charge, a long communiqué about the foreign ministers' trip abroad. *La Tribuna*, the daily organ of the Aprista party, refused and, in consequence, suffered so many fines and demands to pay its debts that it disappeared from the scene.

In March, 1970, there was another illustration of the way the militarists understood freedom of the press. The junta expropriated two important and very popular dailies, *The Express* and *The Extra*—property of a distinguished Belaúndist. What induced it to take this measure, it seems, was that the two dailies had been publishing a series of dispatches about the collaboration of Communist elements with the government, and this irritated the military men all the more since the articles were true. The two expropriated dailies were turned over to a corporation formed by their employees. In February, 1971, the government established state control for all television and radio stations, by expropriating them and

announcing that compensations would be paid. The decision
was explained as an attempt to "Peruvanize" (basically de-
Americanize) the programs and to put the media at the service of the public instead of letting them be just profit-
making enterprises. Such extreme sensibility to the press had
been shown before in the suspension of the magazine *Caretas*
and in the edict against circulation, in Peru, of the American
Spanish-language weekly *Visión.*

By the middle of 1970, it began to look as if this sensitiv-
ity had been extended to other fields. For example, although
there have been no instances of reprisal against the latifundistas who have criticized the agrarian reform law, the military
government revised one part of the law in order to increase
the penalties for those accused of inciting strikes in the rural
areas. Immediately, five non-Communist leaders of the sugar
workers' union were arrested and tried in accordance with
this revision.

That there has been no persecution of the political parties
does not mean, however, that the junta does not try, in de-
vious ways, to make life hard for them. For instance, on
February 8, 1970, the Day of Fraternity—the great annual
APRA fiesta—was celebrated as usual. A football match between Peruvian and Russian teams had been announced for
Wednesday. It was postponed, with the consent of the Rus-
sians, until the following day—when the Apristas were to
hold their rally—in the hope that the game would lure attendance away from the political rally.

Perhaps an idea of the subtle and undramatic methods
used by the military to control the populace (with the advice
of elements of the New Left) can be gleaned from this simple
list of documents every Peruvian must have on his person,
and which may be demanded by anyone in authority: identification card, military card, voter-registration card (even
though there are no elections), tax-payment card, and social-
security card. Whoever cannot show these five identification
cards is liable to arrest and a fine.[23]

Economic Policy

The economic measures adopted by the junta are of three

types: those designed to confront an immediate situation and
the repercussion of political measures on the economy; those
aimed at fortifying the bourgeoisie's influence and hastening
Peru's conversion into a capitalist society (while weakening
the landholding oligarchy); and those designed to increase
foreign investment and create allies for the junta among foreign investors. Most of these measures have been adopted in
secret and announced only when they have already been
passed. The chief exception is agrarian reform with its political implications.

In response to the situation created by the mass emigration
of capital, the closing of firms, and the consequent unemployment that resulted when the junta came to power and
announced its revolutionary line, the government at first decreed that all foreign money should be surrendered and all
capital repatriated. When this decree proved ineffective, the
government ordered the opening of bank vaults in search of
hoarded dollars. Other measures include refinancement of
the external debt, virtual state control over foreign trade, and
price controls on necessities. In 1970, the sole was devalued
and exchange brought under control.

Among measures of the second type, those intended to
weaken the landholding oligarchy and encourage capitalism,
we find, in addition to agrarian reform, diplomatic and commercial treaties with the Soviet Union and its satellites; fiscal
reform and higher income taxes; campaigns to improve the
morale of those in the administrative system and simplify
bureaucratic routine; fishing and mining laws, which, in effect, subject these two industries to government control;
assurances that the government would not nationalize industry; the fusion of thirteen automobile assembly firms into
four; and negotiations for increased foreign investment in
oil and mining.

All these, though for the moment contrary to prevailing
economic custom, are not measures of a socialist type, but
tend, in their long-range effects, to establish a capitalistic system more or less controlled by the state. The 1970 budget—
the first prepared by the military—has this character. It represents an increase of 86 percent over that of 1969, or 31

percent when appropriate adjustments are taken into account. The budget, said the minister of economics, was to be an instrument of expansion. Public investment was to account for 20 percent of the budget, whereas little more than 3 percent was to be devoted to agrarian reform. There was a marked rise in taxes, as much through reform of the fiscal tariffs as through the contributions of certain industries— fishing, mining—subject to *de facto* government control.

In July, 1970, the junta promulgated, after first having submitted it to public discussion, the law of industrial incentive which divided firms into three categories, in accordance with their importance in the national economy, and set guidelines for taxes, credit, exemptions, subsidies, and the extension of credit in each category. Under this law, priority is given to heavy industry and machinery, then to processing firms that serve them and export their own goods. In the third category are industries that produce nonessential goods. Each industry is assigned a category by a complex point system in which even the patriotism of the firms is considered. The law also requires all industrial enterprises to distribute 10 percent of their net profits among their employees and to earmark 15 percent for reinvestment and 2 percent for industrial research. Every board of directors must include a representative of the community or of the workers, but since the law does not specify how they are to be named, the government is free to designate them.

This sort of regulation was all the more logical, since, in 1970, the country was in a precarious economic condition, with a drop in exports, flight of capital, devaluation, a decline in production, a rise in prices, and the closing of some industries—in general, in a state of uneasiness rather than one of active discontent. The only thing that was stabilized was wages; for, although the government did not come into conflict with the unions, it found means, more psychological than legal, to paralyze their agitation in favor of tying wages to the cost of living.

Measures of the third type include the series of agreements signed with foreign firms (nearly all American) during and after the conflict with the IPC—agreements all announced after they were signed. The military government does not want to be dependent on foreign capital and is sincerely nationalistic and even anti-American, but the facts have shown that Peru, at present, has not enough available capital to speed up development of its mining, exploit its oil, and create new industries. Hence these agreements, accepted with the hope that development of other sectors of industry will permit the country to absorb foreign capital without risking its economic independence and sovereignty. These agreements have been discussed in chapter 6. It is sufficient to add here that they offer guarantees and conditions much more favorable to foreign firms than any other agreement signed before 1968. They have even gone so far as to legalize the wage discrimination between Peruvian and foreign workers. It is also odd that, whereas in Bolivia the military government headed by Gen. Alfredo Ovando expropriated the holdings of the Gulf Petroleum Company, in Peru the military government has reached an accord with that firm for extraction of oil in the Sierra in exchange for an investment of $60 million. It is curious, too, that in the decree requiring that a major percentage of water traffic be conveyed in Peruvian vessels (thus ruling out Chilean and Colombian vessels, contrary to the terms of the Andean Pact, of which Peru is a signer), the ships of such American companies as the Grace Line and Gulf Steamship Company are regarded as Peruvian.

The military regime has been extremely pragmatic in the enforcement of its laws. When a decision has proved very impractical or has aroused too much opposition, the government publishes an order modifying such or such an article of the law so as to make it enforceable. In this sense, there has been no dogmatism. The only things the military are dogmatic about are their desire to remain in power, the general orientation—nationalist and capitalist—of their policy, and their insistence upon formulating this policy without consulting the public.

What Kind of Revolution?

We repeat that the military government calls itself the Revolutionary Government of the Armed Forces. But is it really a

revolutionary government? Is it only a government of the
armed forces? In any event, what sort of revolution is this
government bringing about? And, in short, how can its regime be described?

First of all, let us see who are behind the throne. Velasco
Alvarado is something more than a figurehead, but he is less
than an all-powerful dictator. He has on his team the real
policymakers of the regime—those whom the public calls the
"earthquake group." This is formed of elements from the
CAEM. In 1962, elements of the CAEM tried to take advantage of the coup against the APRA's victory at the polls to
direct the government de facto—but international pressure
compelled them to call new elections, and the CAEM group
had to wait and prepare for another opportunity (which
presented itself five years later).

In the CAEM, Marxism-Leninism and the works of Mao and
Ho are studied, and guerrilla warfare and its programs and
tactics are analyzed. Although many of the alumni go to
study in the United States and others are detached to follow
civilian careers, especially technical ones, so that the army
will have men available for all sorts of posts, the officers produced by the CAEM have no respect for democracy; they
know only the kind Peru has experienced, and that is hardly inspiring. They are elitists, paternalists; and their desire
to produce a revolution stems from the conviction that without it the army will be powerless. They are development-
minded, like the young businessmen with whom they see eye
to eye. They are also anti-American, like the Communists and
the New Left. They believe that the answer to Peru's needs is
a revolution that will destroy the power of the oligarchy and
will employ cooperatives as the means of organizing the
people (and, incidentally, of controlling them) and as a replacement for unions controlled by the APRA. They are not
enemies of private property or of capitalism but only of the
great landholders and of feudal survivals. Basically, the
CAEM elements would like to carry out the program of the
APRA that the older military men kept the APRA from putting into effect.

Two factors influence the education of the generations of

the CAEM. On the one hand, there is the consciousness of belonging to the middle class and the obligation, consequently, to protect its interests—not as the middle class understands them, but as the CAEM elements do. On the other hand, there is guilt for the past history of the army, the police, and the oligarchy, and chiefly for the treatment of the guerrillas a few years ago. The activity of the army in 1965–66 was so brutal that many colonels and captains who had witnessed it returned to their quarters with a guilt complex. Apropos of this, the present minister of power and mining, Gen. Jorge Fernandez Maldonado, told the correspondent of *Le Monde,* "We are discovering remote causes of insurrection—poverty, the shameful exploitation of the masses, the social injustice of archaic structures."

These officers from the CAEM had supported Belaúnde against Haya, but the former disappointed them, in spite of his leanings toward development and his planner's rhetoric. They concluded that political action and its impediments would make it impossible to effect the changes that the country needed. And, at the same time, they concluded that the chief enemy was the oligarchy, and that this group would not have had the strength to resist change had it not been for their links to foreign interests (American, in particular). The oligarchy takes its strength from the land; therefore, the land must be taken from the oligarchy. As long as the peasant has no land, he will not be a Peruvian, said Mariátegui. As long as the peasant owns no land, he will not be a good producer or a good consumer, say the young company owners. And the CAEM men say that, as long as the peasant does not own land, he will not be a good soldier.

The key posts in the administration are in the hands of the CAEM elements, who have the majority of the ministries, have charge of agrarian reform, and have won the collaboration of elements of the New Left and even Communist fellow-travelers. This does not imply that the regime is Communist or even anything like it; simply that the young militarists are making use of the Communists and of the New Left as incidental allies, while hoping not to be used by them. The future will tell whether they can do this.

The objectives of these militarists may be summed up as follows:

1. To transform the structure of the state, making it more dynamic and efficient, and to improve the functioning of the government
2. To elevate the least favored elements of the population to a standard of living compatible with human dignity
3. To give a nationalist and independent orientation to the acts of the government, founded on a firm defense of national sovereignty and dignity
4. To reverse the demoralization of the country in all areas of national activity, and to reestablish firmly the principle of authority and respect for the law and the exercise of justice
5. To promote unity, concord, and the integration of all Peruvians in the strengthening of Peru's national consciousness[24]

The publicly stated objectives, obviously, are rather vague and might be those of any party or ideology. What will help us to be more precise is to examine the means employed to reach these ends. The young militarists, whom we may label technocrats, want to produce what they call a revolution, but they want to do it from above, with participation of the masses—that is, through paternalistic methods. There is, for the present, no doubting their good faith or the sincerity of the younger men; as for the older ones, who also hold government posts, nothing leads us to suppose that they are revolutionists or lacking in the intent to keep the young men in check, and even to replace them if opportunity should arise— assuming that this will not cause a division in the armed forces.

These paternalistic, elitist, and technocratic methods presuppose that the revolution that the militarists want to produce—if we can call a change effected by such methods a revolution—shall not be socialist, nor even that vague thing called Castroist, nor is it to destroy private ownership of the means of production or substitute for that a collective or socialized ownership. In a context of semifeudal oligarchy, to want what is desired by the military technocrats is equivalent to wanting what the Marxists would call a bourgeois revolution—that is, to realize from above, paternalistically, the changes necessary to make Peruvian society pass from semi-feudal and oligarchic to capitalist and elitist, with a sincere desire on the part of some that it will become, in the distant future, a capitalist democratic society.

Thus, younger officers want to effect the same things the APRA has wanted—without the participation of the public and without any haste about creating conditions that will make this participation possible.

Naturally, such a capitalism as will emerge from these changes will not be American-style, with free enterprise, private initiative, and limited state intervention in the economy. Peruvian traditions (and Latin American ones, in general) condition the Peruvian capitalism of the future, and the examples furnished by Latin America itself, especially in the case of Mexico, have the same effect. The tradition is one of a managed economy—under the Incas, during the colonial period, and after the coming of independence (although, in the last case, the management by the landholding oligarchy was subtle and concealed). The examples are of a mixed economy, with public and private investment, the former exercising, in effect, a planning and controlling function.

For decades, the armed forces prevented all social change until they finally came to realize that change not only was inevitable but would favor their very status as military forces. This freed them from subjection to the oligarchy. But they did not resign themselves to a passive role, which the military had never had in Peru. And, as there was a power vacuum, with an oligarchy unable to govern without unconditional support from the armed forces, and with political parties incapable of attaining power and effecting change without this same support, the armed forces ended by arrogating to themselves the roles of sole authors of the revolution, of *paterfamilias* of the "great Peruvian family," of tutors of the people and supreme administrators of the national interest.

Can this concept work in practice? A strictly military government can stay in power a long time if opposition is passive and purely verbal, and if it has available a policy system efficient enough to disarm any attempt at active opposition. But, if this military government wants to accomplish reforms that will affect the mass of the population—all social classes—it must count on mass support, or at least on the most powerful segments of society, or have the participation of the masses in reform. Since the military technocrats of Peru have no intention of allowing the masses any participation—even if they wanted to, they would not know how, since military life has not exactly prepared them for that— they have to seek support without offering such participation; which means that they must foster among the people an attitude we may best describe as filial, the attitude of protégés. They have managed to do this, to some extent, thanks to their waving of the nationalist flag and were able to make opposition to the dictatorship appear as support of foreign interests. But, in Peru, it is not easy to prolong deception of this magnitude, because the masses have had some political preparation, thanks to decades of work by the APRA, and because this is not the first time a military man has risen to power while hoisting the revolutionary flag and then deceived those who believed in him (Odría's case is the most recent). On the other hand, the very nature of the changes the regime wants to effect demands that there be an absence of tension with other countries, and even that investment shall be forthcoming from them. (The case of Cuba has shown the extent to which tense relationships with investing countries can handicap social change.) The anti-imperialist flag will not serve for any long-term appeasement of the masses, whose standard of life, far from improving since 1968, has been deteriorating. The masses will demand a part in reform, and the most politically aware among them will also demand a constitutional regime that will formalize these reforms and give them some degree of juridical guarantee.

It is possible that the military in power will, in time, yield to these popular demands, or that the situation will worsen so much that they may see in yielding to such demands a way out of power, which will have become a burden. But, given the outlook of the military technocrats, there is little likelihood of that. There are officers in all the important administration posts, and they are beginning to turn up in key economic posts, too, thanks to intervention by the state in agricultural and cattle-raising enterprises, and undoubtedly they will be in key posts in banking, foreign trade, and other branches of economic activity. In this way, a bureaucracy in uniform is being created—one with interest in the permanency of a regime that gives it this power to make decisions in economic affairs. Therefore, the officers will not want to move out.

If they want to stay, after the profitable exploitation of "opposition equals antinationalism" has been worn out, they will have to create another "enemy," fly another flag for the masses to rally around, and so obtain the latter's submission and support. For a regime of this character, it is not enough to say, like an old-style dictator, "Whoever is not against me is with me." It must proclaim "Whoever is not with me is against me."

This new flag, for a military man, will logically be that of the "foreign enemy." As the "foreign enemy" cannot be one of the major powers—whose help Peru needs, in view of the present situation in the world and the country—it will have to be a neighboring country, perhaps the "traditional enemy" to the south, Chile, or the one to the north, Ecuador. Peru, its military men think, is now prepared to face a war with either of these two countries. In this way, unbelievable though it may seem, the "revolutionary" military dictatorship can bring about another era of frontier wars in Latin America. All that is needed is for one country to take the offensive. The gestures of the OAS will not have the same effect upon Peru as they have had upon the smaller countries, as when Honduras and El Salvador squared off in the "football war" of 1969.

But, if this device to appease and subjugate the masses proves unfeasible, because of international pressure or the economic situation at home, the militarists will still have another card up their sleeves. They could ask for the collaboration of those who know how to organize the masses, how to appeal to them, and how to control them. The old democratic establishments would not be able to accept this role, both on principle and because, in doing so, they would lose what effectiveness they still had; but the junta would find the Communists ready to put at its disposal the party's techniques of organizing and controlling the masses. The Communists do support the military regime—but that is because it is verbally anti-American, and this plays the Soviet policy game. The help they would furnish, however—at the time we are speaking of—would be of a different sort: a support that would absorb from within. This would not be simply out of anti-Americanism, but because the situation would give the Communists key posts—not glamorous, but still posts of great effectiveness—and because it would make them indispensable. To some degree, the same thing could happen as occurred in the case of Castro: when, because of his own blunders, Castro had to organize and control the masses, he turned to the only ones who knew how to do so—the Communists—and finally was absorbed by them. In the case of Peru the affair would be less sweeping, since the country and the technocratic military regime would not depend exclusively for survival on the Soviet Union, as Castro did. But, in any case, such a situation—hypothetical now but quite possible in the future—would, for the first time, give the Communists real influence in Peru. Furthermore, this collaboration would permit the Communists to realize an old dream, one that is almost an obsession—liquidation of the APRA. And, as a bonus, it would offer them the possibility of eliminating all the splinter groups of the New Left that are such an irritation to them and criticize them so much—although most of these groups, for the present, agree with the Communists in supporting the military regime.

The character of this support by the Communists and the New Left—which they call "critical support," an expression they picked up when they backed Perón and other Latin American dictators in the period from 1948 to 1958—has been very well defined in an article in *Pravda*:

> The Peruvian Communist Party has declared
> several times in its documents that agrarian reform,
> despite its limited petit-bourgeois character and its
> slow pace, corresponds to the aspirations of the
> Peruvian peasantry and of the people as a whole.
> This reform has a progressive, antifeudal, and anti-
> imperialist content. . . . it is directed primarily
> against the land barons and against their protective
> allies, the American monopolies.[25]

Apart from some groups of the New Left, the Communists, and those Christian Socialists of the Left, who are able
to furnish some technicians and propagandists but, for the
present, exert no influence upon the public-opinion level or
on the masses—who supports the militarists? No one. At first,
the landholding oligarchy were pleased to see the military
take power, because they were preventing the inevitable victory of the APRA in the 1969 elections, and because the
oligarchy thought the regime's "revolutionary" rhetoric
would remain just rhetoric, as had happened so often in the
past. Now, however, they are trying to persuade some of the
older officers to stage a countercoup, but, at the moment,
they seem to have little chance of succeeding. The APRA and
the other parties are putting up a verbal opposition to the
military, but are not really doing anything.

Indeed, the situation from 1968 to the present has been
such that all groups, except the latifundistas, have been
happy to have the militarists assume the task of doing things
that some of the parties, when they had power, did not dare
to do, and that others could not think of attempting because
the militarists would have then objected. The businessmen
are content, though alarmed at the cost of the operation. The
workers are indifferent. The peasants are satisfied with the
reform—that is, those who have heard about it—even if not
overjoyed because it was effected without taking them into
account. Thus, anything that is done now redounds to the

benefit of the militarist regime in power, and opposition, without posing any threat to them, serves their purpose by showing how "tolerant," "democratic," and "progressive" they are. Of course, how long this placid surface can remain unruffled no one knows.

Are there any alternatives to the present situation? To be sure, some of the things that have been done are irreversible. If the military regime succeeds in dismantling the power of the landholding oligarchy—if they expropriate and redistribute enough lands to make the former landholders understand that there is no possibility of recovering them—then the regime will have eliminated the most immediate possibility of being replaced by a coup on the part of the military traditionalists, who remain alarmed by the measures of their "progressive" counterparts. There is a chance, too, that rivalries may arise in the very bosom of these "progressive" militarists—a possibility present in every regime as authoritarian and personalist as the present one.

Just now, it does not seem as if civilian opposition or the old political parties pose any real threat to the regime, outside of this opposition's constant prodding of the traditionalist military men to stage a coup, which prodding is obviously done privately and most discreetly.

Much more dangerous to the future of the regime is the possibility—almost a probability—that the youth groups and other elements that support the regime (I refer to the non-Communist New Left) will withdraw their support when they are convinced that the regime is less anti-American and less revolutionary than it pretends to be. From these groups, together with young elements of the APRA, could come either the rejuvenation of the APRA itself or a new, truly revolutionary opposition movement—one seeking to give a popular, democratic content to what has been done by the "progressive" militarists by allowing for the people's participation in the reforms. Naturally, no estimate can be made of the power this active and youthful opposition can command, since that will depend largely on the mistakes that the "progressive" militarists will make, on the rapidity with which they become preservers of what they have done, and also on the rapidity with which their regime evolves toward authoritarian forms of collaboration with the Communists, as we have suggested.

Obviously, today's situation in Peru is not quite as black and white (or as critical) as would appear from the press dispatches and from what partisans and adversaries see. It is curious that there is more passionate feeling outside Peru against or in favor of the new regime than there is in the country itself. Among the Latin American New Left, Gen. Valasco Alvarado's regime has been received enthusiastically. Contributing to this, on the one hand, has been the regime's apparent and initial anti-Americanism and, on the other, the growing dissatisfaction with Castro, whose failures have deprived the New Left of an idol. (Velasco, however, lacks Castro's charisma.) Where one finds the most fervent enthusiasm for the Peruvian militarists is in the New Left in the United States, despite its opposition to militarism at home. Perhaps this shows, better than any of its activities, the elitist and paternalistic character of this New Left. Velasco Alvarado and his colonels are doing what, fundamentally, the Latin American and North American New Left would like to do.

Castro has repeatedly praised the Peruvian military junta. In Bolivia, the regime established by Gen. Alfredo Ovando, not dissimilar from Peru's, expressed its solidarity with the Peruvian militarists and its desire to march along the same road. It is probable that Peru's example will strengthen the position of the groups of young technocratic militarists in other Latin American armies; but, for the moment, it does not appear as if Velasco wants to imitate Castro and be converted into a continental figure or to export his "revolution" to other countries. Obviously, a change in circumstances could induce him, nevertheless, to try it.

No one can foretell what road Peru is going to follow. For good or evil—and without being able to decide their own destiny—today's young Peruvians are going to live in a Peru different from that of their fathers. No one can know whether it will be a truer nation than the present one, united in outlook and with its own distinct identity, or whether it will be but an archipelago of capitalistic cities sharing only a common administration that is controlled by an oligarchy of military officers and capitalistic technocrats. Nor can one know whether the forms of capitalistic democracy will evolve in the Peru of tomorrow. Yet, one thing is certain: in ten years, this book will no longer be a valid description of Peru.

10

The Coup within the Coup

After the first two years of spectacular measures, the military regime slid into a routine broken only, from time to time, by certain decisions—purported to be dramatic by the propaganda apparatus—which were made when the economic situation deteriorated or when rivalries and discrepancies appeared within the establishment. The point was not so much to add something substantial to the regime's image as to divert public attention. The only substantial measures adopted were those meant to prevent criticism of the government, which along with its supporters, had always shown signs of susceptibility in that respect.

By 1970 the official dynamism was gone. It is difficult to speak in terms of enthusiasm or faith, since these were always absent in Peru itself, even among the military. However, outside of Peru, among the New Left and the anti-American middle class, that nation had been cited as an example many times. In all truth, there was more enthusiasm for the Peruvian "revolution" outside Peru than inside it.

The "Normal" Government

In order to understand the regime's late evolution, it is necessary to summarize those years of routine, of "normal" government. This we will do rather briefly, as if to present a list of provisions adopted by the government.

In May, 1973, equality between white-collar workers and manual laborers was decreed, along with a retirement system establishing fifty-five as the minimum retirement age for women and sixty for men. (It must be remembered, when these ages are considered, that in Peru, as in most Andean countries, life expectancy does not go far beyond sixty.) This system does away with the idea of requiring a certain number of years of work, which allowed for retirement when a person had worked continuously for twenty-five years, even if he had begun work at the age of fifteen or twenty.

In January of 1974, Gen. José Graham, chief of the Presidential Advisory Commission, declared: "We have established the juridical basis for our revolution, which intends to change the social structure; but the most difficult part remains: to convince the people of the need for change." At the same time, he announced that Peru was going to buy more tanks and planes, because Chile and Ecuador had made similar arms purchases. Among the Peruvian acquisitions were 100 Soviet mid-weight tanks of the 55-T model, 24 American Northrop model A-37B jet planes for training, 1 Italian and 2 British destroyers, a Dutch cruiser, and several German submarines.

Commenting on these purchases, the foreign minister, Gen. Miguel Angel de la Flor, said that "we are not part in an arms race, but we need a dissuasive force." He added that Peru was still faithful in its attempts to obtain the readmission of Cuba to the O.A.S., its support for the reassumption of Panamanian sovereignty over the canal, and the restructuring of the "out-dated inter-American system." At the same time he noted that there was a better understanding of the "independent policies of Peru" in Washington. Nonetheless, he said, there was a feeling of diplomatic isolation because Lima lost the tactical alliance of Allende when he was overthrown and of Perón when the president of the *descamisados* ("shirtless ones") started switching to more conservative positions. This isolation increased after the ultraconservative military assumed de facto control of the Uruguayan government and after the victory in the Venezuelan elections of the Acción Democrática party, which had sheltered many Peruvian exiles.

This isolation was being felt also within the country. The measures adopted during the government's first two years, even though they answered long-standing aspirations of many Peruvians, were applied from the top, and this alienated the masses, who were not permitted to participate in what they were told was being done for their benefit . . . but without them. The teachers, always very active, organized their own union in 1972; they carried out several 24-hour long strikes demanding better conditions, and a general strike in the fall of 1973 that paralyzed the academic life of the country, especially in the south. The government for the first time reacted with violence and proclaimed a state of emergency. The demonstrators were fired upon and many were arrested (twenty dead in Puno and Cuzco and some five hundred arrested, many of whom could not be found after two months). Ninety-one teachers were interned in the El Sepa penal colony in the southeast. The teachers were headed by extreme Left groups that had supported the military junta but were against it after it became a stable government, and by APRA elements. "We oppose the government," declared one of the teachers' leaders, "because it is proimperialist, antipopular and repressive." He added: "Although they talk about eliminating the old oligarchy, they are creating a new bourgeoisie formed by army officers." Popular support for the teachers was large. Miners, students, small-business owners, and some industrial workers showed their sympathy for them.

The government was not successful with what was called, as explained, the social mobilization. This was headed by Carlos Delgado, a former member of APRA, who used his knowledge as an activist among the peasants to try to organize, with government support, 500 cooperatives, 70 peasant coalitions, and 2,500 worker communities. But the system turned into a traditional bureaucracy, and since there was no allowance for initiative from below, it found very little response.

It was in order to detract attention from those failures that the government nationalized the Cerro de Pasco mining company. Soon afterward, in an effort to gain support from the workers, the government issued the Law of Social Property in July, 1974, which according to Velasco Alvarado was "the most decisive move of the revolution" and which would require "readjustments in the state apparatus."

The purpose of the law was to put into practice the premise formulated by members of the military in order to justify, theoretically, the coup: the building of a "democracy of social participation." Up to that moment there had been no widespread participation in the government, nor in the application of the agrarian reform or the administration of the nationalized businesses, all of which were in the hands of the military. The law was to demonstrate that the final objective of the coup had not been forgotten.

The decree, in very vague terms, asserted that its purpose was "to recognize the creative work of man in society as the original source of wealth" (which was, of course, nothing original) and to "secure the solidarity of man as well as guarantee the process of social accumulation." In order to achieve this, the law established the concept of the publically owned firm (*empresa de propiedad social*, or EPS), which was to be made up entirely of workers, who would make decisions and participate in the enterprise's operations and benefits. The National Commission of Social Property was created to authorize the EPSs. These were not old companies that would be transformed and whose workers would be given participation in their operations and benefits, but rather new enterprises formed by workers. It was not, thus, a matter, in spite of the official rhetoric, of socializing property, but rather one of creating a sector of "social" property alongside that of private property.

How are the new enterprises financed? The Corporation for Financing Development gives official credits, once the National Commission of Social Property and the National City Planning Institute approve their formation. Actually, the new firms are production cooperatives financed by the state. All the EPSs must be organized following the model provided in the law (which calls for a workers' assembly and head, management, and honor committees). The positions are of limited duration, except those in management, which are unlimited. The benefits are awarded in the form of wage increases, retirement pensions, and so forth. A national social property fund is created also, out of contributions from the EPSs.

Even though in all appearance the law was more propaganda than reality, the industrialists became alarmed. There even was an attempted coup on the part of the navy, the most conservative of the armed forces, seeking to stop the application of the law. But in fact, the law had very few repercussions. Very few EPSs were established, and always in such branches of industry where they would not represent dangerous competition for the existing private enterprises.

Shortly before the issuance of this law the government had suspended the popular magazine *Caretas* and jailed its director, and at the same time had exiled two leaders of former President Belaúnde Terry's Acción Popular party and closed the party's local offices. In November, 1974, the leftist weekly *Oiga* and the rightist *Opinión Libre*, as well as the English-language newspaper for businessmen, *The Peruvian Times*, were suspended for criticizing the law. In addition, ten journalists were exiled for their criticism of a contract made with a multinational Japanese company to build an oil pipeline. What the journalists objected to was that the military government, after consistently rejecting the arbitration clause customary in international contracts, would have accepted this one, but hidden it from the public. Two ministers affirmed that the exiling of the journalists was due to the discovery of a counterrevolutionary conspiracy. Five lawyers, directors of the Lima Lawyers' Association, were arrested because they declared, in a juridical report, that the contract with the Japanese was not valid because it contained the arbitration clause. At the same time, Lima signed an agreement with Washington creating a mixed Peruvian-American enterprise in order to develop the food-fishing industry. This agreement was also criticized.

It has been suggested that the social property law was intended to draw public attention away from the expropriation
of big newspapers decreed in July of 1974. For some time
the government, irritated by the papers' criticisms, had been
threatening to expropriate the dailies and allow only the
weeklies to continue (and we have seen that even these would
be subject to many interferences. Among the five expropriated papers were two very old ones, *La Prensa* and *El Comercio*. In order to soften the measure, the government handed
over the first one to the workers' communities and the second to the peasants' organizations. *Ojo* was given to the intellectuals and artists and *Ultima Hora* to the transportation
workers and banking employees. The measure only affected
those newspapers with a circulation in excess of 20,000
copies, and, according to the government, "it was not a matter of expropriation, but rather of handing over those media
for social communication to the social organization of the
country." A month later, other dailies were expropriated and
a press statute was published. Actually, the transfer to social
organizations was effected only on paper, since the special
committees created by the government to take charge of each
paper had, as of 1975, not yet transferred the ownership of
the papers to the social organizations, nor had the organizations in question been specifically identified. Many journalists resigned and the press stopped criticizing the government.
Though during the first few weeks after the expropriation the
news media appeared more free than before, this was tem-
porary and quite possibly an intentional deceit. It must be
said that the Peruvian press has never been free from governmental and financial influences.

One can easily understand the government's interest in
silencing the papers' criticisms. Although political parties can
continue to function (despite the absence of elections) without access to the dailies, they can only express themselves
through low-circulation weeklies, which do not reach the
masses. The majority of the population derive their information from the dailies, and the government, when forced
by economic and social conditions to make international

concessions, saw the need to hide the contradiction between its rhetoric and its actions.

Concessions to Investors

We have already mentioned two or three of the concessions to foreign investors. There were others that were necessary because of the deterioration of the economy, the growing inflation, and the resulting dissatisfaction among business-men. These feel very nationalistic when things are going well, but as soon as there are signs of recession, they immediately start thinking about ways of obtaining foreign aid, especially about increasing investments coming from other countries.

In 1974 the nationalization of the International Petroleum Company had almost been forgotten, above all because it did not cause any dramatic reaction from the Nixon administration. This made it possible for the military government to try to attract foreign capital, especially American, Japanese and European, and to direct it to the prospecting and eventual exploitation of the oil reserves that the geologists affirm exist in the Amazon basin. The worldwide energy crisis, of course, aided the Peruvian government in "seducing" the companies which, in different circumstances, would have been more cautious because of the fear of future nationalizations. Any misgivings were also overcome because of the fact that the government established clearcut regulations for foreign capi-tal: one-half of the oil production must come from the na-tional petroleum enterprise, Petroperú, the other half to be allotted to foreign companies. The first one to accept these conditions was the Occidental Petroleum Company. Then, in other contracts with other companies, Petroperú's share was set at 56 percent of the extracted oil. The contracts are for seven years, at the end of which all territory granted goes to Petroperú. Taxes are exempted during that period and a mini-mum number of drillings is established for each year. A Japa-nese company will build, with Japanese credit and German pipes, the line that will link the coast with the Amazon jun-gle. The Soviet Union will contribute storage tanks for the sum of $7 million. It is believed that a total of 1,500 million barrels in reserves have already been discovered, according to government figures (about 450 million according to the companies). (In order to compare, let us say that 1 billion barrels are extracted each year in Venezuela; and in Ecuador, where the most important discoveries in Latin American have been made, there are 5 billion barrels in reserves, which cost Texaco $300 million in prospecting investments to locate.)

The development of oil zones in the Amazon would of course contribute to economic progress in the region. Populated largely by Indians, the area has been much neglected until now. The 135,000 inhabitants of Iquitos, its capital, live among the city's old palaces—relics from the rubber "boom" era that ended abruptly in 1935, after which the city was reduced to a simple administrative center, linked to Lima only by air. For the moment the Iquiteños suffer the highest inflation rate in the country, while not receiving benefits from the oil yet, although many businessmen, young people, prostitutes, gamblers, and local gangsters invade the streets of the city which the Amazon River floods from time to time.

The oil fields are isolated and everything has to be brought in by helicopter, from water and food to unassembled machinery. One thousand helicopter flights are necessary (at $10 per flying minute) in order to complete the drilling of a well. Iquitos and the Peruvian Amazon are probably among the few places in the world where adventure is still possible.

Another concession to foreign capital—to attract it rather than to placate the American State Department—has been the indemnification granted for oil expropriations. Since the IPC, which belonged to Esso, was accused of robbing the country, the government could not pay it any compensation. But a way of surmounting this juridical obstacle was found. In February, 1974, the two countries agreed that Peru would pay the American government $76 million to compensate the expropriated companies, upon the condition that no indemnification be given to IPC. But in December of 1974, after receiving the money, Washington paid $22 million to Esso, the IPC owner. This violation of the agreement infuriated the Peruvians, merited accusations of disloyalty in the Lima press, and met only with silence on the part of the military government, which probably had taken for granted that things would happen that way and had saved its prestige by including in the agreement a clause that it knew would not be fulfilled. In any case, it imposed an 18-month jail sentence upon a journalist, Enrique Zileri, for "damaging the honor and the reputation of high military officers" when he commented on the American payments to Esso, and it suspended his magazine *Caretas*.

Probably in order to make public opinion forget the bad impression it had received from all this, the government announced in December of 1974 that it would nationalize the telegraphic service, including the ITT services, beginning in March of the following year. Years before, the telephone services—owned by ITT and a Swiss company—had been nationalized. All radio and telephone communication services came thus to be controlled by one government enterprise, Entel.

Undoubtedly, it was also with the goal of placating public opinion that government organs and the press undertook a campaign against the Peace Corps, whch had 137 members in Peru. The government requested that the United States recall those volunteers, after a newspaper accused them of espionage. Many missionaries—mostly American—feared that this campaign would engulf them also, but it did not turn out to do so. The town of Yarinacocha, on the banks of the Ucayali River, right on the Andes, has become the most important missionary center in all of Latin America, with some 550 families participating in numerous linguistic and anthropological investigations.

It was partially because of those studies and the pressure from the missionaries that the government decided to declare Quechua an official language on the same footing with Spanish (obviously, this is only in theory, since in practice very few bureaucrats speak Quechua and even fewer can write it). This decision was part of the Inca Plan announced by the military when they assumed power, in keeping with which they withdrew the Pizarro statue from Lima's Plaza Mayor and declared Tupac Amaru, an Indian rebel from the eighteenth century, an official hero.

But this sort of measure could not hide facts that were affecting the daily lives of the people, such as the fact tht inflation could not be stopped in spite of the control that the military government had, toward the end of 1974, over 75 percent of all banking and over a large part of industrial and agricultural production. Nor could the promise of 50 percent worker participation in the companies in which they were employed hide the fact that economic nationalism had to be abandoned for practical reasons when the copper mining complex of Cuajone, in the south, was under development. For five years, the government sought a way of financing this plan, and finally arrived at an agreement with four American companies that formed the Southern Peru Copper Company. These companies were the ones that had traditionally dominated Peruvian mining: American Smelting and Refining, Cerro de Pasco, Phelps Dodge, and Newmont Mining. In 1969 the government gave them the Cuajone concession, with the condition that they had to start exploiting it in six-and-a-half years. By the end of 1976, it was expected to produce 170,000 tons of copper yearly. The paradox is that this concession and the production of oil from the Amazon—exploited also by foreign companies—are the basis, in the eyes of the government, for the development of Peruvian industry. The abandonment of economic nationalism in this instance was motivated by pragmatic reasons: the weakness in the investments offered by Communist countries, the delay in developing the projects of the government body Minero Perú (whose Cerro Verde ore was a few years behind schedule), and the reduction for several years of low-interest loans granted by the Export-Import Bank of the United States.

The Cuajone project is technically impressive: two cities will be built, with clinics, schools, and other services for the 2,000 employees and workers in the enterprise; and 240 million tons of dirt will be removed before they reach the copper vein. This operation is being done by ten enormous mechanical shovels, each one of which can fill a ten-ton truck in one minute. The work is being done twenty-four hours a day at an altitude of 10,000 feet, where the thin air reduces the engines' efficiency by 30 percent and just as much, if not more, the men's longevity. Seventeen miles of railroad will be laid in order to transport the gangue to an already-existing railroad station. Financially speaking, the project will cost about $600 million, provided by some fifty-four banks in fifteen countries. The government will collect a 47.5 percent tax on the profits until the company has recovered its investment (within five to seven years), and afterwards this tax will go up to 54.5 percent.

This agreement and the indemnity payment to Esso softened international financial reticence. In 1975 Peru had requested $3,500 million in credits for its development plans. A group of eleven countries, members of the Consultative Group of the World Bank, resolved to offer it $2,850 million, at the rate of $950 million annually for three years. With this money they plan to establish a complex for petrochemical refining and another one for zinc and copper, along with irrigation, transportation, and heavy industry programs; in other words, plans that, in the long run, will produce capital.

People, nevertheless, mistrust such plans because they have the impression that, presently, their daily lives are deteriorating. These suspicions manifested themselves in a violent form in February of 1975, when the Lima policemen went on strike asking for a raise in salaries and the army attacked their headquarters. There were armed riots in the street with much vandalism, and the government declared a state of siege for thirty days and closed banks and businesses for twenty-four hours. There were fifty killed and several hundred wounded. Two newspapers, the most progovernment, were set on fire and the flames also destroyed a large part of the civic center, built in the commercial section of the city. The Officers' Club on the Plaza de San Martín was also set on fire. Tanks in the streets were not enough to disperse the groups of youths who were vandalizing and demonstrating.

The controlled press attributed the riots to "reactionary and counterrevolutionary elements," but the truth is that thousands of people threw themselves on the streets. It was not a middle class protest, organized and coordinated, such as those in Chile against Allende, but a spontaneous eruption. Some wanted to blame the APRA for the problem, but soon this theory was discarded when it was seen that, in the eyes of the people, it favored rather than damaged the old party. Although when the crisis was over there were organized demonstrations in support of the government, and although the instigation of the protests, as usual, was attributed to the CIA (and this at a moment when the American companies were beginning to recover part of their influence), the truth is that that outburst reflected the unhappiness of the urban population—especially that of Lima. Accustomed to intervening in politics and now left out of the decision-making process, the people of Lima had been overwhelmed by a 20 percent annual inflation the last two years and were exasperated by the spectacle of "the leading circles of the revolution" improving their standard of living while the masses saw theirs stagnating and even receding. The striking policemen were asking a $46 per month increase in salary—the government offered less than $10—but declared that they were ready to make sacrifices as long as "those who are above" made them too. Apparently it was this phrase that caused Gen. Enrique Ibáñez, chief of the guard of the presidential palace, to lose control of himself and slap a police officer. This news sparked the flames.

The regime could have been in danger if the protest had spread throughout the country, but it was limited to Lima, which proves that it was spontaneous and not organized. However, it left a great deal of malaise not only among the population, but even among the military. They used to boast that in almost seven years they "had made a revolution without bloodshed," and in fact, although there were frequent persecutions against journalists, there had been neither violence nor systematic political persecution nor mass detention, which constituted, in Peru, a novelty. But Velasco Alvarado's reaction in the face of the protest was hard and inflexible, and many among his own supporters believed that the general had been unnecessarily rigorous. For instance, he deported two journalists of the Reuters agency, and forbade the auxiliary bishop of Lima from entering the police headquarters in order to mediate and to avoid an attack from the troops. The image of the peaceful revolution by consensus had been destroyed.

The "establishment" attributed it to Velasco Alvarado. A rumor began that since one of his legs was amputated he had shown more and more rigidity. From there to suggesting that it was necessary to substitute him as leader of the "revolution" there was just one step. Perhaps it would not have been taken if Velasco, after the Lima riots, had tried to heal the wounds. But he did the opposite.

The Final Tension

The second half of 1975 was a period of tension and repression all over Peru, with the by-then habitual policy of the carrot and the stick, one demonstration and one expropriation, one repression and one expropriation. When a high official of Gulf Oil admitted before the American Senate that he had paid $4 million in bribes to foreign functionaries with the aim of obtaining concessions, the Peruvian government decided to expropriate all the assets of that company in Peru because, as the foreign minister, Gen. Miguel Angel de la Flor Valle, said, "He who was corrupting yesterday may try to corrupt tomorrow." The expropriated company was to be compensated and Peruvian courts would determine the amount of the indemnification.

Since there was malcontent and agitation among the peasants, who several times had elected among their representatives elements belonging to the APRA, the minister of agriculture accused the "raving ultra-left groups of dragging the peasants outside the margins of the law." Gen. Enrique Gallegos announced that in 1976 the agrarian reform would be finished and expropriations would end, but admitted that up to that moment only half of the reformation plan had been carried out. In fact, the peasants, fearing that distribution would come to an end, rushed to occupy land—sometimes spurred by leftist groups, sometimes spontaneously. At any rate, the ending of the agrarian reform before it was completed indicated a desire to placate foreign investors and conservative elements within Peru itself, who were recovering their influence as inflation fomented popular malcontent. The latter was manifested in July with a general strike in

Arequipa, called by the local unions; 50,000 workers abandoned their jobs demanding salary increases, freezing of
prices, lowering of transportation costs, and the return to the
unions of one of the expropriated newspapers in the city.
Union leaders were arrested, barricades were erected, and a
state of siege was declared. A week later, the government
nationalized the metal-mining complex Marcona Mining
Company, owned by Americans, which had been operating
in the country for twenty-two years, extracting iron 320
miles south of Lima.

A breathing spell in the protests was provided several days
later, by the fifth meeting of the foreign ministers of non-
aligned countries, whose presence in Lima flattered the
Peruvians' nationalism. But as soon as the meeting was over,
in August, the government exiled twenty-seven journalists
and politicians, most of them belonging to the APRA. This
old party, in spite of being immobilized because of lack of
elections, continued to be popular and strong enough that
the government did not dare dissolve it (as it did, for instance, with Belaúnde's party), and was gaining support from
the popular discontent. Their members were winning elections in unions, cooperatives, and agrarian leagues, vis-à-vis
the Communists and the other candidates supported by the
government. The politicians were accused of something as
vague as "negative attitudes after the president of the republic's calling for unity in the job of building up the new Peru."
These negative attitudes consisted of "trips in the countryside, handing out watchwords, inciting to strikes and lock-
outs, and attempting to subvert the order." As for the
journalists of a new leftist weekly, *Marka,* they were accused
of having published "expressions unacceptable to the Chilean
government" (of General Pinochet). Lima, after having pas-
sively supported Allende, started getting close to Pinochet in
1975 out of fear that the Chilean government would reach
an agreement with Bolivia to give that country a strip of
coast it had lost a century ago which allied with Peru in a war
against Chile. According to international agreements, any
outlet to the sea given to Bolivia would have to have the
acquiescence of Peru, and it seems that Lima does not want

to grant its consent. But so as not to find itself in the position of having to veto it, it is approaching Santiago with the intention of torpedoing the negotiations before any agreement is reached that would put the Lima chancellery in a bind. This rapprochement was evident in August of 1975 with the signing of a preliminary non-aggression agreement between Peru, Bolivia, and Chile.

The deportations funneled protests from the unions, APRA, and the journalists' association. The Communist party at the same time protested the deportation of the reporters and approved that of the APRA leaders, saying that "it was a true patriotic necessity to adopt firm measures against the counterrevolutionary sedition of APRA."

Communist Support

The Communist reaction reflects the systematic support that Moscow and its organizations have given to the Peruvian military, a support more open now as the military continue to lose that of the New Left groups that welcomed them with joy in 1968. It cannot be said that the military government entered into a feudal-type relationship with Moscow, as Castro did in Cuba. But Moscow's support not only strengthened trade between Peru and the USSR and its satellites, but it also allowed the Peruvian government to use its gestures toward the USSR and China to placate a segment of the Marxist Left—to neutralize it and attract the Communists. The latter were not sufficiently strong, by themselves, for their support to be decisive to the military. But as it had happened under the dictator Odría, they could be used, if assisted underhandedly, to counteract the influence of the APRA in the unions and among the peasants. We have seen now how the Communists were in charge of organizing a union to rival the dominant workers' union. In the countryside, they applauded the methods with which the agrarian reform was put into effect, as compared to the APRA criticisms of those measures.

Since the Peruvian Communist party is highly bureaucratized and figures among the most addicted to Moscow, its support to the military was conditioned by Lima's policy with respect to Moscow and by Moscow's position regarding Lima. For the first time in its history, the *International Magazine* (the Communist party organ edited in Prague) published, in January of 1975, an interview with a non-Communist chief of state, Velasco Alvarado. The magazine affirmed that "the entire world has its eyes set on the profound transformations initiated by the people and the armed forces' revolutionary government of Peru." In one of his answers, Velasco said that "Peru, since the beginning of the revolutionary process, established relations in all fields with diverse countries, in particular with those whose governments declare themselves in favor of socialism. Our relations with those countries are totally satisfactory up to now."

When, in 1974, there was strong repression of the press, the minister of the navy, Vice Admiral Vargas Caballero, declared that criticisms of the government could not be considered "as expressions of a counterrevolutionary spirit." When Velasco demanded Vargas' resignation, the navy—a more traditionalist and "aristocratic" branch than the army— answered by sending its ships out to the high seas, and the two branches were at the verge of a confrontation. But the navy chiefs did not dare go all the way, and Vargas resigned, as previously indicated. Velasco learned the lesson. He asked Moscow for a team of advisers to help him reorganize the armed forces. Beginning in July, 1975, Soviet arms shipments started to arrive at Callao: 250 thirty-ton tanks, 500 armored cars, SAM 3 rockets, and other types of materiel. Raúl Castro was the guest of honor in the parade where this materiel was exhibited. The Soviet military advisers did not show up, on the other hand. Even after the army was reorganized, Velasco wanted to be sure; he reached an agreement with Aeroflot, the Soviet airline, to establish a base in Lima; in article thirteen of the agreement it is stipulated that "in case of international conflict, internal disorder or public calamity, the Peruvian government will be able to use, in order to achieve its specific ends, all the resources at the disposal of Aeroflot of the Soviet Union."

In spite of the policies of coexistence and "détente," the USSR is thus trying to establish a "special friendship" with the Peru of the military. For this reason the Communists have supported them from the beginning of their regime, as has been explained. This support has not diminished in spite of the regime's changes of direction and the protests against it. In 1974, for example, the Moscow magazine *Latin America* published an interview with the Peruvian Communist party boss Jorge del Prado, in which he declared that the Communist party had supported the military since before 1970. This support was confirmed by the Sixth Congress of the Communist Party, in November of 1973, which resolved to "spell out the alliance between the workers that is, the Communist Party and the armed forces in the building of the revolutionary process; to develop friendly ties with the USSR, Cuba, and the socialist countries in Europe, and to carry out the unification of the Peruvian syndicated movement" (the latter which it did not achieve). For Jorge del Prado, what is happening in Peru constitutes "a brilliant confirmation of Lenin's thesis about the diverse ways and forms of the revolutionary struggle." Thanks to the participation of the Communist party, "a grouping of class forces is taking place which carries with it qualitative changes in the revolutionary process."

According to this statement, the Communists not only supported those measures that appeared to be most revolutionary—nationalizations, agrarian reform, and so on—but also the more controversial ones, such as the expropriations of newspapers. "We are sure that the restructured press, whatever form it may adopt, will serve the ends of the anti-imperialist and anti-oligarchical revolution."[26]

Thus was abandoned the cautious position taken by the Communists in 1968, who took no sides for several months and approved of some measures while criticizing others. Del Prado, when he modified this position a year later, adopting one of systematic support after Lima had given some signs of wanting to get closer to Moscow, explained that "at first glance it was not clear that the military coup was of a new kind." And the same Communists who protest the arms purchase agreements signed with the United States applaud when, as in April of 1975, one is concluded with East

Germany whereby this country grants a $140 million credit to Peru destined to acquire military materiel.

Support for the military has come also from other sectors of the New Left that are rivals of the Communists: Maoists and Trotskyites. But one of the three factions in the latter group soon started to criticize the generals until, in October of 1973, the government suppressed its magazine *Sociedad y Política* (Society and Politics).

In a political gathering that took place behind closed doors in Lima's Frontón in 1970, the "non-Communist Marxist Left declared its opposition to the military, decided not to collaborate with them, and to analyze their policies with severity." However, there were divisions in most of the groups that had upheld this attitude. Some members of these groups—especially technicians and intellectuals, because they belonged to elite rather than mass groups—gave their support to the military, while others tried to go from vocal to active opposition. In order to attract these groups , the government in 1970 released the political prisoners, among them the famous Trotskyite Hugo Blanco, jailed since 1962. Blanco attempted to go back to his job of organizing the peasants of Cuzco, but the government did not allow him to do so and deported him to Chile, ruled then by Allende. The MIR (Movement of the Revolutionary Left) split when one of its bosses, Gonzalo Fernández Gasco, started a guerrilla movement, albeit unsuccessfully. Ricardo Lenz, of the Vanguardia group (Maoist), was exiled. But toward 1974 the government allowed the return of many of these New Left elements, because by then their comrades in Lima were actively collaborating. In spite of this collaboration, the social mobilization system has lacked efficiency and has met with no success, because, as a Mexican political science professor says, "The genuine social mobilization has, by implication, autonomy, critical reserve, and in the end, the sharing of responsibility in important decisions and the coparticipation in power. Up to now, the Peruvian military do not seem ready to go that far; on the contrary, through the speeches of the chief of state, they reiterate a certain willful position, according to which it is the armed forces which exclusively determine the content, reaches, and limits of the revolutionary movement."[27]

Scandals and Repression

The support of the New Left, of many intellectuals, and of businessmen—the main beneficiaries of the "revolution" along with the military—decreased in the same measure as the disillusionment of the masses increased, and as certain shady aspects of the regime were discovered.

For instance, "Everywhere one can hear juicy comments regarding the different scandals recently discovered: in the nationalized mines, in the Central Bank, and, above all, in the EPSA, the government's body for agricultural sales. Here someone disposed of agricultural surpluses by way of foreign sales totalling $120 million, which would explain why it was so difficult to find a kilogram of sugar in a country that harvests this product abundantly. The Agriculture Ministry was accused of these misdeeds, but the government explained nothing and did not apologize. President Velasco Alvarado, in a press conference, limited himself to saying that he had heard about those scandals 'on the street.'

"One can see corruption appearing in other less important bodies. The revolutionary military groups constitute now a new class, in the sense referred to by Milovan Djilas some twenty years ago, when he described Titoist Yugoslavia. Numerous members of the armed forces exercise, besides their commands, a civilian position, receiving two salaries. A certain resentment can be felt toward some officers that dwell in sumptuous residences in front of which one could see, during days of meat scarcity, a limousine that stopped and proceeded to deliver meat packages. Someone said to me: 'Could one really expect the military to conduct themselves modestly and with full awareness of their economic responsibilities?' "[28]

Precisely because of the increase, not only in corruption, but also in rumors about it—something inevitable when there is not true press freedom or surveillance by an independent body—discontent increased, the government kept restricting liberties more and more, and repression became sharper and increasingly brutal. "Nowhere is the regime's hysteria more visible than in its attempts at oppressing the freedom of political opinion. It is true that political parties still exist, but in a state ruled by a 'revolutionary direction,' which is not responsible before any parliament, those parties have no influence at all. When the College of Lawyers and the College of Magistrates asserted that the new regulations for the so-called cooperation were illegal and unconstitutional, their members were accused of 'treason' and 'sabotage,' and at the same time a certain number of eminent jurists were forced to go into exile." When the newspapers were expropriated, "a hundred outstanding journalists were dismissed, without wasting any time in curtsies, and replaced by a new class of 'free correspondents.' I did not find anybody who later on would find that the newspapers were better or more interesting. The bureaucracy caused a paralysis phenomenon and newspaper circulation diminished. Only one weekly, *Oiga*, gained new readers all of a sudden, since the 'expropriated readers' of the socialized press were looking for a paper that could be a source of information and would show a certain critical judgment. Another weekly, *Opinión Libre*, conducted, for a while, the struggle to fill the same vacuum. 'We continue to support the revolution,' declared *Oiga's* director, 'but a peaceful revolution, a socialism with freedom.'

"With these feelings, no one can make friends with the government. The advertisers in *Oiga* suffered all sorts of pressures, while the printers received innumerable visits from the police. . . . As for *Opinión Libre*, it was accused of being a 'bunch of extreme Right opponents,' to which this newspaper answered: 'Our fundamental principle is freedom, freedom for each citizen to express himself without curtailing his opinions, to be able to organize political parties, to participate in elections for the selection of his government, to express his opinion concerning public affairs, to be protected by civilized laws.'

"Toward the end of November 1974, *Oiga* and *Opinión Libre* were suspended, while a significant number of their editors were expulsed from the country.

"In February, 1975, the offices of two of the most impor-

tant newspapers among those expropriated by the government were the target of the Lima rioters and were completely
burned. The other government-controlled papers attributed
this violence to 'reactionary and counterrevolutionary elements.' The following day two British correspondents of the
Reuter Agency were expulsed.

"The revolution was getting nervous. There were many
demonstrations by young people demanding freedom of the
press, as well as disturbances among the farmers. Educators
were unhappy. At the university, the professors side with
Moscow, while the students side with Peking. It is easy to
hear, anywhere, the most diverse jokes and political rumors
that are highly insidious. The memory of elections has not
disappeared and the middle class has not been eliminated. Up
to now, the revolution has treated its adversaries with a
degree of indulgence, and in its catalogue for punishments
the worst one was exile."[29] Starting toward the end of 1974,
repression became harsher, and rumors were circulated about
secret detentions and torture.

Only one free magazine was left, the bimonthly *Caretas*.
In March of 1975, its turn arrived. "It was a holiday. The
editors of *Caretas* were in a restaurant celebrating the freeing
of Juana, a young collaborator jailed as a result of the February riots. While the guests were tasting the traditional seafood
seasoned with lemon juice, the girl was telling about her mis-
fortunes in the women's prison, in the prostitutes' gallery.
The dinner was coming to an end in the midst of all the
noise, when three very serious gentlemen appeared.

"Policemen, like funeral home employees, need not be
introduced; one can recognize them a hundred miles away.
Before the PIP (political police) commissar bent toward
Enrique Zileri to whisper in his ear, everybody knew what he
was going to say to the *Caretas* director: 'Sir, we have an
order to arrest you; please follow us.' The appearance of a
dozen agents, who had kept at a distance, put an end to the
protests very quickly. It was useless to resist, so Mr. Zileri,
after paying the bill, not knowing whether to cry or to laugh,
climbed in the commissar's car.

"*Caretas* was banned and its director forced to leave Lima

on Friday the twenty-first of March, early in the morning, headed for Buenos Aires. The event would not warrant additional comments if it were not the last Peruvian publication independent from the government, and if the daily press, presently at the exclusive service of the armed forces' 'revolution' for all practical purposes, had not considered it necessary to ignore the event or even, in certain cases, to be glad about it."[30]

The Morales Government

All of these repressions increased the discontent. The fact that the parties or the citizens could not express themselves openly, that legal channels of expression did not exist, did not stop the jokes, the rumors, and did not prevent the echoes of this tension among the people from reaching the armed forces and its chiefs. When this happens in a military regime, whether it calls itself conservative or revolutionary, there are two possible outlets: the chief is forced to call upon the civilians in order to hand over the package of mistakes; or the chief is replaced so as to concentrate the unhappiness on his head, to use him as a scapegoat, and to find a substitute that maintains the army in power.

In Peru the situation had not deteriorated to the point of having to resort to the first solution, especially since repression had been, for four years, light and not cruel. But precisely for this reason, the relative toughness shown by Velasco Alvarado starting in 1974 exasperated many people and surprised even his fellow military men. These, in the discreet, oblique, and secret way that the Latin American armed forces have of expressing their will (the will of their bosses, which frequently reflects that of most of the officers), let Velasco Alvarado know that he had to change his procedures. So many interests had been created of an ideological, prestigious nature, as well as those that were personal and financial, that it was unthinkable that the army would risk losing what it had because its chief allowed his nerves to get the best of him.

On the other hand there were alternatives, since political parties existed, some legally, and others, even though outlawed, in the conscience and memory of their leaders and adherents. Those parties had seen how the military had put into practice programs—especially of the APRA—that had never before been carried out because of military opposition. Peruvians realized this and also what the military government had done: distributed land to some 200,000 peasants (in a country where, in 1968, 3,780 landholders owned 76 percent of all arable land and 708,000 small landowners just 24 percent), put under state control 30 percent of the gross national production and 80 percent of basic industries, maintained the economic growth rate (that barely descended to 5.6 and 6.3 percent in such critical years as 1973 and 1974, and a little less than 5 percent in 1975), and nationalized a good portion of the country's mining and oil industry. None of those could be ignored, and quite a few Peruvians thought that to be deprived of a press that was corrupt and lacked objectivity anyway, and of elections, that, in the end, the military would frustrate when an Aprista was elected, was not such a high price to pay.

They had to take advantage of that minimal amount of confidence, that sort of resignation to the lesser evil, in order to modify the direction without changing the goal. In February of 1975, Velasco Alvarado, heeding the suggestions of his fellow military, changed the government and appointed as its president Gen. Francisco Morales Bermúdez, who kept for himself the position of war minister and supreme commander of the army. People immediately saw him as an eventual successor to Velasco. The event was carried out without scandal, taking advantage of the fact that the head of the government since the beginning of the "revolution," Gen. Edgardo Mercado Jarrín, had reached retirement age. What may have forced Velasco to yield (and undoubtedly what had made him get tougher before) was his poor state of health. In a short time he had undergone surgery twice— in one operation his right leg had been amputated. If his health forced him to resign, Morales would succeed him, at least until 1978 when his own turn for retirement would come, something that is sacred in any army.

Morales had been part of the team that prepared the 1968

coup, and between 1969 and 1973 was minister of finance. However, he never made any ideological statements, being satisfied with such rhetorical phrases as were being used at the moment. He was considered a realist who, without disagreeing openly with Velasco, considered that he was going too fast. The government relied on copper sales to finance new advances in agrarian reform, as an answer to land seizures that occurred in 1974 and the beginning of 1975 in areas not too far from Lima. However, world copper prices fell.

Shortly after his accession to power Morales put through a law, in July of 1975, creating the Consultative Board to the Prime Minister. It was to be made up of workers, technicians, military personnel, and intellectuals, and its mission would be to give the prime minister "varied opinions" concerning government policies. It was an attempt to give the impression that the people were being listened to, to extricate the government from its political isolation and at the same time furnish the armed forces with a vehicle with which to put pressure on Velasco without giving the impression that they were in disagreement with him.

Since Velasco persisted in his show of toughness, army pressures increased. There were comments about exhaustion brought by power and about the president's health. The machinery was ready.

Velasco's Successor

On the twenty-ninth of August, 1975, the chiefs of the armed forces advised Velasco that his state of health warranted his resignation. Velasco addressed the country, asking it to continue on its "revolutionary path." Upon leaving the presidential palace, he said to the journalists: "I am going home." He had been in power for seven years. The armed forces chiefs appointed the prime minister, Francisco Morales Bermúdez, to be Velasco's successor. Morales was thought of as a technocrat—that is to say, in this case, more pragmatic than his predecessor. At any rate, he was not a counterrevolutionary to the Peruvian military "revolution."

There are many apparently irreversible changes in Peru,

such as nationalizations and agrarian reform, and other innovations, that will probably change in due time, such as popular mobilization, the takeover of newspapers, and authoritarianism.

Morales, whose grandfather was president toward the end of the last century, finds himself isolated as Velasco was after September of 1968, because although he has done a few things desired by the people—and put forth by the parties, above all APRA, for decades—he did them without asking the people and without giving them any participation in the administration of the country and its economy. Morales, without a doubt, will try to come out of this isolation. He finds himself in a situation similar to that of Sadat after the death of Nasser, but without the help of an Israeli problem that helped the former avoid very deep dissensions. The first thing Morales did was to appoint a new government that included, for the first time since 1968, two civilians, one as minister of finance. The other ministers were almost all military men in office, and did not come from the ranks of the staff.

Morales was rather ambiguous. He said that the revolutionary process would be "strengthened," that the mistakes made would be corrected, and that the "ideological guidelines of the revolution" would be followed. This ambiguity, as it could be forecasted in such a personalistic regime, immediately caused many to hope that things would return to the situation prior to 1968. Landholders began to apply pressure right away, seeking support in the United States and among the local middle class. In October, the minister of agriculture was forced to warn in a speech that a reversal in the agrarian reform would not be permitted.

Popular opinion began to attribute to Velasco all the mistakes and to call Morales "the exorcist," believing that he would free Peru from the demon that the general retired from the presidency was becoming. Morales exorcised with his first measures: he returned the Partido de Acción Democrática to its offices; and its boss, whom the president had deposed in 1968, Belaúnde Terry, returned to Peru from exile in American universities. He granted two amnesties in a few months, which brought out of jail the condemned journalists and almost all political prisoners, and allowed the return of almost all the exiled. He authorized the publication of some nonofficial newspapers and magazines, even opposition ones.

The ministers in the new government started to point, with discretion, to the real situation of the country, noting the decrease in production (especially in mining and agriculture), in exports, and in money reserves. They pointed out the slump, during the last three years, in the fish flour industry, so vital for the country. At the same time, the press began to criticize the agrarian reform. It was not, as it had been before, to complain about the peasants not being educated, but rather to say, with some exaggeration, that there were a million farmers without work and to suggest that only with the devolution of the lands to the former holders could they find employment. The influence of the former landholders was evident. Morales announced that "urgent and drastic measures aimed at modifying the quasi inactivity that the countryside suffers will be adopted." The problem—and there seem to exist disparaties among the military—was in whether these measures should consist of allowing the peasants to participate in the administration of their lands, instead of leaving it in the hands of bureaucrats that were almost all military, or whether the former big landholders should be called upon. It must not be forgotten that there remain in the army many active soldiers who, for decades, considered the idea of agrarian reform to be "Communism."

An area where Morales has won general support has been in the fight against corruption. Not quite two months had passed after his ascension to power when he started a "moralization campaign." He replaced the labor and sanitation ministers and the chief of the air force. A dozen very rich people who were close to Velasco either were arrested or fled, accused of illegal enrichment, fraud, bribery, and of improperly using their influence. Among the detainees were chiefs in the 1968 coup, such as the former minister of fisheries, Gen. Javier Tantaleán, and minister of agriculture, Gen. Enrique Valdéz, along with the presidents of the

Mining Bank and Lima's Department of Public Welfare, the mayors of certain cities and of three of the capital's districts, and the principal executives of the most important insurance companies. It became known that they were investigating people such as Eduardo Bruce, head of Pescaperú, the fishing monopoly with 25,000 workers; and Luis González Posada, Velasco's brother-in-law, director of *La Crónica,* who went into exile in Mexico. The same was done by Augusto Zimmerman, Velasco's chief of the press, who had apparently inspired the repressive measures against journalists. The head of the government's information system and the chief of Velasco's advisory body, two generals, were retired "for institutional reasons." At the same time, in an attempt to show that it was not a matter of going back, Gen. Jorge Fernández Maldonado was designated as successor to the chief of government appointed by Morales, Gen. Oscar Prietti, who was to retire soon. General Fernández inspired and wrote the code which regulates mining investments. Morales, to whom people attributed the desire to surround himself with men he could trust, declared that those changes did not reflect a "state of paralysis in the revolution's momentum."

Morales' task is not easy. In 1975 there was a deficit of $800 million in trade balance, $36 million had to be allotted to pay the increases obtained by the copper miners after a six-week strike, and the search for $3.5 billion in the foreign market was disappointing.

In fact, then, a second phase in the "revolution" was begun, the conservative phase, aimed at the consolidation of achievements. The achievements were, fundamentally, of a nationalist character: the Peruanization of part of the American investments, and the turning over of land to the peasants (land found, in no small degree, in the hands of Peruvians residing abroad). The regime had begun a process of "arteriosclerosis" similar to the one that was literally afflicting its "leader," Velasco Alvarado. The foreign businessmen, who have been active in Peru for decades—among them the Americans, who were never secure under Velasco—seemed to feel comfortable with Morales. They even admitted that the "revolution's" methods had increased the Peruvians' purchasing power—but only for 25 percent of them. The landholding oligarchy has lost its power and this, in the long run, is perhaps the most important thing done by the very army that for a century protected it and prevented it from being destroyed politically and economically.

At the same time that he conducted his moralizing campaign, Morales ordered the replacement of Gen. Leónidas Rodríguez Figueroa, who had supported his coup against Velasco but who was considered as the most radical of the generals. Velasco had entrusted him with the confiscated press, which now contemplated his relief with anxiety. The National Agrarian Confederation and Peru's Revolutionary Youth, two organizations created by Velasco's government that sheltered both the Communists and their rivals the Maoists, Trotskyites, and others, showed their "surprise and preoccupation" and asked the people to "maintain their vigilance in defense of the revolutionary achievements and against the traditional enemies of the process of transformation."

The Communist party, in turn, during a session of its central committee shortly after the presidential change, declared that Morales' program was "a dialectic appreciation that coincides in essence with our characterization of the present situation." The Communists admitted that "one of the characteristics and weaknesses [of the Peruvian revolution] consists of the fact that it has been taking form without the full popular support that it needs." The Communist party blames Velasco for it, although it supported him unconditionally when he was in power, and affirms: "But all work [Velasco's] was punctuated by manipulating practices, implemented through public administration and using ideological pseudocounselors, pseudopromoters and pseudoactivists, and yellow union leaders, virtual political mercenaries coming from APRA and Trotskyism."[31] Thus, in explaining its transfer of support to Velasco's successor, the party took advantage of the fact that a few Apristas and several Trotskyites, expulsed by their organizations, had served Velasco.

APRA continues to watch the situation, demands that

elections take place, and maintains its cadres and strong popularity in the unions and peasant organizations. It is probably the only Latin American party that, after getting old and becoming more moderate, has not lost popular support. This constitutes an unexplainable phenomenon in its continental context.

Morales, however, cannot devote much time to politics. He has overwhelming economic problems: he found only $300 million in the treasury and a $3 billion debt, mostly short-term (which he managed to defer at a high cost), a balance of payments for 1975 in which exports had decreased by 20 percent and imports had increased 50 percent, nationalized industries in which production had decreased under the direction of the military (a pound of copper costs seventy-five cents in state mines and fifty-five cents in private ones), 40 percent price hikes in 1975, and the prospect of a total copper production of 440,000 tons in 1977 as the market keeps descending and shrinking.

At the same time, after spending $600 million, on an oil pipeline from the Amazon to the coast (currently under construction), it turns out that the prospects have been more or less disappointing and that several foreign companies have decided to lose their investment rather than to continue (as they think) hopelessly looking for oil. The fishing industry is going through a crisis: large number of anchovies, due to shifts in ocean currents, are moving away, fish flour production has gone down from 2.3 million tons annually to 1 million, and the cost per ton is $230, whereas on the world market they only pay $200.

Evidently, these data support those who say that the blame for the situation does not fall on bad administration, paternalism, and lack of popular participation, but on the very nature of the reforms. It is possible that Morales will be forced, perhaps with intimate satisfaction, to reform the reforms themselves if he wants to get out of this economic mire—not to make the measures popular, but to return to the executives and technicians the businessman role that the military has arrogated. The new military team seems to inspire confidence in Europe and in the United States (and even in

the Soviet Union, where they feared that Velasco's demagogy
would put Moscow in a bind and cost it a lot of money).
Kissinger, during his trip through Latin America in February
of 1976, stopped in Lima and, after praising Peru's policy of
nonalignment, reminded, without euphemisms, that Peru is
part of the Western hemisphere. The State Department did
not get upset when Lima put pressure, along with the democratic government of Venezuela, to gain Castroist Cuba's readmission to the Organization of American States, but had
no sympathy for Velasco's aspiration that his country should
turn into a third world leader. Morales, who evidently does
not share this expensive fantasy, hopes the United States will
facilitate credits and promote investments that will help the
country come out of its difficult economic situation, without
necessarily abandoning the nationalist rhetoric (which in
Latin American inevitably sounds anti-American).

One way out of this economic situation would be the scal-
ing down of military spending and especially the purchases
from the USSR, France, Great Britain, and the United States;
for Peru, under the military government, has become very
ecumenical concerning arms. In a country where the annual
per capita income is still $350, where one out of every three
citizens is illiterate and one out of every eight lives in a slum,
the army absorbs 10 percent of the national budget and 2.4
percent of the gross national product ($226 million for the
military in 1974 and a few more million the following years).
With 16 million people, there are 56,000 men in the military
(39,000 in the army in ten brigades, with French and Soviet
tanks and American artillery; 8,000 in the navy with units
purchased from Sweden and the United States; and 9,000 in
the air force with ninety-four French Mirage planes, British
Camberras, and some American models). These figures are
modest compared to those in countries belonging to NATO
or to the Warsaw Pact, but in the Latin American context
they are the highest and put Peru right behind Cuba as the
two most well-armed countries.[32] The military men talk privately about threats on the frontiers: Ecuador and Colombia
to the north, Chile to the south, and the possible alliance—
they say sponsored by the Pentagon—between Brazil, Chile,

and Bolivia; and with this they justify their arms expenditures. One should not forget that the Peruvian army has not digested yet two fundamental facts about its history: that independence was won by Bolívar and San Martín and not by Peruvian arms, and that it lost the two important wars in which it became involved.

In order to reconcile all those pressures—economic, political, military, and international—Morales, in April of 1976, put forth a six-year plan and named it after the ancient head of the indigenous eighteenth-century rebellion, Tupac Amaru. The objective of the plan is to "correct" the "revolution's" mistakes, and, most of all, to face up to the economic crisis stemming from those mistakes and worsened by the world crisis. In this plan, private enterprises without worker management are authorized, and a transfer to private hands of nonprofitable state enterprises is predicted. This is a confession of failure in nationalization, when directed by the military. The National Confederation of Commerce applauded the plan and the radical groups criticized it, saying that this "could be the diving board for capitalism in Peru." This last comment indicates how little the Peruvian radicals, so enthusiastic about nationalism, have understood that the military "revolution" was meant precisely to free capitalism from feudal shackles, and that nationalizations were, simply, a drastic way of encouraging state capitalism. The rest—participation and so forth—were simply attempts to mask this reality so that it would be accepted and supported by the radicals.

However, the plan keeps worker representation in administrative councils and the obligation of distributing 25 percent of the profits among the workers. The plan, prepared before Kissinger's visit and published afterwards, made possible an improvement of diplomatic and economic relations with the United States, which were never really cold other than in public.

The change of presidents encouraged the traditional parties to ask for a return to an elective system. In May, Morales retorted by affirming that this ever-increasing demand for elections was untimely in view of the economic crisis. The

calling for harmony and the granting of amnesties did not
mean that the government's intention was to seek an electoral outlet, although it is not unusual for the Latin American military to call upon the civilians once they have created
economic chaos with their dictatorship, so that it is the
civilians who have to adopt unpopular measures. But this
time the material and bureaucratic interests of the military
are so deeply rooted that this will possibly be the exception.
For elections to take place, Morales said, first *caciquismo*
("bossism"), demagogy, and manipulation have to cease.
Finally, Morales affirmed that those radicals who accuse the
government of having turned right do so because they think
that those who are not Marxist-Leninists have to be necessarily capitalists. "The revolution," he said, "is humanistic
and Christian, but not Marxist or totalitarian." According to
the president, then, even though he did not say it in so many
words, his policies are comparable to those of Lenin's New
Economic Policy, not referring to Communism, of course,
but rather to the "goals of the Peruvian revolution."

World Opinion

What do those who are foreigners, and have followed closely
the military experiment, think about the situation? Let us
summarize some points of view, following the same chrono-
logical order in which they were listed.

After one-and-one-half years of military government, the
American professor Grayson wrote that the American diplomats who think that socially-conscious military are the
key to Latin American development were showing an opti-
mism "which will be premature until the Peruvian generals
satisfactorily solve the economic problems which they
face."[33]

A year later, French journalist Marcel Niedergang affirmed
that the Peruvian experiment was part of a complex of social
experiments, together with those of Allende in Chile and the
military in Bolivia, which he referred to as "nationalistic
revolutionary regimes," and noted that the concessions that
the Peruvian regime had to make, for practical reasons, were
linked to a "world system with which Peru could not break

without resorting to drastic measures that it refused to adopt."[34]

Still, two years later, Spanish correspondent Guerrero Martín wondered what was going on in Peru, and himself answered that only time would tell if it was a matter of reform or revolution. But he pointed out that "a very important apsect remains: the political outlet that will permit the Peruvian people to truly participate in its destiny by electing its own rulers. In this respect," he ended, "an upcoming solution does not seem to be in sight."[35]

French professor Joxe, the same year, stated that the Peruvian army applied the Kennedy model, which remained a utopia in its political aspect, but which was applied in its military aspect in several countries. This model attempted to prove wrong the 1961 Havana declaration that talked about "coup d'etat armies and civil war" and creating power elites that could overthrow old feudal elites. "In this respect, the Peruvian army is, then, not a creation, but a discovery of American imperialism."[36]

A Guatemalan professor living in Mexico, Monteforte Toledo, considered, at about the same time, that "judging from its theoretical basis and from its political practice, the Peruvian armed forces movement is, fundamentally, a revolution" that had the options of becoming a bourgeois revolution, a democratic one, or a socialist one.[37]

The Mexican political journalist Hernando Pacheco, after the bloody events in Lima in 1975, wrote in turn that the reforms carried about by the army were methods of "modernization, autonomy and sovereignty of a modern state." But he continued that a political discipline and an ideological line were lacking, and were being shaped from reaction and not from decision. On the other hand, the "populist and Aprista historical memory" was against the military process and there were, besides, military arrogance and simplification on the part of the Apristas, so that the latter could not give the former the theory that they (the military) lacked.[38]

Theo Sommer, director of *Die Zeit,* a great German paper, pointed out also in 1975 that a new class of corrupt leaders was being formed, and that press freedom had been completely suppressed, and, with it, freedom of criticism. These two features seemed to be the two essential results of the Peruvian "revolution" for him.[39]

Finally, a French-Chilean, Mercier Vega, assessed in 1971 that "there is absolutely no paradox in seeing in the armed forces, if one takes into account the way they actually behave, a particular aspect of the great movement of Latin American 'intelligentisia,' an expression of a superdeveloped sector—equivalent to the famous middle classes—which seeks to shape society according to its dimensions and responding to its needs."[40]

A Latin American, Julio Cotler, considers that what there is in Peru is a "populist military" regime, different from Perónism, Varguism, or the Venezuelan Acción Popular. The main difference consists of the absence of a party to mobilize the masses; the party, at any rate, is the armed forces. This leads to a lack of participation that will frustrate modernization and create "bottlenecks" in the development process.[41]

One Italian author believes that the Peruvian government has unleashed a process that "is evidently giving a new shape to society." It is a process without precedents. The legal changes can be reversed, but the social ones, those which affect the way of life and the distribution of power and prestige within the society are irreversible. The Peruvian experiment proves that the strategy of change coming from within, as opposed to that coming from without, has more effective results.[42] It will also be useful to see what those Peruvians think who, because of residing outside of their country, have a certain perspective from which to evaluate Peruvian events.

Sociologist Castro Contreras was a professor at Peru's Center for High Military Studies (CAEM), where the 1968 coup was conceived and where the revolution's ideas originated. Contreras wrote a document in which he explained what the center was: "The armed forces' nationalism, expressed through their recent participation in the political life of the country, responds, and is the result of, the analytical study of the national situation carried out by CAEM; it is besides, a statement of awareness concerning the national problem, and an expresion of nationalism that differs from the traditional concept based solely on the differences among peoples. It is, lastly, a kind of nationalism tied to the general welfare and to the integral security that the country must possess."[43]

Another sociologist, who belongs to the New Left, Anibal Quijano, without denying the immediate role played by the CAEM, their investigations, and their teachings, has a broader concept of the events in his country. To Quijano, the bourgeoisie had shown itself impotent in dominating the protest movements of the peasants and the urban workers; this situation was the result of the "struggles for hegemony among the oligarchical and modernistic factions of the bourgeoisie." The armed forces, which had used repression against the peasants, and the technical-bureaucratic groups had "enlarged their relative autonomy within their general subordination to the capitalistic interests." After the 1968 coup, these middle-ground groups had their hands freed, due to this autonomy and to the failure of the bourgeoisie. First they tried to arbitrate among the classes, and then kept adopting a more and more development-oriented, technocratic posture, which ended in a phase of growing tensions which, in turn, forced "a purification of the ideological and social content of the military regime." The military government arrived, thus, at establishing as its own basis "an association between state capital and the monopolistic international capital, with which is integrated, in a minor and subordinated position, the capital of the most powerful groups of the dependent bourgeoisie."[44]

World-famous novelist Mario Vargas Llosa, upon returning to Lima in 1975 after several years of absence, protested against the newspaper expropriations and the suffocation of all politically dissenting attitudes. "With the growing lack of freedom of expression, the revolution is risking fossilization. I do not think that the press was outstanding when it was in private hands, and it defended the class interests of a minority. But now the government has moved away from any political debate."[45] Vargas Llosa, who defended Fidel Castro before the latter started the persecution of intellectual dissidents and whose first novel, *The City and the Dogs,* takes place in a military academy (where the students conducted an auto-da-fé with a thousand copies of it), considered the military's agrarian reform and their establishment of profit-sharing for workers unexpected. But the suffocation of all criticism seemed to him to correspond to military mentality.

An American economist who has worked in Peru since 1971, Peter T. Knight,[46] considered that the 1974 law that created the "social property" enterprises reflected an old aspiration in the Aprista and anarcho-syndicalist movement, which only a military government dared to put into practice. Even though their application was difficult and mistakes were made, Knight considered that "the military rulers of Peru have proved themselves to be as pragmatic as they are creative in responding to the correlation of changing forces, while they continue to deepen the revolution."

An Argentinian anarcho-syndicalist, Ernesto Ramos, affirmed: "Our position is not stemming from precipitous and unconditional support, because it is not lost on us that [the revolution] is being controlled and directed by a military group that, even if they are imbued with ideas for over-coming the defects of the capitalist system, make you wonder because of their peculiar professional condition and because of the fluctuation of the forces involved."[47] One must say that most of the elements in the Latin American, American, and even European New Left lacked this cautious-ness, and, forgetting their old mistrust of the military, blindly applauded any measure adopted by the military in Peru, provided they classified it as "revolutionary" and "anti-imperialist." None of them, anyway, were able to foresee that in the very midst of the "revolutionary" military forces there would arise elements capable both of slowing down the impulse toward gradual change and of staging a coup within a coup.

Notes

1. David Chaplin, *Industrialization and the Distribution of Wealth in Peru* (Madison, Wis., 1966), p. 22.

2. Louis Baudin, *La vie quotidienne au temps des derniers Incas* [Daily life at the time of the last Incas] (Paris, 1956), p. 19.

3. *Tenencia de la tierra y desarrollo socio-económico del sector agrícola: Perú* (Washington, D.C., 1966), p. 19.

4. CIT—Confederación Interamericana de Trabajadores (Inter-American Confederation of Workers).

5. ORIT—Organización Regional Interamericana de Trabajadores (Regional Inter-American Organization of Workers).

6. CTAL—Confederación Trabajadores de América Latina (Confederation of Latin American Workers).

7. Edgardo Seoane, *Surcos de paz* (Lima, 1963), p. 33.

8. The highways have a total length of about 65,000 miles, of which 7,000 are asphalt. There are 124,000 pleasure cars, 85,000 trucks, and 10,000 autobuses—more than half of them in Lima and Callao.

9. The railways have about 5,500 miles of track, about 1,100 of which belong to the government. They carry an average of 8 million passengers and 6 million metric tons of freight a year.

10. The first Peruvian airline went into operation in 1957. Today, more than 700,000 passengers travel by air every year.

11. In recent years, an average of 12,000 ships with 21 million tons of total displacement have visited Peruvian ports. Coastal freight traffic is reserved to Peruvian vessels—about 2.3 million tons a year—with Peruvian crews. International shipping has a displacement of 6,000 tons; coasting vessels, 23,000 tons; and riverboats, 5,000 tons.

12. There are 2,000 post offices, 320 telegraph offices, 400 telephone central offices, and 80 radio-telegraph offices. Telephone lines extend over 45,000 miles. The telephone system consists of 136,000 instruments, two-thirds of which are in Lima alone. Communication with distant cities is carried on by radio-telephone. A submarine cable connects Lima with Chile, and another with the countries to the north on the Pacific coast.

There are also 152 radio broadcasting stations, 19 of which belong to the government. Television is broadcast by 23 stations (5 in Lima and 18 in the provinces) and the rest by "relay," with about 900,000 receivers.

13. Humberto Espinoza Uriarte, "La inversión privada norteamericana en el Perú," in *Desarrollo,* Bogotá, May 1969, p. 19.

14. Facts such as these have been reported in the press in May 1966 and on September 9, 1968. The figures referring to illegitimacy, abortion, and illegitimate unions are found in a pastoral letter from the archbishop of Lima, Msgr. Leonardo José Rodriguez Ballón, quoted in *La Prensa,* Lima, August 5, 1968.

15. Ana Maria Portugal, "La peruana, tapada sin manto?" in *Mundo Nuevo,* Buenos Aires–Paris, April 1970, p. 24.

16. In addition to the million transistor radios, there are another million of the regular kind. There are about 400,000 television receivers, mostly imported, although these are often manufactured in small shops, using imported parts. There are 450 motion picture theaters in about 200,000 localities, with an average annual attendance of 7.6 per capita. There are also several small operations of the traveling type, using trucks, generators, and portable projectors, which, from time to time, show films in villages that lack electricity. There are no use taxes on radio or television receivers. The offical Radio Nacional station is maintained by paid announcements and by a tax on imported receivers. It is compulsory for every film program to include one Peruvian-produced film (in general, these are documentaries or educational). Several small companies produce this material for short-term local consumption and also publicity films. On the other hand, there are various firms of some importance, operating on a national scale, that produce films and programs intended for television.

17. Speech of July 14, 1969, about the sugar crop.

18. *The Economist* (Spanish ed.) 3, no. 16.

19. From June 1969, when the agrarian reform law was promulgated, to June 1970, payments in compensation for expropriations have amounted to $4.5 million in cash and $28.5 million in bonds. In the same period, $18.3 million was paid for cattle expropriated along with seized land. On the other hand, the director of Cattle Raising (Banco de

Fomento Agropecuario), Edgardo Seoane—Belaúnde's vice president who had broken with him shortly before the coup—announced that, in 1969, small landholders had been lent $96.6 million, and that the World Development Bank and the World Bank had been asked for credits of $23 million and $30 million respectively. Finally, in May, 1970, it was decreed that all agricultural firms should distribute not less than 50 percent of their net profits among their permanent employees.

20. Rolland G. Paulston, "Educación y cambio social en el Perú," in *Mundo Nuevo,* Buenos Aires–Paris, July 1970, p. 14.

21. Ibid.

22. In December, 1969, a few days before publication of the Statute of Freedom of the Press, the junta ordered a reorganization of the judicial system, replaced sixteen members of the Supreme Tribunal, and set a term of ninety days for this tribunal to clean up and reorganize the lower courts. The replacement of the sixteen justices was illegal, for they had been appointed by the Congress for life. Under the military's reorganization, justices will be appointed for five-year terms—by the junta.

23. *Latin American Newsletter,* Albuquerque, March 1969.

24. Dirección General de Informaciones, *Noventa días después: La Revolución está en marcha por un Perú para todos los peruanos* (Lima, 1969).

25. B. Listov, "Peru: Reform Goes Forward," in *Pravda,* Moscow, June 24, 1970.

26. An editorial in *Unidad,* the organ of the Peruvian Communist party, Lima, July 25, 1974.

27. Mario Monteforte Toledo, "El guerrillero solitario del Perú," *Siempre,* Mexico, D. F., October 20, 1972.

28. Theo Sommer, "Parameters of the Revolution," *Encounter,* London, April 1975, p. 54.

29. Ibid.

30. The following story was told by a special envoy of *Le Monde,* Paris, March 23-24, 1975.

31. *Unidad,* Lima, Oct. 4, 1975.

32. Hugh O'Shaughnessy, "Little Peru Spends Big for Arms," in *The New York Times,* New York, March 7, 1976.

33. George W. Grayson, Jr., "Peru's Military Government," in *Current History,* New York, February 1970.

34. Marcel Niedergant, "Revolutionary Nationalism in Peru," in *Foreign Affairs,* New York, April 1971.

35. José Guerrero Martín, "Qué pasa en Peru," in *La Vanguardia Española,* April 25 and May 2, 1973.

36. Alain Joxe, "Para qué sirven essos generales," in *Ahora,* Santo Domingo, July 30, 1973.

37. Mario Monteforte Toledo, *La solución militar a la peruana* (Mexico, D. F., 1973), p. 182.

38. Hernando Pacheco, "El sangriento aviso del Perú," in *El Dien,* Mexico, D. F., Feb. 8, 1975.

39. Theo Sommer, "The Peruvian Revolution," in *Encounter,* London, April 1975.

40. Luis Mercier Vega, "¿Hacia la unión?" in *Interrogations,* Paris, December 1975.

41. Julio Cotler, "Political Crisis and Military Populism in Peru," in *Militarism in Developing Countries* (New Brunswick, N. J., 1975), pp. 219 ff.

42. Luigi R. Einaudi, "Revolution from Within? Military Rule in Peru since 1968," in *Militarism in Developing Countries,* pp. 283 ff.

43. Jaime Castro Contreras, "The Center for High Military Studies, or the Origins of the New Mentality Towards Change," in *Interrogations,* Paris, December 1975.

44. He expounds it in detail in his book *Nationalism and Capitalism in Peru* (New York, 1971), and in an article, "The Political Juncture in Peru," in *Siempre,* Mexico, D. F., Nov. 28, 1973, written shortly before he had to leave his country when his magazine *Sociedad y Politica* was confiscated. When he was still in Peru, he gave an interview to Rolando Cordera ("Peru, Four Years after the Reform Project," in *Siempre,* Mexico, D. F., Nov. 8, 1972). Quijano's opinions as presented in this chapter are based on these materials.

45. Jonathan Kandell, "A Reluctant Antagonist in Peru," in the *New York Times,* Feb. 20, 1975.

46. Peter T. Knight, *Perú, ¿Lacia la autosugestión?,* Buenos Aires, 1975, p. 101.

47. Ibid., p. 7.

For Further Reading

The literature about Peru in English is not very abundant compared to that devoted to other Latin American countries. But neither is it so scarce that the reader will have to be content with what can be found in this book.

Several Peruvian novels have been translated into English, but, unfortunately, not very much poetry. Graphic reproductions of the remains of pre-Hispanic culture are plentiful, but those of colonial works of art are more rare, and those of the art of our time are very rare.

At any rate, the reader will be able to find, in the following list, books about the outstanding aspects of Peru at various periods in history.

Acha V., J. W. *Art in Peru.* Washington, D.C.: Organization of American States, 1961.

Astriz, Carlos A. *Pressure Groups and Power Elites in Peruvian Politics.* Ithaca, N. Y.: Cornell University Press, 1969.

Baudin, Louis. *Daily Life in Peru under the Incas.* New York: Macmillan, 1962.

Beals, Carleton. *Fire on the Andes.* Philadelphia, 1934.

Bejen, Hector. "Peru 1965: Notes on a Guerrilla Experience." *Monthly Review,* 1969.

Bourricaud, François. *Power and Society in Contemporary Peru.* New York: Praeger, 1970.

Brundage, B. C. *Empire of the Inca.* Norman: University of Oklahoma Press, 1963.

Buck, Alfred A., et al. *Health and Disease in Four Peruvian Villages.* Baltimore, Md.: Johns Hopkins Press, 1968.

Bushnell, G. H. S. *Ancient Peoples and Places: Peru.* New York: Praeger, 1963.

Carey, James C. *Peru and the United States, 1900-1962.* Notre Dame, Ind.: University of Notre Dame Press, 1964.

Chaplin, David. *Industrialization and the Distribution of Wealth in Peru.* Madison: University of Wisconsin Land Tenure Center, 1966.

——————. "Peruvian Nationalism, A Corporatist Revolution." *Transaction,* 1975.

Coutu, A. J., et al. *The Agricultural Development of Peru.* New York: Praeger, 1969.

Dew, Edward. *Politics in the Altiplano.* Austin: University of Texas Press, 1969.

Doughty, Paul L. *Huaylas. An Andean District in Search of Progress.* Ithaca, N. Y.: Cornell University Press, 1968.

Fischer, Lillian Estelle. *The Last Inca Revolt.* Norman: University of Oklahoma Press, 1966.

Ford, Thomas R. *Man and Land in Peru.* Gainesville: University of Florida Press, 1955.

Hopkins, Jack W. *The Government Executive of Modern Peru.* Gainesville: University of Florida Center for Latin American Studies, 1967.

Kantor, Harry. *The Ideology and Program of the Peruvian Aprista Movement.* Washington, D. C.: Savile Books, 1966.

Larco Hoyle, Rafael. *Checan.* Geneva: Nägel, 1965.

Lieserson, A. *Notes on the Process of Industrialization of Argentina, Chile and Peru.* Berkeley: University of California Press: 1966.

Marett, Robert. *Peru.* New York: Praeger, 1969.

Mason, J. Alden. *The Ancient Civilisations of Peru.* London: Penguin, 1957.

Metraux, Alfred. *The History of the Incas.* New York, 1969.

Osborne, Harold. *Indians of the Andes: Aymara and Quechuas.* Cambridge, Mass., 1952.

Owens, R. J. *Peru.* New York: Oxford University Press, 1963.

Payne, James L. *Labor and Politics in Peru.* New Haven, Conn.: Yale University Press, 1966.

Pike, Frederick B. *The Modern History of Peru.* New York: Praeger, 1967.

Prescott, William H. *History of the Conquest of Peru.* Philadelphia, Penn., 1847.

Primov, George P., and Van den Berghe, Pierre L. *Inequality in the Peruvian Andes.* Columbia: University of Missouri Press, 1977.

Quijano, Anibal. "Nationalism and Capitalism in Peru." *Monthly Review,* 1971.

Shapiro, S. *Invisible Latin America.* Boston: Beacon Press, 1963.

Stewart, Watt. *Henry Meiggs, Yankee Pizarro.* Durham, 1966.

United States Department of Labor. *Labor in Peru.* Washington, D. C.: United States Department of Labor, 1964.

Woodcock. *Incas and Other Men.* London, 1967.

Zarate, Agustin de. *The Discovery and Conquest of Peru.* London: Penguin, 1968.